The Island of
the Colour-blind

ALSO BY OLIVER SACKS

Migraine

Awakenings

A Leg to Stand On

The Man Who Mistook His Wife for a Hat

Seeing Voices

An Anthropologist on Mars

The Island of
the Colour-blind

and

Cycad Island

OLIVER SACKS

PICADOR

First published 1996 by Picador

an imprint of Macmillan Publishers Ltd
25 Eccleston Place, London SW1W 9NF
and Basingstoke

Associated companies throughout the world

ISBN 0 330 35081 1

Grateful acknowledgement is made to Douglas Goode for permission
to reproduce the illustration on pages 309–10, John Johnston Ltd. for
permission to reproduce the drawing by Stephen Wiltshire on page 68,
and to the library of the New York Botanical Garden, Bronx, New York,
for permission to reproduce illustrations on pages 134 and 135.

1 3 5 7 9 8 6 4 2

A CIP catalogue record for this book is available from
the British Library.

Typeset by CentraCet Limited, Cambridge
Printed and bound in Great Britain by
Mackays of Chatham plc, Chatham, Kent

For Eric

Contents

List of Illustrations

List of Illustrations

Psilotum, or 'whisk fern', from Bower's *Origin of a Land Flora*, page 214

Grove of *Cycas circinalis*, from Warming's *Systematic Botany*, page 220

Humboldt's Dragon-Tree, page 228

Reading by the light of phosphorescent sea, from Holder's *Living Lights*, page 248

Gosse's 'horrid' *Encephalartos*, from his *Omphalos*, page 295

Commemorative stamps from China depicting native cycad species, including the last known living *Cycas multipinnata*, by Zeng Xiaolian, page 298

Phyllotaxis of a fir cone, from Henslow, page 300

Encephalartos woodii, the cycad Ishi, from Goode's *Cycads of Africa*, page 309

Preface

This book is really two books, independent narratives of two parallel but independent journeys to Micronesia. My visits to these islands were brief and unexpected, not part of any programme or agenda, not intended to prove or disprove any thesis, but simply to observe. But if they were impulsive and unsystematic, my island experiences were intense and rich, and ramified in all sorts of directions which continually surprised me.

I went to Micronesia as a neurologist, or neuroanthropologist, intent on seeing how individuals and communities responded to unusual endemic conditions – a hereditary total colour-blindness in Pingelap and Pohnpei; a progressive, fatal neurodegenerative disorder in Guam and Rota. But I also found myself riveted by the cultural life and history of these islands, their unique flora and fauna, their singular geological origins. If seeing patients, visiting archaeological sites, wandering in rainforests, snorkelling in the reefs, at first seemed to bear no relation to each other, they then fused into a single unpartitionable experience, a total immersion in island life.

But perhaps it was only on my return, when the experiences recollected and reflected themselves again and again, that their connection and meaning (or some of their meanings) started to grow clear; and with this, the impulse to put pen to paper. Writing, in these past months, has allowed me, forced me, to revisit these islands in memory. And since memory, as Edelman reminds us, is never a simple recording or reproduction, but an active process of recategorization – of reconstruction, of imagination, determined by our own values and perspectives – so remembering has caused me to reinvent these visits, in a sense, constructing a personal, idiosyncratic, perhaps eccentric view of these islands, informed in part by a lifelong romance with islands and island botany.

From my earliest years I had a passion for animals and plants, a biophilia nurtured in the first place by my mother and my aunt, then by favourite teachers and the companionship of school friends who shared these passions – Eric Korn, Jonathan Miller, and Dick Lindenbaum. We would go plant-hunting together, vascula strapped to our backs; on frequent freshwater expeditions, at dawn; and for a fortnight of marine biology at Millport each spring. We discovered and shared books – I got my favourite Strasburger's *Botany* (I see from the flyleaf) from Jonathan in 1948, and innumerable books from Eric, already a bibliophile. We spent hundreds of hours at the zoo, at Kew Gardens, and in the Natural History Museum, where we could be vicarious naturalists, travel to our favourite islands, without leaving Regent's Park or Kew or South Kensington.

Many years later, in the course of a letter, Jonathan looked back on this early passion, and the somewhat Victorian character which suffused it: 'I have a great hankering for that sepia-tinted era,' he wrote. 'I regret that the people and the furniture about me are so brightly coloured and clean. I long endlessly for the whole place suddenly to be plunged into the gritty monochrome of 1876.'

Eric felt similarly, and this is surely one of the reasons why he has come to combine writing, book collecting, book buying, book selling with biology, becoming an antiquarian with a vast knowledge of Darwin, of the whole history of biology and natural science. We were all Victorian naturalists at heart.

In writing about my visit to Micronesia, then, I have gone back to old books, old interests and passions I have had for forty years, and fused these with the later interests, the medical self, which followed. Botany and medicine are not entirely unallied. The father of British neurology, W. R. Gowers, I was delighted to learn recently, once wrote a small botanical monograph – on Mosses. In his biography of Gowers, Macdonald Critchley remarks that Gowers 'brought to the bedside all his skill as a natural historian. To him the neurological sick were like the flora of a tropical jungle. . . .'

*

In writing this book, I have travelled into many realms not my own, and I have been greatly helped by many people, especially those people of Micronesia, of Guam and Rota and Pingelap and Pohnpei – patients, scientists, physicians, botanists – whom I encountered on the way. Above all, I am grateful to Knut Nordby, John Steele, and Bob Wasserman for sharing the journey with me, in many ways. Among those who welcomed me to the Pacific, I must thank in particular Ulla Craig, Greg Dever, May Okahiro, Bill Peck, Phil Roberto, Julia Steele, Alma van der Velde, and Marjorie Whiting. I am grateful also to Mark Futterman, Jane Hurd, Catherine de Laura, Irene Maumenee, John Mollon, Britt Nordby, the Schwartz family, and Irwin Siegel for their discussions of achromatopsia and of Pingelap. Special thanks are due to Frances Futterman, who, among other things, introduced me to Knut and provided invaluable advice on selecting sunglasses and equipment for our expedition to Pingelap, in addition to sharing her own experience of achromatopsia.

I am likewise indebted to many researchers who have played a part in investigating the Guam disease over the years: Sue Daniel, Ralph Garruto, Carleton Gajdusek, Asao Hirano, Leonard Kurland, Andrew Lees, Donald Mulder, Peter Spencer, Bert Weiderholt, Harry Zimmerman. Many others have helped in all sorts of ways, including my friends and colleagues Kevin Cahill (who cured me of amoebiasis contracted in the islands), Elizabeth Chase, John Clay, Allen Furbeck, Stephen Jay Gould, G. A. Holland, Isabelle Rapin, Gay Sacks, Herb Schaumburg, Ralph Siegel, Patrick Stewart, and Paul Theroux.

My visits to Micronesia were greatly enriched by the documentary film crew which accompanied us there in 1994, and shared all of these experiences with us (and got a great many of them on film, despite often difficult conditions). Emma Crichton-Miller, first, provided a great deal of research on the islands and their people, and Chris Rawlence produced and directed the filming with infinite sensitivity and intelligence. The film crew – Chris and Emma, David Barker, Greg Bailey, Sophie Gardiner, and Robin Probyn – enlivened our visit with skill and camaraderie, and not least as friends, who have now accompanied me on many different adventures.

I am grateful to those who have helped in the course of writing and publishing this book, particularly Nicholas Blake, Suzanne Gluck, Jacqui Graham, Schellie Hagan, Carol Harvey, Claudine O'Hearn, and Heather Schroder; and especially Juan Martinez, who has skilfully and intelligently organized in innumerable ways.

Though the book was written in a sort of swoop, a single breath, in July 1995, it then grew, like an unruly cycad, to many times its original size, putting out offshoots and bulbils in all directions. Since the offshoots, in volume, now started to vie with the text, and since I felt it crucial to keep the narrative unencumbered, I have placed many of these additional thoughts together, as endnotes. The complexities of what to put in and leave out, of how to orchestrate the five parts of this narrative, owe a great deal to the sensitivity and judgement of Dan Frank, my editor at Knopf, and to Kate Edgar.

For sharing their expertise and enthusiasm on botanical subjects, most especially on ferns and cycads, I am grateful to Bill Raynor, Lynn Raulerson, and Agnes Rinehart in Micronesia, to Chuck Hubbuch at the Fairchild Tropical Garden in Miami and to John Mickel and Dennis Stevenson at the New York Botanical Garden. And finally, for their patient and careful readings of the manuscript of this book, I am indebted to Stephen Jay Gould and Eric Korn. It is to Eric, my oldest and dearest friend and companion in all sorts of scientific enthusiasms over the years, that I dedicate this book.

O. W. S.

New York
August 1996

Book One

The Island of
the Colour-blind

Island Hopping

Islands have always fascinated me; perhaps they fascinate everyone. The first summer holiday I remember – I was just three years old – was a visit to the Isle of Wight. There are only fragments in memory: the cliffs of many-coloured sands, the wonder of the sea, which I was seeing for the first time – its calmness, its gentle swell, its warmth, entranced me; its roughness, when the wind rose, terrified me. My father told me that he had won a race swimming round the Isle of Wight before I was born, and this made me think of him as a giant, a hero.

Stories of islands, and seas, and ships and mariners entered my consciousness very early – my mother would tell me about Captain Cook, about Magellan and Tasman and Dampier and Bougainville, and all the islands and peoples they had discovered, and she would point them out to me on a globe. Islands were special places, remote and mysterious, intensely attractive, yet frightening too. I remember being terrified by a children's encyclopaedia with a picture of the great blind statues of Easter Island looking out to sea, as I read that the islanders had lost the power to sail away from the island and were totally cut off from the rest of humanity, doomed to die in utter isolation.[1]

I read about castaways, desert islands, prison islands, leper islands. I adored *The Lost World*, Conan Doyle's splendid yarn about an isolated South American plateau full of dinosaurs and Jurassic life-forms – in effect, an island marooned in time (I knew the book virtually by heart, and dreamed of growing up to be another Professor Challenger).

I was very impressionable and readily made other people's imaginings my own. H. G. Wells was particularly potent – all desert islands, for me, became his Aepyornis Island or, in a nightmare mode, the Island of Dr Moreau. Later, when I came to read Herman Melville and Robert Louis Stevenson, the real and the imaginary fused in my mind. Did the Marquesas actually exist? Were *Omoo* and *Typee* actual adventures? I felt this uncertainty most especially about the Galapagos, for long before I read Darwin, I knew of them as the 'evilly enchanted' isles of Melville's 'Encantadas'.

Later still, factual and scientific accounts began to dominate my reading – Darwin's *Voyage of the Beagle*, Wallace's *Malay Archipelago*, and my favourite, Humboldt's *Personal Narrative* (I loved especially his description of the six-thousand-year-old dragon tree on Tenerife) – and now the sense of the romantic, the mythical, the mysterious, became subordinated to the passion of scientific curiosity.[2]

For islands were, so to speak, experiments of nature, places blessed or cursed by geographic singularity to harbour unique forms of life – the aye-ayes and pottos, the lorises and lemurs of Madagascar; the great tortoises

of the Galapagos; the giant flightless birds of New Zealand – all singular species or genera which had taken a separate evolutionary path in their isolated habitats.[3] And I was strangely pleased by a phrase in one of Darwin's diaries, written after he had seen a kangaroo in Australia and found this so extraordinary and alien that he wondered if it did not represent a second creation.[4]

*

As a child I had visual migraines, where I would have not only the classical scintillations and alterations of the visual field, but alterations in the sense of colour too, which might weaken or entirely disappear for a few minutes. This experience frightened me, but tantalized me too, and made me wonder what it would be like to live in a completely colourless world, not just for a few minutes, but permanently. It was not until many years later that I got an answer, at least a partial answer, in the form of a patient, Jonathan I., a painter who had suddenly become totally colour-blind following a car accident (and perhaps a stroke). He had lost colour vision not through any damage to his eyes, it seemed, but through damage to the parts of the brain which 'construct' the sensation of colour. Indeed, he seemed to have lost the ability not only to see colour, but to imagine or remember it, even to dream of it. Nevertheless, like an amnesiac, he in some way remained conscious of having *lost* colour, after a lifetime of chromatic vision, and complained of his world feeling impoverished, grotesque, abnormal – his art, his food, even his wife looked 'leaden' to him. Still, he could not assuage my curiosity on the allied, yet totally different, matter of what it might be like *never* to have seen colour, never to have had the least sense of its primal quality, its place in the world.

Ordinary colour-blindness, arising from a defect in the retinal cells, is almost always partial, and some forms are very common: red-green colour-blindness occurs to some degree in one in twenty men (it is much rarer in women). But total congenital colour-blindness, or achromatopsia, is surpassingly rare, affecting perhaps only one person in thirty or forty thousand. What, I wondered, would the visual world be like for those born totally colour-blind? Would they, perhaps, lacking any sense of something missing, have a world no less dense and vibrant than our own? Might they even have developed heightened perceptions of visual tone and texture and movement and depth, and live in a world in some ways more intense than our own, a world of heightened reality – one that we can only glimpse echoes of in the work of the great black-and-white photographers? Might they indeed see *us* as peculiar, distracted by trivial or irrelevant aspects of the visual world, and insufficiently sensitive to its real visual essence? I could only guess, as I had never met anyone born completely colour-blind.

*

Many of H. G. Wells's short stories, it seems to me, fantastical as they are, can be seen as metaphors for certain neurological and psychological realities. One of my favourites is 'The Country of the Blind', in which a lost traveller, stumbling into an isolated valley in South America, is struck by the strange 'parti-coloured' houses that he sees. The men who built these, he thinks, must have been as blind as bats – and soon he discovers that this *is* the case, and indeed that he has come across an entire blind society. He finds that their blindness is due to a disease contracted three hundred years before, and that over the course of time, the very concept of seeing has vanished:

For fourteen generations these people had been blind and cut off from all the seeing world; the names for all the things of sight had faded and changed. . . . Much of their imagination had shrivelled with their eyes, and they had made for themselves new imaginations with their ever more sensitive ears and finger-tips.

Wells's traveller is at first contemptuous of the blind, seeing them as pitiful, disabled – but soon the tables are reversed, and he finds that they see *him* as demented, subject to hallucinations produced by the irritable, mobile organs in his face (which the blind, with their atrophied eyes, can conceive only as a source of delusion). When he falls in love with a girl in the valley and wants to stay there and marry her, the elders, after much thought, agree to this, provided he consent to the removal of those irritable organs, his eyes.

Forty years after I first read this story, I read another book, by Nora Ellen Groce, about deafness on the island of Martha's Vineyard. A sea captain and his brother from Kent, it seems, had settled there in the 1690s; both had normal hearing, but both brought with them a recessive gene for deafness. In time, with the isolation of the Vineyard, and the intermarriage of its close community, this gene was carried by the majority of their descendants; by the mid-nineteenth century, in some of the up-island villages, a quarter or more of the inhabitants were born totally deaf.

Hearing people were not so much discriminated against here as assimilated – in this visual culture, everyone in the community, deaf and hearing alike, had come to use sign language. They would chat in Sign (it was much better than spoken language in many ways: for communicating across a distance, for instance, from one fishing boat to another, or for gossiping in church), debate in Sign, teach in Sign, think and dream in Sign. Martha's Vineyard was an island where everyone spoke sign language, a veritable country of the deaf. Alexander Graham Bell, visiting in the 1870s, wondered indeed whether it might not come to harbour an entire 'deaf variety of the human race', which might then spread throughout the world.

And knowing that congenital achromatopsia, like this form of deafness, is also hereditary, I could not help wondering whether there might also be, somewhere on the planet, an island, a village, a valley of the colour-blind.

*

When I visited Guam early in 1993, some impulse made me put this question to my friend John Steele, who has practised neurology all over Micronesia. Unexpectedly, I received an immediate, positive answer: there *was* just such an isolate, John said, on the island of Pingelap – it was relatively close, 'barely twelve hundred miles from here,' he added. Just a few days earlier, he had seen an achromatopic boy on Guam, who had journeyed there with his parents from Pingelap. 'Fascinating,' he said. 'Classical congenital achromatopsia, with nystagmus, and avoidance of bright light – and the incidence on Pingelap is extraordinarily high, almost ten per cent of the population.' I was intrigued by what John told me, and resolved that – sometime – I would come back to the South Seas and visit Pingelap.

When I returned to New York, the thought receded to the back of my mind. Then, some months later, I got a long letter from Frances Futterman, a woman in Berkeley who was herself born completely colour-blind. She had read my original essay on the colour-blind painter and was at pains to contrast her situation with his, and to emphasize that she herself, never having known colour, had no sense of loss, no sense of being chromatically defective. But congenital achromatopsia, she pointed out, involved far more than colour-blindness as such. What was far more disabling was the painful hypersensitivity to light and poor visual acuity which also affect congenital achromatopes. She had grown up in a relatively shadeless part of Texas, with a constant squint, and preferred to go outside only at night. She was intrigued by the notion of an island of the colour-blind, but had not heard of one in the Pacific. Was this a fantasy, a myth, a daydream generated by lonely achromatopes? But she had read, she told me, about another island mentioned in a book on achromatopsia – the little island of Fuur, in a Jutland fjord – where there were a large number of congenital achromatopes. She wondered if I knew of this book, called *Night Vision* – one of its editors, she added, was an achromatope too, a Norwegian scientist named Knut Nordby; perhaps he could tell me more.

Astounded at this – in a short time, I had learned of not one but *two* islands of the colour-blind – I tried to find out more. Knut Nordby was a physiologist and psycho-physicist, I read, a vision researcher at the University of Oslo and, partly by virtue of his own condition, an expert on colour-blindness. This was surely a unique, and important, combination of personal and formal knowl-edge; I had also sensed a warm, open quality in his brief autobiographical memoir, which forms a chapter of *Night Vision*, and this emboldened me to write to him in Norway. 'I would like to meet you,' I wrote. 'I would also like to visit the island of Fuur. And, ideally, to visit the island *with* you.'

Having fired off this letter impulsively, to a complete stranger, I was surprised and relieved by his reaction, which arrived within a few days: 'I should be delighted to accompany you there for a couple of days,' he wrote. Since the original studies on Fuur had been done in the 1940s and '50s, he added, he would get some more up-to-date information. A month later, he contacted me again:

> I have just spoken to the key specialist on achromatopsia in Denmark, and he told me that there are no known achromats left on the island of Fuur. All of the cases in the original studies are either dead ... or have long since migrated. I am sorry – I hate to bring you such dis-appointing news, as I would much have fancied travelling with you to Fuur in search of the last surviving achromat there.

I too was disappointed, but wondered whether we should go none the less. I imagined finding strange residues, ghosts, of the achromatopes who had once lived there – parti-coloured houses, black-and-white vegetation, documents, drawings, memories and stories of the colour-blind by those who once knew them. But there was still Pingelap to think of; I had been assured there were still 'plenty' of achromatopes there. I wrote to Knut again, asking how he might feel about coming with me on a ten-thousand-mile journey, a sort of scientific adventure to Pingelap, and he replied yes, he would love to come, and could take off a few weeks in August.

Colour-blindness had existed on both Fuur and Pingelap for a century or more, and though both islands had been the subject of extensive genetic studies, there had been no human (so to speak, Wellsian) explorations of them, of what it might be like to be an achromatope in an achromatopic community – to be not only totally colour-blind oneself, but to have, perhaps, colour-blind parents and grandparents, neighbours and teachers, to be part of a culture where the entire concept of colour might be missing, but where, instead, other forms of perception, of attention, might be amplified in compensation. I had a vision, only half fantastic, of an entire achromatopic culture with its own singular tastes, arts, cooking, and clothing – a culture where the sensorium, the imagination, took quite different forms from our own, and where 'colour' was so totally devoid of referents or meaning that there were no colour names, no colour metaphors, no language to express it; but (perhaps) a heightened language for the subtlest variations of texture and tone, all that the rest of us dismiss as 'grey'.

Excitedly, I began making plans for the voyage to Pingelap. I phoned up my old friend Eric Korn – Eric is a writer, zoologist, and antiquarian bookseller – and asked him if he knew anything about Pingelap or the Caroline Islands. A couple of weeks later, I received a parcel in the post; in it was a slim leather-bound volume entitled *A Residence of Eleven Years in New Holland and the Caroline Islands, being the Adventures of James F. O'Connell*. The book was published, I saw, in Boston in 1836; it was a little dilapidated (and stained, I wanted to think, by heavy Pacific seas). Sailing from McQuarrietown in Tasmania, O'Connell had visited many of the Pacific islands, but his ship, the *John Bull*, had come to grief in the Carolines, in a group of islands which he calls Bonabee. His description of life there filled me with delight – we would be visiting some of the most remote and least-known islands in the world, probably not much changed from O'Connell's time.

I asked my friend and colleague Robert Wasserman if he would join us as well. As an ophthalmologist, Bob sees many partially colour-blind people in his practice. Like myself, he had never met anyone born totally colour-blind; but we had worked together on several cases involving vision, including that of the colour-blind painter, Mr I. As young doctors, we had done fellowships in neuropathology together, back in the 1960s, and I remembered him telling me then of his four-year-old son Eric, as they drove up to Maine one summer, exclaiming, 'Look at the beautiful orange grass!' No, Bob told him, it's not orange – 'orange' is the colour of an orange. Yes, cried

Eric, it's orange like an orange! This was Bob's first intimation of his son's colour-blindness. Later, when he was six, Eric had painted a picture he called *The Battle of Grey Rock*, but had used pink pigment for the rock.

Bob, as I had hoped, was fascinated by the prospect of meeting Knut and voyaging to Pingelap. An ardent wind-surfer and sailor, he has a passion for oceans and islands and is reconditely knowledgeable about the evolution of outrigger canoes and proas in the Pacific; he longed to see these in action, to sail one himself. Along with Knut, we would form a team, an expedition at once neurological, scientific, and romantic, to the Caroline archipelago and the island of the colour-blind.

*

We converged in Hawaii: Bob looked completely at home in his purple shorts and bright tropical shirt, but Knut looked distinctly less so in the dazzling sun of Waikiki – he was wearing two pairs of dark glasses over his normal glasses: a pair of Polaroid clip-ons, and over these a large pair of wraparound sunglasses – a darkened visor such as a cataract patient might wear. Even so, he tended to blink and squint almost continuously, and behind the dark glasses we could see that his eyes showed a continual jerking movement, a nystagmus. He was much more comfortable when we repaired to a quiet (and, to my eyes, rather dimly lit) little café on a side street, where he could take off his visor, and his clip-ons, and cease squinting and blinking. I found the café much too dark at first, and groped and blundered, knocking down a chair as we went in – but Knut, already dark adapted from wearing his double dark glasses, and more adept at night vision to begin with, was perfectly at ease in the dim lighting, and led us to a table.

Knut's eyes, like those of other congenital achromatopes, have no cones (at least no functional cones): these are the cells which, in the rest of us, fill the fovea – the tiny sensitive area in the centre of the retina – and are specialized for the perception of fine detail, as well as colour. He is forced to rely on the more meagre visual input of the rods, which, in achromatopes as in the rest of us, are distributed around the periphery of the retina, and though these cannot discriminate colour, they are much more sensitive to light. It is the rods which we all use for low-light, or scotopic, vision (as, for instance, walking at night). It is the rods which provide Knut with the vision he has. But without the mediating influence of cones, his rods quickly blanch out in bright light, becoming almost nonfunctional; thus Knut is dazzled by daylight, and literally blinded in bright sunlight – his visual fields contract immediately, shrinking to almost nothing – unless he shields his eyes from the intense light.

His visual acuity, without a cone-filled fovea, is only about a tenth of normal – when we were given menus, he had to take out a four-power magnifying glass and, for the special items chalked on a blackboard on the opposite wall, an eight-power monocular (it looked like a miniature telescope); without these, he would barely be able to read small or distant print. His magnifying glass and monocular are always on his person, and like the dark glasses and visors, they are essential visual aids. And, with no functioning fovea, he has difficulty fixating, holding his gaze on target, especially in bright light – hence his eyes make groping, nystagmic jerks.

Knut must protect his rods from overload and, at the same time, if detailed vision is needed, find ways of enlarging the images they present, whether by optical devices or peering closely. He must also, consciously or unconsciously, discover ways of deriving information from other aspects of the visual world, other visual cues which, in the absence of colour, may take on a heightened importance. Thus – and this was apparent to us right away – his intense sensitivity and attention to form and texture, to outlines and boundaries, to perspective, depth, and movements, even subtle ones.

Knut enjoys the visual world quite as much as the rest of us; he was delighted by a picturesque market in a side street of Honolulu, by the palms and tropical vegetation all around us, by the shapes of clouds – he has a clear and prompt eye for the range of human beauty too. (He has a beautiful wife in Norway, a fellow psychologist, he told us – but it was only after they married, when a friend said, 'I guess you go for redheads,' that he learned for the first time of her flamboyant red hair.)

Knut is a keen black-and-white photographer – indeed his own vision, he said, by way of trying to share it, has some resemblance to that of an orthochromatic black-and-white film, although with a far greater range of tones. 'Greys, you would call them, though the word "grey" has no meaning for me, any more than the term "blue" or "red".' But, he added, 'I do not experience my world as "colourless" or in any sense incomplete.' Knut, who has never seen colour, does not miss it in the least; from the start, he has experienced only the positivity of vision, and has built up a world of beauty and order and meaning on the basis of what he has.[5]

As we walked back to our hotel for a brief night's sleep before our flight the next day, darkness began to fall, and the moon, almost full, rose high into the sky until it was silhouetted, seemingly caught, in the branches of a palm tree. Knut stood under the tree and studied the moon intently with his monocular, making out its seas and shadows. Then, putting the monocular down and gazing up at the sky all around him, he said, 'I see thousands of stars! I see the whole galaxy!'

'That's impossible,' Bob said. 'Surely the angle subtended by a star is too small, given that your visual acuity is a tenth of normal.'

Knut responded by identifying constellations all over the sky – some looked quite different from the configurations he knew in his own Norwegian sky. He wondered if his nystagmus might not have a paradoxical benefit, the jerking movements 'smearing' an otherwise invisible point image to make it larger – or whether this was made possible by some other factor. He agreed that it was difficult to explain how he could see stars with such low visual acuity – but none the less, he did.

'Laudable nystagmus, eh?' said Bob.

*

By sunrise, we were back at the airport, settling in for the long flight on the 'Island Hopper', which calls twice a week at a handful of Pacific islands. Bob, jet-lagged, wedged himself in his seat for more sleep. Knut, dark-glassed already, took out his magnifying glass and began to pore over our bible for this trip – the admirable *Micronesia Handbook*, with its brilliant, sharp descriptions of the islands that awaited us. I was restless, and decided to keep a journal of the flight:

> An hour and a quarter has passed, and we are steadily flying, at 27,000 feet, over the trackless vastness of the Pacific. No ships, no planes, no land, no boundaries, nothing – only the limitless blue of sky and ocean, fusing at times into a single blue bowl. This featureless, cloudless vastness is a great relief, and reverie-inducing – but, like sensory deprivation, somewhat terrifying, too. The Vast thrills, as well as terrifies – it was well called by Kant 'the terrifying Sublime'.

After almost a thousand miles, we at last saw land – a tiny, exquisite atoll on the horizon. Johnston Island! I had seen it as a dot on the map, and thought, 'What an idyllic place, thousands of miles from anywhere.' As we descended it looked less exquisite: a huge runway bisected the island, and to either side of this were storage bins, chimneys, and towers: eyeless buildings, all enveloped in an orange-red haze . . . my idyll, my little paradise, looked like a realm of hell.

Landing was rough, and frightening. There was a loud grinding noise and a squeal of rubber as the whole plane veered suddenly to one side. As we skewed to a halt on the tarmac, the crew informed us that the brakes had locked and we had torn much of the rubber off the tyres on the left – we would have to wait here for repairs. A bit shaken from the landing, and cramped from hours in the air, we longed to get off the plane and stroll around a bit. A stair was pushed up to the plane, with 'Welcome to Johnston Atoll' written on it. One or two passengers started to descend, but when we tried to follow, we were told that Johnston atoll was 'restricted' and that non-military passengers were not allowed to disembark. Frustrated, I returned to my seat and borrowed the *Micronesia Handbook* from Knut, to read about Johnston.

It was named, I read, by a Captain Johnston of HMS *Cornwallis*, who landed here in 1807 – the first human being, perhaps, ever to set foot on this tiny and isolated spot. I wondered if it had somehow escaped being seen altogether before this, or whether perhaps it had been visited, but never inhabited.

Johnston, considered valuable for its rich deposits of guano, was claimed by both the United States and the Kingdom of Hawaii in 1856. Migratory fowl stop here by the hundreds of thousands, and in 1926 the island was designated a federal bird reserve. After the Second World War it was acquired by the US Air Force, and 'since then', I read, 'the US military has converted this formerly idyllic atoll into one of the most toxic places in the Pacific.' It was used during the 1950s and '60s for nuclear testing, and is still maintained as a standby test site; one end of the atoll remains radioactive. It was briefly considered as a test site for biological weapons, but this was precluded by the huge population of migratory birds, which, it was realized, might easily carry lethal infections back to the mainland. In 1971 Johnston became a depot for thousands of tons of mustard and nerve gases, which are periodically incinerated, releasing dioxin and furan into the air (perhaps this was the reason for the cinnamon haze I had seen from above). All personnel on the island are required to have their gas masks ready. Sitting in the now-stuffy plane as I read this – our ventilation had been shut off while we were on the ground – I felt a prickling in my throat, a tightness in my chest, and wondered if I was breathing some of Johnston's lethal air. The 'Welcome' sign now seemed blackly ironic; it should at least have had a skull and crossbones added. The crew members themselves, it seemed to me, grew more uneasy and restless by the minute; they could hardly wait, I thought, to shut the door and take off again.

But the ground crew was still trying to repair our damaged wheels; they were dressed in shiny, aluminized suits, presumably to minimize skin contact with the toxic air. We had heard in Hawaii that a hurricane was on its way towards Johnston: this was of no special importance to us when we were on schedule, but now, we started to think, if we were further delayed, the hurricane might indeed catch up with us on Johnston, and maroon us there with a vengeance – blowing up a storm of poison gases and radioactivity too. There were no planes scheduled to arrive until the end of the week; one flight, we heard, had been detained in this way the previous December, so that the passengers and crew had to spend an unexpected, toxic Christmas on the atoll.

The ground crew worked for two hours, without being able to do anything; finally, with many anxious looks at the sky, our pilot decided to take off again, on the remaining good tyres. The whole plane shuddered and juddered as we accelerated, and seemed to heave and flap itself into the air like some giant ornithopter – but finally (using almost the entire mile-long runway) we got off the ground, and rose through the brown, polluted air of Johnston into the clear empyrean above.

*

Now another lap of more than 1,500 miles to our next stop, Majuro atoll, in the Marshall Islands. We flew endlessly, all of us losing track of space and time, and dozing fitfully in the void. I was woken briefly, terrifyingly, by an air pocket which dropped us suddenly, without warning; then I dozed once more, flying on and on, till I was woken again by altering air pressure. Looking out the window, I could see far below us the narrow, flat atoll of Majuro, rising scarcely ten feet above the waves; scores of islands surrounded the lagoon. Some of the islands looked vacant and inviting, with coconut palms fringing the ocean – the classic desert-island look; the airport was on one of the smaller islands.

Knowing we had two badly damaged tyres, we were all a little fearful about landing. It was indeed rough – we were flung around quite a bit – and it was decided we should stay on Majuro until some repairs could be made;

this would take at least a couple of hours. After our long immurement in the plane (we had travelled nearly three thousand miles now from Hawaii), all of us burst off it, and scattered, explosively.

Knut, Bob, and I stopped first at the little shop in the airport – they had souvenir necklaces and mats, strung together from tiny shells, but also, to my delight, a postcard of Darwin.[6]

While Bob explored the beach, Knut and I walked out to the end of the runway, which was bounded by a low wall overlooking the lagoon. The sea was an intense light blue, turquoise, azure, over the reef, and darker, almost indigo, a few hundred yards out. Not thinking, I enthused about the wonderful blues of the sea – then stopped, embarrassed. Knut, though he has no direct experience of colour, is very erudite on the subject. He is intrigued by the range of words and images other people use about colour and was arrested by my use of the word 'azure'. ('Is it similar to cerulean?') He wondered whether 'indigo' was, for me, a separate, seventh colour of the spectrum, neither blue nor violet, but itself, in between. 'Many people,' he added, 'do not see indigo as a separate spectral colour, and others see light blue as distinct from blue.' With no direct knowledge of colour, Knut has accumulated an immense mental catalogue, an archive, of vicarious colour knowledge about the world. He said that he found the light of the reef extraordinary – 'A brilliant, metallic hue,' he said of it, 'intensely luminous, like a tungsten bronze.' And he spotted half a dozen different sorts of crabs, some of them scuttling sideways so fast that I missed them. I wondered, as Knut himself has wondered, whether his perception of motion might be heightened, perhaps to compensate for his lack of colour vision.

I wandered out to join Bob on the beach, with its fine-grained white sand fringed by coconut palms. There were breadfruit trees here and there and, hugging the ground, low tussocks of zoysia, a beach grass, and a thick-leaved succulent which was new to me. Driftwood edged the strand, admixed with bits of cardboard carton and plastic, the detritus of Darrit-Uliga-Delap, the three-islanded capital of the Marshalls, where twenty thousand people live in close-packed squalor. Even six miles from the capital, the water was scummy, the coral bleached, and there were huge numbers of sea cucumbers, detritus feeders, in the turbid water. None the less, with no shade and the humid heat overwhelming, and hoping there would be clearer water if we swam out a bit, we stripped down to our underwear and walked carefully over the sharp coral until it was deep enough to swim. The water was voluptuously warm, and the tensions of the long hours in our damaged plane gradually eased away as we swam. But just as we were beginning to enjoy that delicious timeless state, the real delight of tropical lagoons, there came a sudden shout from the airstrip – 'The plane is ready to leave! Hurry!' – and we had to clamber out hastily, clutching wet clothes around us, and run back to the plane. One wheel, with its tyre, had been replaced, but the other was bent and difficult to remove, and was still being worked on. So having rushed back to the plane, we sat for another hour on the tarmac – but the other wheel finally defeated all efforts at repair, and we took off again, bumping, noisily clattering over the runway, for the next lap, a short one, to Kwajalein.

Many passengers had left at Majuro, and others had got on, and I now found myself sitting next to a friendly woman, a nurse at the military hospital in Kwajalein, her husband part of a radar tracking unit there. She painted a less than idyllic picture of the island – or, rather, the mass of islands (ninety-one in all) that form Kwajalein atoll, surrounding the largest lagoon in the world. The lagoon itself, she told me, is a test target for missiles from US Air Force bases on Hawaii and the mainland. It is also where countermissiles are tested, fired from Kwajalein at the missiles as they descend. There were nights, she said, when the whole sky was ablaze with light and noise as missiles and antimissiles streaked and collided across it, and reentry vehicles crashed into the lagoon. 'Terrifying,' she said, 'like the night sky in Baghdad.'

Kwajalein is part of the Pacific Barrier radar system, and there is a fearful, rigid, defensive atmosphere in the place, she said, despite the ending of the Cold War. Access is limited. There is no free discussion of any sort in the (military-controlled) media. Beneath the tough exterior there is demoralization and depression, and one of the highest suicide rates in the world. The authorities are not unaware of this, she added, and bend over backward to make Kwajalein more palatable with swimming pools, golf course, tennis courts, and whatnot – but none of it helps, the place remains unbearable. Of course, civilians can leave when they want, and military postings tend to be brief. The real sufferers, the helpless ones, are the Marshallese themselves, stuck on Ebeye, just three miles from Kwajalein: nearly fifteen thousand labourers on an island a mile long and two hundred yards wide, a tenth of a square mile. They come here for the jobs, she said – there are not many to be had in the Pacific – but end up stuck in conditions of unbelievable crowding, disease, and squalor. 'If you want to see hell,' my seatmate concluded, 'make a visit to Ebeye.'[7]

I had seen photographs of Ebeye – the island itself scarcely visible, with virtually every inch of it covered by tar-paper shacks – and hoped we might get a closer look as we descended; but the airline, I learned, was at some pains to keep the sight of it from passengers. Like Ebeye, the other infamous Marshallese atolls – Bikini, Eniwetak, Rongelap – many of them still uninhabitable from radio-activity, are also kept from ordinary eyes; as we got closer to them, I could not help thinking of the horror stories from the 1950s: the strange white ash that had rained down on a Japanese tuna fishing vessel, the *Lucky Dragon*, bringing acute radiation sickness to the entire crew; the 'pink snow' that had fallen on Rongelap after one blast – the children had never seen anything like it, and they played with it delightedly.[8] Whole populations had been evacuated from some of the nuclear test islands; and some of the atolls were still so polluted, forty years later, that they were said to glow eerily, like a luminous watch dial, at night.

Another passenger who had got on at Majuro – I got to

chatting with him when we were both stretching our legs at the back of the plane – was a large, genial man, an importer of canned meats with a far-flung business in Oceania. He expatiated on 'the terrific appetite' the Marshallese and Micronesians have for Spam and other canned meats, and the huge amount he was able to bring into the area. This enterprise was not unprofitable, but it was, above all, to his mind, philanthropic, a bringing of sound Western nutrition to benighted natives who, left alone, would eat taro and breadfruit and bananas and fish as they had for millennia – a thoroughly un-Western diet from which, now, they were happily being weaned. Spam, in particular, as my companion observed, had come to be a central part of the new Micronesian diet. He seemed unaware of the enormous health problems which had come along with the shift to a Western diet after the war; in some Micronesian countries, I had heard, obesity, diabetes, and hypertension – previously quite rare – now affected huge percentages of the population.[9]

Later, when I went for another stretch, I got to talking to another passenger, a stern-looking woman in her late fifties. She was a missionary who had got on the plane at Majuro with a gospel choir composed of a dozen Marshallese in flowered shirts. She spoke of the importance of bringing the word of God to the islanders; to this end she travels the length and breadth of Micronesia, preaching the gospel. She was rigid in her self-righteousness and posture, her hard, aggressive beliefs – and yet there was an energy, a tenacity, a single-mindedness, a dedication which was almost heroic. The double valence of religion, its complex and often contradictory powers and effects, especially in the collision of one culture, one spirit, with another, seemed embodied in this formidable woman and her choir.

*

The nurse, the Spam baron, the self-righteous missionary, had so occupied me that I had scarcely noticed the passage of time, the monotonous sweep of the ocean beneath us, until suddenly I felt the plane descending toward the huge, boomerang-shaped lagoon of Kwajalein. I strained to see the shantied hell of Ebeye, but we were approaching Kwajalein from the other side, its 'good' side. We made the now-familiar sickening landing, crashing and bouncing along the huge military runway; I wondered what would be done with us while the bent wheel was finally mended. Kwajalein is a military encampment, a test base, with some of the tightest security on the planet. Civilian personnel, as on Johnston, are not allowed off the plane – but they could hardly keep all sixty of us on it for the three or five hours which might be needed to replace the bent wheel and do whatever other repairs might be needed.

We were asked to line up in single file and to walk slowly, without hurrying or stopping, into a special holding shed. Military police directed us here: 'PUT YOUR THINGS DOWN,' we were told, 'STAND AGAINST THE WALL.' A slavering dog, which had lain panting on a table (it seemed to be at least a hundred degrees in the shed) was now led down by a guard, first to our luggage, which it sniffed carefully, and then to us, each of whom it sniffed in turn. Being herded in this way was deeply chilling – we had a sense of how helpless and terrified one could be in the hands of a military or totalitarian bureaucracy.

After this 'processing', which took twenty minutes, we were herded into a narrow, prisonlike pen with stone floors, wooden benches, military police, and, of course, dogs. There was one small window, high up on a wall, and by stretching and craning I could get a glimpse through it – of the manicured turf, the golf course, the country club amenities, for the military stationed here. After an hour we were led out into a small compound at the back, which at least had a view of the sea, and of the gun emplacements and memorials of the Second World War. There was a signpost here, with dozens of signs pointing in all directions, giving the distances to major cities all over the world. Right at the top was a sign saying 'Lillehammer, 9716 miles' – I saw Knut scrutinizing this with his monocular, perhaps thinking how far he was from home. And yet the sign gave a sort of comfort, by acknowledging that there was a world, another world, out there.

The plane was repaired in less than three hours, and though the crew was very tired – with the long delays in Johnston and Majuro, it was now thirteen hours since we had left Honolulu – they opted to fly on rather than spend the night here. We got on our way, and a great sense of lightness, relief, seized us as we left Kwajalein behind. Indeed there was a festive air on the plane on this last lap, everyone suddenly becoming friendly and voluble, sharing food and stories. We were united now by a heightened consciousness of being alive, being free, after our brief but frightening confinement.

Having seen the faces of all my fellow passengers on the ground, in Kwajalein, I had become aware of the varied Micronesian world represented among them: there were Pohnpeians, returning to their island; there were huge, laughing Chuukese – giants, like Polynesians – speaking a liquid tongue which, even to my ears, was quite different from Pohnpeian; there were Palauans, rather reserved, dignified, with yet another language new to my ears; there was a Marshallese diplomat, on his way to Saipan, and a family of Chamorros (in whose speech I seemed to hear echoes of Spanish), returning to their village in Guam. Back in the air, I now felt myself in a sort of linguistic aquarium, as my ears picked up different languages about me.

Hearing this mix of languages started to give me a sense of Micronesia as an immense archipelago, a nebula of islands, thousands in all, scattered across the Pacific, each as remote, as space surrounded, as stars in the sky. It was to these islands, to the vast contiguous galaxy of Polynesia, that the greatest mariners in history had been driven – by curiosity, desire, fear, starvation, religion, war, whatever – with only their uncanny knowledge of the ocean and the stars for guidance. They had migrated here more than three thousand years ago, while the Greeks were exploring the Mediterranean and Homer was telling the wanderings of Odysseus. The vastness of this other odyssey, its heroism, its wonder, perhaps its desperation, seized my imagination as we flew on endlessly over the Pacific. How many of these wanderers just perished in the vastness, I wondered, never even sighting the lands they hoped for; how many canoes were dashed to pieces by savage surf on reefs and rocky shores; how many arrived at islands which, appearing hospitable at first, proved too small to support a living culture and community, so that their habitation ended in starvation, madness, violence, death?

*

Again the Pacific, now at night, a vast lightless swell, occasionally illuminated, narrowly, by the moon. The island of Pohnpei too was in darkness, though we got a faint sense, perhaps a silhouette, of its mountains against the night sky. As we landed, and decamped from the plane, we were enveloped in a huge humid warmth and the heavy scent of frangipani. This, I think, was the first sensation for us all, the smell of a tropical night, the scents of the day eluted by the cooling air – and then, above us, incredibly clear, the great canopy of the Milky Way.

But when we awoke the next morning, we saw what had been intimated in the darkness of our arrival: that Pohnpei was not another flat coral atoll, but an island mountain, with peaks rising precipitously into the sky, their summits hidden in the clouds. The steep slopes were wreathed in thick green jungle, with streams and water-falls tracing down their sides. Below this we could see rolling hills, some cultivated, all about us, and, looking toward the coastline, a fringe of mangroves, with barrier

reefs beyond. Though I had been fascinated by the atolls
– Johnston, Majuro, even Kwajalein – this high volcanic
island, cloaked in jungle and clouds, was utterly different,
a naturalist's paradise.

I was strongly tempted to miss our plane and strand
myself in this magical place for a month or two, or
perhaps a year, the rest of my life – it was with reluctance,
and a real physical effort, that I joined the others for our
flight onward to Pingelap. As we took off, we saw the
entire island spread out beneath us. Melville's description
of Tahiti in *Omoo,* I thought, could as well have been
Pohnpei:

> From the great central peaks ... the land radiates on all
> sides to the sea in sloping green ridges. Between these are
> broad and shadowy valleys – in aspect, each a Tempe –
> watered with fine streams and thickly wooded. . . . Seen
> from the sea, the prospect is magnificent. It is one mass of
> shaded tints of green, from beach to mountain top;
> endlessly diversified with valleys, ridges, glens, and cas-
> cades. Over the ridges, here and there, the loftier peaks
> fling their shadows, and far down the valleys. At the head
> of these, the water-falls flash out into the sunlight as if
> pouring through vertical bowers of verdure. . . . It is no
> exaggeration to say, that to a European of any sensibility,
> who, for the first time, wanders back into these valleys –
> the ineffable repose and beauty of the landscape is such,
> that every object strikes him like something seen in a
> dream.

Pingelap

Pingelap is one of eight tiny atolls scattered in the ocean around Pohnpei. Once lofty volcanic islands like Pohnpei, they are geologically much older and have eroded and subsided over millions of years, leaving only rings of coral surrounding lagoons, so that the combined area of all the atolls – Ant, Pakin, Nukuoro, Oroluk, Kapingamarangi, Mwoakil, Sapwuahfik, and Pingelap – is now no more than three square miles. Though Pingelap is one of the farthest from Pohnpei, 180 miles (of often rough seas) distant, it was settled before the other atolls, a thousand years ago, and still has the largest population, about seven hundred. There is not much commerce or communication between the islands, and only a single boat plying the route between them: the MS *Microglory*, which ferries cargo and occasional passengers, making its circuit (if wind and sea permit) five or six times a year.

Since the *Microglory* was not due to leave for another month, we chartered a tiny prop plane run by the Pacific Missionary Aviation service; it was flown by a retired commercial airliner pilot from Texas who now lived in Pohnpei. We barely managed to squeeze ourselves in, along with luggage, ophthalmoscope and various testing materials, snorkelling gear, photographic and recording equipment, and special extra supplies for the achromatopes: two hundred pairs of sunglass visors, of varying darkness and hue, plus a smaller number of infant sunglasses and shades.

The plane, specially designed for the short island runways, was slow, but had a reassuring, steady drone, and we flew low enough to see shoals of tuna in the water. It was an hour before we sighted the atoll of Mwoakil, and another hour before we saw the three islets of Pingelap atoll, forming a broken crescent around the lagoon.

We flew twice around the atoll to get a closer view – a view which at first disclosed nothing but unbroken forest. It was only when we skimmed the trees, two hundred feet from the ground, that we could make out paths intersecting the forest here and there, and low houses almost hidden in the foliage.

Very suddenly, the wind rose – it had been tranquil a few minutes before – and the coconut palms and pandanus trees began lashing to and fro. As we made for the tiny concrete airstrip at one end, built by the occupying Japanese a half century before, a violent tailwind seized us near the ground, and almost blew us off the side of the runway. Our pilot struggled to control the skidding plane, for now, having just missed the edge of the landing strip, we were in danger of shooting off the end. By main force, and luck, he just managed to bring the plane around – another six inches and we would have been in the lagoon. 'You folks OK?' he asked us, and then, to himself, 'Worst landing I ever had!'

Knut and Bob were ashen, the pilot too – they had

visions of being submerged in the plane, struggling, suffo-
cating, unable to get out; I myself felt a curious indiffer-
ence, even a sense that it would be fun, romantic, to die
on the reef – and then a sudden, huge wave of nausea. But
even in our extremity, as the brakes screamed to halt us, I
seemed to hear laughter, sounds of mirth, all around us.
As we got out, still pale with shock, dozens of lithe brown
children ran out of the forest, waving flowers, banana
leaves, laughing, surrounding us. I could see no adults at
first, and thought for a moment that Pingelap was an
island of children. And in that first long moment, with the
children coming out of the forest, some with their arms
around each other, and the tropical luxuriance of vegetation in all directions – the beauty of the primitive, the
human and the natural, took hold of me. I felt a wave of
love – for the children, for the forest, for the island, for
the whole scene; I had a sense of paradise, of an almost
magical reality. I thought, I have arrived. I am here at last.
I want to spend the rest of my life here – and some of
these beautiful children could be mine.

'Beautiful!' whispered Knut, enraptured, by my side,
and then, 'Look at that child – and that one, and that . . .'
I followed his glance, and now suddenly saw what I had
first missed: here and there, among the rest, clusters of
children who squinted, screwed up their eyes against the
bright sun, and one, an older boy, with a black cloth over
his head. Knut had seen them, identified them, his achromatopic brethren, the moment he stepped out of the plane
– as they, clearly, spotted him the moment he stepped out,
squinting, dark-glassed, by the side of the plane.

Though Knut had read the scientific literature, and though he had occasionally met other achromatopic people, this had in no way prepared him for the impact of actually finding himself surrounded by his own kind, strangers half a world away with whom he had an instant kinship. It was an odd sort of encounter which the rest of us were witnessing – pale, Nordic Knut in his Western clothes, camera around his neck, and the small brown achromatopic children of Pingelap – but intensely moving.[10]

Eager hands grabbed our luggage, while our equipment was loaded onto an improvised trolley – an unstable contraption of rough-hewn planks on trembling bicycle wheels. There are no powered vehicles on Pingelap, no paved roads, only trodden-earth or gravelled paths through the woods, all connecting, directly or indirectly, with the main drag, a broader tract with houses to either side, some tin-roofed, and some thatched with leaves. It was on this main path that we were now being taken, escorted by dozens of excited children and young adults (we had seen no one, as yet, over twenty-five or thirty).

Our arrival – with sleeping bags, bottled water, medical and film equipment – was an event almost without precedent (the island children were fascinated not so much by our cameras as by the sound boom with its woolly muff, and within a day were making their own booms out of banana stalks and coconut wool). There was a lovely festive quality to this spontaneous procession, which had no order, no programme, no leader, no precedence, just a raggle-taggle of wondering, gaping people (they at us, we at them and everything around us), making our way, with many stops and diversions and detours, through the forest-village of Pingelap. Little black-and-white piglets darted across our path – unshy, but unaffectionate, unpetlike too, leading their own seemingly autonomous existence, as if the island were equally theirs. We were struck by the fact that the pigs were black and white and wondered, half seriously, if they had been specially bred for, or by, an achromatopic population.

None of us voiced this thought aloud, but our interpreter, James James, himself achromatopic – a gifted young man, who (unlike most of the islanders) had spent a considerable time off-island and been educated at the University of Guam – read our glances and said, 'Our ancestors brought these pigs when they came to Pingelap a thousand years ago, as they brought the breadfruit and yams, and the myths and rituals of our people.'

Although the pigs scampered wherever there was food (they were evidently fond of bananas and rotted mangoes and coconuts), they were all, James told us, individually owned – and, indeed, could be counted as an index of the owner's material status and prosperity. Pigs were originally a royal food, and no one but the king, the nahnmwarki, might eat them; even now they were slaughtered rarely, mostly on special ceremonial occasions.[11]

Knut was fascinated not only by the pigs but by the richness of the vegetation, which he saw quite clearly, perhaps more clearly than the rest of us. For us, as colour-normals, it was at first just a confusion of greens, whereas to Knut it was a polyphony of brightnesses, tonalities, shapes, and textures, easily identified and distinguished from each other. He mentioned this to James, who said it was the same for him, for all the achromatopes on the island – none of them had any difficulty distinguishing the plants on the island. He thought they were helped in this, perhaps, by the basically monochrome nature of the landscape: there were a few red flowers and fruits on the island, and these, it was true, they might miss in certain lighting situations – but virtually all else was green.[12]

'But what about bananas, let's say – can you distinguish the yellow from the green ones?' Bob asked.

'Not always,' James replied. ' "Pale green" may look the same to me as "yellow".'

'How can you tell when a banana is ripe, then?'

James's answer was to go to a banana tree, and to come back with a carefully selected, bright green banana for Bob.

Bob peeled it; it peeled easily, to his surprise. He took a small bite of it, gingerly; then devoured the rest.

'You see,' said James, 'we don't just go by colour. We look, we feel, we smell, we *know* – we take everything into consideration, and you just take colour!'

*

I had seen the general shape of Pingelap from the air – three islets forming a broken ring around a central lagoon perhaps a mile and a half in diameter; now, walking on a narrow strip of land, with the crashing surf to one side and the tranquil lagoon only a few hundred yards to the

other, I was reminded of the absolute awe which seized the early explorers who had first come upon these alien land forms, so utterly unlike anything in their experience. 'It is a marvel,' wrote Pyrard de Laval in 1605, 'to see each of these atolls, surrounded by a great bank of stone involving no human artifice at all.'

Cook, sailing the Pacific, was intrigued by these low atolls, and could already, in 1777, speak of the puzzlement and controversy surrounding them:

> Some will have it they are the remains of large islands, that in remote times were joined and formed one con-tinued track of land which the Sea in process of time has washed away and left only the higher grounds. . . . Others and I think . . . that they are formed from Shoals or Coral banks and of consequence increasing; and there are some who think they have been thrown up by Earth quakes.

But by the beginning of the nineteenth century it had become clear that while coral atolls might emerge in the deepest parts of the ocean, the living coral itself could not

grow more than a hundred feet or so below the surface and had to have a firm foundation at this depth. Thus it was not imaginable, as Cook conceived, that sediments or corals could build up from the ocean floor.

Sir Charles Lyell, the supreme geologist of his age, postulated that atolls were the coral-encrusted rims of rising submarine volcanoes, but this seemed to require an almost impossible serendipity of innumerable volcanoes thrusting up to within fifty or eighty feet of the surface to provide a platform for the coral, without ever actually breaking the surface.

Darwin, on the Chilean coast, had experienced at first hand the huge cataclysms of earthquakes and volcanoes; these, for him, were 'parts of one of the greatest phenomena to which this world is subject' – notably, the instability, the continuous movements, the geological oscillations of the earth's crust. Images of vast risings and sinkings seized his imagination: the Andes rising thousands of feet into the air, the Pacific floor sinking thousands of feet beneath the surface. And in the context of this general vision, a specific vision came to him – that such risings and fallings could explain the origin of oceanic islands, and their subsidence to allow the formation of coral atolls. Reversing, in a way, the Lyellian notion, he postulated that coral grew not on the summits of rising volcanoes, but on their submerging slopes; then, as the volcanic rock eventually eroded and subsided into the sea, only the coral fringes remained, forming a barrier reef. As the volcano continued to subside, new layers of coral polyps could continue to build upward, now in the characteristic atoll shape, toward the light and warmth they depended on. The development of such an atoll would require, he reckoned, at least a million years.

Darwin cited short-term evidence of this subsidence – palm trees and buildings, for instance, formerly on dry land, which were now under water; but he realized that conclusive proof for so slow a geologic process would be far from easy to obtain. Indeed, his theory (though accepted by many) was not confirmed until a century later, when an immense borehole was drilled through the coral of Eniwetak atoll, finally hitting volcanic rock 4,500 feet below the surface.[13] The reef-constructing corals, for Darwin, were

> wonderful memorials of the subterranean oscillations of level . . . each atoll a monument over an island now lost. We may thus, like unto a geologist who had lived his ten thousand years and kept a record of the passing changes, gain some insight into the great system by which the surface of this globe has been broken up, and land and water interchanged.

PINGELAP

Looking at Pingelap, thinking of the lofty volcano it once was, sinking infinitesimally slowly for tens of millions of years, I felt an almost tangible sense of the vastness of time, and that our expedition to the South Seas was not only a journey in space, but a journey in time as well.

*

The sudden wind which had almost blown us off the landing strip was dying down now, although the tops of the palms were still whipping to and fro, and we could still hear the thunder of the surf, pounding the reef in huge rolling breakers. The typhoons which are notorious in this part of the Pacific can be especially devastating to a coral atoll like Pingelap (which is nowhere more than ten feet above sea level) – for the entire island can be inundated, submerged by the huge wind-lashed seas. Typhoon Lengkieki, which swept over Pingelap around 1775, killed ninety per cent of the island's population outright, and most of the survivors went on to die a lingering death from starvation – for all the vegetation, even the coconut palms and breadfruit and banana trees, was destroyed, leaving nothing to sustain the islanders but fish.[14]

At the time of the typhoon, Pingelap had a population of nearly a thousand, and had been settled for eight hundred years. It is not known where the original settlers came from, but they brought with them an elaborate hierarchical system ruled by hereditary kings or nahnmwarkis, an oral culture and mythology, and a language which had already differentiated so much by this time that it was hardly intelligible to the 'mainlanders' on Pohnpei.[15] This thriving culture was reduced, within a few weeks of the typhoon, to twenty or so survivors, including the nahnmwarki and other members of the royal household.

The Pingelapese are extremely fertile, and within a few decades the population was reapproaching a hundred. But with this heroic breeding – and, of necessity, inbreeding – new problems arose, genetic traits previously rare began to spread, so that in the fourth generation after the typhoon a 'new' disease showed itself. The first children with the Pingelap eye disease were born in the 1820s, and within a few generations their numbers had increased to more than five per cent of the population, roughly what it remains today.

The mutation for achromatopsia may have arisen among the Carolinians centuries before; but this was a recessive gene, and as long as there was a large enough population the chances of two carriers marrying, and of the condition becoming manifest in their children, were very small. All this altered with the typhoon, and genealogical studies indicate that it was the surviving nahnmwarki himself who was the ultimate progenitor of every subsequent carrier.

Infants with the eye disease appeared normal at birth, but when two or three months old would start to squint or blink, to screw up their eyes or turn their heads away in the face of bright light; and when they were toddlers it became apparent that they could not see fine detail or small objects at a distance. By the time they reached four or five, it was clear they could not distinguish colours. The term *maskun* ('not-see') was coined to describe this strange condition, which occurred with equal frequency in both male and female children, children otherwise normal, bright, and active in all ways.

Today, over two hundred years after the typhoon, a third of the population are carriers of the gene for maskun, and out of some seven hundred islanders, fifty-seven are achromats. Elsewhere in the world, the incidence of achromatopsia is less than 1 in 30,000 – here on Pingelap it is 1 in 12.

*

Our ragged procession, tipping and swaying through the forest, with children romping and pigs under our feet, finally arrived at the island's administration building, one of the three or four two-storey cinder-block buildings on the island. Here we met and were ceremoniously greeted by the nahnmwarki, the magistrate, and other officials. A Pingelapese woman, Deleta, acted as interpreter, introducing us all, and then herself – she ran the medical dispensary across the way, where she treated all sorts of injuries and illnesses. A few days earlier, she said, she had delivered a breech baby – a difficult job with no medical equipment to speak of – but both mother and child were doing fine. There is no doctor on Pingelap, but Deleta had been educated off-island and was often assisted by trainees from Pohnpei. Any medical problems which she cannot handle have to wait for the visiting nurse from Pohnpei, who makes her rounds to all the outlying islands once a month. But Deleta, Bob observed, though kind and gentle, was clearly a 'real force to be reckoned with'.

She took us on a brief tour of the administration building – many of the rooms were deserted and empty, and the old kerosene generator designed to light it looked as if it had been out of action for years.[16] As dusk fell, Deleta led the way to the magistrate's house, where we would be quartered. There were no street lights, no lights anywhere, and the darkness seemed to gather and fall very rapidly. Inside the house, made of concrete blocks, it was dark and small and stiflingly hot, a sweatbox, even after nightfall. But it had a charming outdoor terrace, over which arched a gigantic breadfruit tree and a banana tree. There were two bedrooms – Knut took the magistrate's room below, Bob and I the children's room above. We gazed at each other fearfully – both insomniacs, both heat intolerant, both restless night readers – and wondered how we would survive the long nights, unable even to distract ourselves by reading.

I tossed and turned all night, kept awake in part by the heat and humidity; in part by a strange visual excitement such as I am sometimes prone to, especially at the start of a migraine – endlessly moving vistas of breadfruit trees and bananas on the darkened ceiling; and, not least, by a sense of intoxication and delight that now, finally, I had arrived on the island of the colour-blind.

None of us slept well that night. We gathered, tousled, on the terrace at dawn, and decided to reconnoitre a bit. I took my notebook and made brief notes as we walked (though the ink tended to smudge in the wet air):

Six o'clock in the morning, and though the air is blood-hot, sapping, doldrum-still, the island is already alive with activity – pigs squealing, scampering through the under-growth; smells of fish and taro cooking; repairing the roofs of houses with palm fronds and banana leaves as Pingelap prepares itself for a new day. Three men are working on a canoe – a lovely traditional shape, sawn and shaved from a single massive tree trunk, using materials and methods which have not changed in a thousand or more years. Bob and Knut are fascinated by the boat building, and watch it closely, contentedly. Knut's attention is also drawn to the other side of the road, to the graves and altars beside some of the houses. There is no communal burial, no graveyard, in Pingelap, only this cosy burying of the dead next to their houses, so that they still remain, almost palpably, part of the family. There are strings, like clothes lines, hung around the graves, upon which gaily coloured and patterned pieces of cloth have been hung – perhaps to keep demons away, perhaps just for decoration; I am not sure, but they seem festive in spirit.

My own attention is riveted by the enormous density of vegetation all around us, so much denser than any temper-ate forest, and a brilliant yellow lichen on some of the trees. I nibble at it – many lichens are edible – but it is bitter and unpromising.

Everywhere we saw breadfruit trees – sometimes whole groves of them, with their large, deeply lobed leaves; they were heavy with the giant fruits which Dampier, three hundred years ago, had likened to loaves of bread.[17] I had never seen trees so generous of themselves – they were very easy to grow, James had said, and each tree might yield a hundred massive fruits a year, more than enough to sustain a man. A single tree would bear fruit for fifty years or more, and then its fine wood could be used for lumber, especially for building the hulls of canoes.

Down by the reef, dozens of children were already swimming, some of them toddlers, barely able to walk, but plunging fearlessly into the water, among the sharp corals, shouting with excitement. I saw two or three achromatopic kids diving and romping and yelling with the rest – they did not seem isolated or set apart, at least at this stage of their lives, and since it was still very early, and the sky was overcast, they were not blinded as they would be later in the day. Some of the larger children had tied the rubber soles of old sandals to their hands, and had developed a remarkably swift dog paddle using these. Others dived to the bottom, which was thick with huge, tumid, sea cucumbers, and used these to squeeze jets of water at each other . . . I am fond of holothurians, and I hoped they would survive.

I waded into the water, and started diving for sea cucumbers myself. At one time, I had read, there had been a brisk trade exporting sea cucumbers to Malaya, China, and Japan, where they are highly esteemed as trepang or bêche-de-mer or namako. I myself love a good sea cucumber on occasion – they have a tough gelatinousness, an animal cellulose in their tissues, which I find most appealing. Carrying one back to the beach, I asked James whether the Pingelapese ate them much. 'We eat them,' he said, 'but they are tough and need a lot of cooking –

though this one,' he pointed to the *Stichopus* I had dredged up, 'you can eat raw.' I sank my teeth into it, wondering if he was joking; I found it impossible to get through the leathery integument – it was like trying to eat an old, weathered shoe.[18]

*

After breakfast, we visited a local family, the Edwards. Entis Edward is achromatopic, as are all three of his children, from a babe in arms, who was squinting in the bright sunlight, to a girl of eleven. His wife, Emma, has normal vision, though she evidently is a carrier of the gene. Entis is well educated, with little command of English but a natural eloquence; he is a minister in the Congregationalist Church and a fisherman, a man well respected in the community. But this, his wife told us, was far from the rule. Most of those born with the maskun never learn to read, because they cannot see the teacher's writing on the board; they have less chance of marrying – partly because it is recognized that their children are likelier to be affected, partly because they cannot work outdoors in the bright sunlight, as most of the islanders do.[19] Entis was an exception here, on every count, and very conscious of it: 'I have been lucky,' he said. 'It is not easy for the others.'

Apart from the social problems it causes, Entis does not feel his colour-blindness a disability, though he is often disabled by his intolerance of bright light and his inability to see fine detail. Knut nodded as he heard this; he had been deeply attentive to everything Entis said, and identified with him in many ways. He took out his monocular to show Entis – the monocular which is almost like a third eye for him, and always hangs round his neck. Entis's face lit up with delight as, adjusting the focus, he could see, for the first time, boats bobbing on the water, trees on the horizon, the faces of people on the other side of the road, and, focusing right down, the details of the skin whorls on his own fingertips. Impulsively, Knut removed the monocular from around his neck, and presented it to Entis. Entis, clearly moved, said nothing, but his wife went into the house and came out bearing a beautiful necklace she had made, a triple chain of matched cowrie shells, the most precious thing the family had, and this she solemnly presented to Knut, while Entis looked on.

Knut himself was now disabled, without his monocular – 'It is like giving half my eye to him, because it is necessary to my vision' – but deeply happy. 'It will make all the difference to him,' he said. 'I'll get another one later.'

*

The following day we saw James, squinting against the sunlight, watching a group of teenagers playing basketball. As our interpreter and guide, he had seemed cheerful, sociable, knowledgeable, very much part of the community – but now, for the first time, he seemed quiet, wistful, and rather solitary and sad. We got to talking, and more of his story emerged. Life and school had been difficult for him, as for the other achromatopes on Pingelap – unshielded sunlight was literally blinding for him, and he could hardly go out into it without a dark cloth over his eyes. He could not join the rough-and-tumble, the open-air games the other children enjoyed. His acuity was very poor, and he could not see any of the schoolbooks unless he held them three inches from his eyes. None the less he was exceptionally intelligent and resourceful, and he learned to read early, and loved reading, despite this handicap. Like Deleta, he had gone to Pohnpei for further schooling (Pingelap itself has a small elementary school, but no secondary education). Clever, ambitious, aspiring to a larger life, James went on to get a scholarship to the University of Guam, spent five years there, and got a degree in sociology. He had returned to Pingelap full of brave ideas: to help the islanders market their wares more efficiently, to obtain better medical services and child care, to bring electricity and running water into every house, to improve standards of education, to bring a new political consciousness and pride to the island, and to make sure that every islander – the achromatopes especially – would get as a birthright the literacy and education he had had to struggle so hard to achieve.

None of this had panned out – he encountered an enormous inertia and resistance to change, a lack of ambition, a laissez-faire, and gradually he himself had ceased to strive. He could find no job on Pingelap appropriate to his education or talents, because Pingelap, with its subsistence economy, *has* no jobs, apart from those of the health worker, the magistrate, and a couple of teachers. And now, with his university accent, his new manners and outlook, James no longer completely belonged to the small world he had left, and found himself set apart, an outsider.

*

We had seen a beautifully patterned mat outside the Edwards' house, and now noticed similar ones everywhere, in front of the traditional thatched houses, and equally the newer ones, made of concrete blocks with corrugated aluminium roofs. The weaving of these mats was a craft unchanged from 'the time before time', James told us; the traditional fibres, made from palm fronds, were still used (although the traditional vegetable dyes had been replaced by an inky blue obtained from surplus carbon paper, for which the islanders otherwise had little need). The island's finest weaver was a colour-blind woman, who had learned the craft from her mother, who was also colour-blind. James took us to meet her; she was doing her intricate work inside a hut so dark we could hardly see anything after the bright sunlight. (Knut, on the other hand, took off his double sunglasses and said it was, visually, the most comfortable place he had yet encountered on the island.) As we adapted to the darkness, we began to see her special art of brightnesses, delicate patterns of differing luminances, patterns that all but disappeared as soon as we took one of her mats into the sunlight outside.

Recently, Knut told her, his sister Britt, to prove it could be done, had knitted a jacket in sixteen different colours. She had devised her own system for keeping track of the skeins of wool, by labelling them with numbers. The jacket had marvellous intricate patterns and images drawn from Norwegian folktales, he said, but since they were done in dim browns and purples, colours without much chromatic contrast, they were almost invisible to normal eyes. Britt, however, responding to luminances only, could see them quite clearly, perhaps even more clearly than colour normals. 'It is my special, secret art,' she says. 'You have to be totally colour-blind to see it.'

*

Later in the day, we went to the island's dispensary to meet more people with the maskun – almost forty people were there, more than half the achromatopes on the island. We set up in the main room – Bob with his ophthalmo-scope, his lenses and acuity tests, and I with a mass of coloured yarns and drawings and pens, as well as the standard colour-testing kits. Knut had brought along a set of Sloan achromatopsia cards. I had never seen these before, and Knut explained the test to me: 'Each of these cards has a range of grey squares which vary only in tone, progressing from a very light grey to a very dark grey, almost black, really. Each square has a hole cut out in the centre, and if I place a sheet of coloured paper behind these – like this – one of the squares will be a match for the colour; they will have an equal density.' He pointed to an orange dot, surrounded by a medium grey background. 'For me the internal dot and the surround here are exactly the same.'

Such a match would be completely meaningless for a colour normal, for whom no colour can ever 'match' a grey, and extremely difficult for most – but quite easy and natural for an achromatope, who sees all colours, and all greys, only as differing luminances. Ideally, the test should be administered with a standard source of illumination, but since there was no electricity to run lights on the island, Knut had to use himself as a standard, comparing each achromatope's responses to his own. In nearly every case, these were the same, or very close.

Medical testing is usually rather private, but here it was very public, and with dozens of youngsters peering in through the windows, or wandering among us as we tested, took on a communal and humorous and almost festive quality.

Bob wanted to check refraction in each person, and to examine their retinas closely – by no means easy, when the eyes are continually jerking with nystagmus. It was not possible, of course, to see the microscopic rods and cones (or lack thereof) directly, but he could find nothing else amiss on inspection with his ophthalmoscope. It had been suggested by some earlier researchers that the maskun was linked with severe myopia; but Bob found that although many of the achromatopes were near-sighted, many were not (Knut himself is rather far-sighted) – and he also found that a similar proportion of the island's colour-normals were near-sighted as well. If there were a genetic form of myopia here, Bob felt, it was transmitted independently of the achromatopsia.[20] It was possible as well, he added, that reports of near-sightedness had been exaggerated by earlier researchers who had observed so many of the islanders squinting and bringing small objects closer to view – behaviours which might appear to indicate myopia but actually reflected the intolerance of bright light and poor acuity of the achromatopes.

I asked the achromatopes if they could judge the colours of various yarns, or at least match them one with another. The matching was clearly done on the basis of brightness and not colour – thus yellow and pale blue might be grouped with white, or saturated reds and greens with black. I had also brought the Ishihara pseudoisochromatic test plates for ordinary partial colour-blindness, which have numbers and figures formed by coloured dots, distinguishable only by colour (and not luminosity) from the dots surrounding them. Some of the Ishihara plates, paradoxically, cannot be seen by colour normals, but only by achromatopes – these have dots which are identical in hue, but vary slightly in luminance. The older children with the maskun were particularly excited by these – it turned the tables on me, the tester – and they jostled to take their turns pointing out the special numbers that I could not see.

Knut's presence while we were examining those with maskun, his sharing of his own experiences, was crucial, for it helped remove our questions from the sphere of the inquisitive, the impersonal, and bring us all together as fellow creatures, making it easier for us, finally, to clarify and reassure. For although the lack of colour vision in itself did not seem to be a subject of concern, there were many misapprehensions about the maskun – in particular, fears that the disease might be progressive, might lead to complete blindness, might go along with retardation, madness, epilepsy, or heart trouble. Some believed that it could be caused by carelessness during pregnancy, or transmitted through a sort of contagion. Though there was some sense of the fact that the maskun tended to run in certain families, there was little or no knowledge about recessive genes and heredity. Bob and I did our best to stress that the maskun was non-progressive, affected only certain aspects of vision, and that with a few simple optical aids – dark sunglasses or visors to reduce bright light, and magnifying glasses and monoculars to allow reading and sharp distance vision – someone with the maskun could go through school, live, travel, work, in much the same way as anyone else. But more than words could, Knut himself brought this home, partly by using his own sunglasses and magnifier, partly by the manifest achievement and freedom of his own life.

Outside the dispensary, we began to give out the wraparound sunglasses we had brought, along with hats and visors, with varying results. One mother, with an achromatopic infant squalling and blinking in her arms, took a pair of tiny sunglasses and put them on the baby's nose, which seemed to calm him, and led to an immediate change in his behaviour. No longer blinking and squinting, he opened his eyes wide and began to gaze around with a lively curiosity. One old woman, the oldest achromatope on the island, indignantly refused to try any sunglasses on. She had lived eighty years as she was, she said, and was not about to start wearing sunglasses now. But many of the other achromatopic adults and teenagers evidently liked the sunglasses, wrinkling their noses at the unaccustomed weight of them, but manifestly less disabled by the bright light.

*

It is said that Wittgenstein was either the easiest or the most difficult of house-guests to accommodate, because though he would eat, with gusto, whatever was served to him on his arrival, he would then want exactly the same for every subsequent meal for the rest of his stay. This is seen as extraordinary, even pathological, by many people – but since I myself am similarly disposed, I see it as perfectly normal. Indeed, having a sort of passion for monotony, I greatly enjoyed the unvarying meals on Pingelap, whereas Knut and Bob longed for variety. Our first meal, the model which was to be repeated three times daily, consisted of taro, bananas, pandanus, breadfruit, yams, and tuna followed by papaya and young coconuts full of milk. Since I am a fish and banana person anyhow, these meals were wholly to my taste.

But we were all revolted by the Spam which appeared with each meal – invariably fried; why, I wondered, should the Pingelapese eat this filthy stuff when their own basic diet was both healthy and delicious? Especially when they could hardly afford it, because Pingelap has only the small amount of money it can raise from the export of copra, mats, and pandanus fruits to Pohnpei. I had talked with the unctuous Spam baron on the plane; and now, on Pingelap, I could see the addiction in full force. How was it that not only the Pingelapese, but all the peoples of the

Pacific, seemingly, could fall so helplessly, so voraciously, on this stuff, despite its intolerable cost to their budgets and their health? I was not the first to puzzle about this; later, when I came to read Paul Theroux's book *The Happy Isles of Oceania*, I found his hypothesis about this universal Spam mania:

> It was a theory of mine that former cannibals of Oceania now feasted on Spam because Spam came the nearest to approximating the porky taste of human flesh. 'Long pig' as they called a cooked human being in much of Melanesia. It was a fact that the people-eaters of the Pacific had all evolved, or perhaps degenerated, into Spam-eaters. And in the absence of Spam they settled for corned beef, which also had a corpsy flavour.

So far as I knew, though, there was no tradition of cannibalism in Pingelap.[21]

*

Whether or not Spam is, as Theroux suggests, a sublimate of cannibalism, it was a relief to visit the taro patch, the ultimate source of food, which covers ten swampy acres in the centre of the island. The Pingelapese speak of taro with reverence and affection, and sooner or later everyone takes a turn at working in the communally owned patch. The ground is carefully cleaned of debris, and turned over by hand, and the soil is then planted with shoots about eighteen inches long. The plants grow with extraordinary speed, soon reaching ten feet or more in height, with broad triangular leaves arching overhead. The upkeep of the patch devolves traditionally on the women, working barefoot in the ankle-high mud, and different parts of the patch are tended and harvested by them each day. The deep shade cast by the huge leaves makes it a favourite meeting place, particularly for those with the maskun.

A dozen or more varieties of taro are grown in the patch, and their large, starchy roots range in taste from bitter to sweet. The roots can be eaten fresh, or dried and stored for later use. Taro is the ultimate crop for Pingelap, and there is still a vivid communal memory of how, during typhoon Lengkieki two centuries ago, the taro patch was inundated with salt water and totally destroyed – and that it was this which brought the remaining islanders to starvation.

Coming back from the taro patch, we were approached by an old man in the woods, who came up to us diffidently, but determinedly, and asked if he could get Bob's advice, as he was going blind. He had clouded eyes, and Bob, examining him later at the dispensary with his ophthalmoscope, confirmed that he had cataracts, but could find nothing else amiss. Surgery could probably help him, he told the old man, and this could be done in the hospital on Pohnpei, with every chance of restoring good vision. The old man gave us a big smile and hugged Bob. When Bob asked Deleta, who coordinates with the visiting nurse from Pohnpei, to put the man's name down for cataract surgery, she commented that it was a good thing he had approached us. If he had not, she said, he would have been allowed to go completely blind. Medical services in Pingelap are spread very thin, already overstretched by more pressing conditions. Cataracts (like achromatopsia) are a very low priority concern here; and cataract surgery, with the added costs of transport to Pohnpei, is generally considered too expensive to do. So the old man would get treatment, but he would be the exception to the rule.

*

I counted five churches on Pingelap, all Congregationalist. I had not seen so great a density of churches since being in the little Mennonite community of La Crete in Alberta; here, as there, churchgoing is universal. And when there is not churchgoing, there is hymn singing and Sunday school.

The spiritual invasion of the island began in earnest in the mid-nineteenth century, and by 1880, the entire population had been converted. But even now, more than five generations later, though Christianity is incorporated into the culture, and fervently embraced in a sense, there is still a reverence and nostalgia for the old ways, rooted in the soil and vegetation, the history and geography, of the island. Wandering through the dense forest at one point, we heard voices singing – voices so high and unexpected and unearthly and pure that I again had a sense of Pingelap as a place of enchantment, another world, an island of spirits. Making our way through the thick undergrowth, we reached a little clearing, where a dozen children stood with their teacher, singing hymns in the morning sun. Or were they singing *to* the morning sun? The words were Christian, but the setting, the feeling, were mythical and pagan. We kept hearing snatches of song as we walked about the island, usually without seeing the singer or singers – choirs, voices, incorporeal, on the air. They seemed innocent at first, almost angelic, but then to take on an ambiguous, mocking note. If I had thought first of Ariel, I thought now of Caliban; and whenever voices, hallucination-like, filled the air, Pingelap, for me, took on the quality of Prospero's isle:

> Be not afeard: the isle is full of noises
> Sounds and sweet airs, that give delight, and hurt not.

When Jane Hurd, an anthropologist, spent a year on Pingelap in 1968 and '69, the old nahnmwarki was still able to give her, in the form of an extended epic poem, an entire oral history of the island – but with his death a good deal of this knowledge and memory died.[22] The present nahnmwarki can give the flavour of old Pingelapese belief and myth, but no longer has the detailed knowledge his grandfather had. None the less, he himself, as a teacher at the school, does his best to give the children a sense of their heritage and of the pre-Christian culture which once flourished on the island. He spoke nostalgically, it seemed to us, of the old days on Pingelap, when everyone knew who they were, where they came from, and how the island came into being. At one time, the myth went, the three islets of Pingelap formed a single piece of land, with its own god, Isopaw. When an alien god came from a distant island and split Pingelap into two, Isopaw chased him away – and the third islet was created from a handful of sand dropped in the chase.

We were struck by the multiple systems of belief, some

seemingly contradictory, which co-exist among the Pinge-lapese. A mythical history of the island is maintained alongside its secular history; thus the maskun is seen simultaneously in mystical terms (as a curse visited upon the sinful or disobedient) and in purely biological terms (as a morally neutral, genetic condition transmitted from generation to generation). Traditionally, it was traced back to the Nahnmwarki Okonomwaun, who ruled from 1822 to 1870, and his wife, Dokas. Of their six children, two were achromatopic. The myth explaining this was recorded by Irene Maumenee Hussels and Newton Morton, geneticists from the University of Hawaii who visited Pingelap (and worked with Hurd) in the late 1960s:

> The god Isoahpahu became enamoured of Dokas and instructed Okonomwaun to appropriate her. From time to time, Isoahpahu appeared in the guise of Okonomwaun and had intercourse with Dokas, fathering the affected children, while the normal children came from Okonom-waun. Isoahpahu loved other Pingelapese women and had affected children by them. The 'proof' of this is that persons with achromatopsia shun the light but have rela-tively good night vision, like their ghostly ancestor.

There were other indigenous myths about the maskun: that it might arise if a pregnant woman walked upon the beach in the middle of the day – the blazing sun, it was felt, might partly blind the unborn child in the womb. Yet another legend had it that it came from a descendant of the Nahnmwarki Mwahuele, who had survived typhoon Lengkieki. This descendant, Inek, was trained as a Christian minister by a missionary, Mr Doane, and was assigned to Chuuk, as Hussels and Morton write, but refused to move because of his large family on Pingelap. Mr Doane, 'angered by this lack of evangelical zeal', cursed Inek and his children with the maskun.

There were also persistent notions, as always with disease, that the maskun had come from the outside world. The nahnmwarki spoke, in this vein, of how a number of Pingelapese had been forced to labour in the German phosphate mines on the distant island of Nauru, and then, on their return, had fathered children with maskun. The myth of contamination, ascribed (like so many other ills) to the coming of the white man, took on a new form with our visit. This was the first time the Pingelapese had ever seen another achromatope, an achromatope from outside, and this 'confirmed' their brooding suspicions. Two days after our arrival, a revised myth had already taken root in the Pingelapese lore: it must have been achromatopic white whalers from the far north, they now realized, who had landed on Pingelap early in the last century – raping and rampaging among the island women, fathering dozens of achromatopic children, and bringing their white man's curse to the island. The Pingelapese with maskun, by this reckoning, were partly Norwegian – descendants of people like Knut. Knut was awed by the rapidity with which this not entirely jocular, fantastic myth emerged, and by finding himself, or his people, 'revealed' as the ultimate origin of the maskun.

*

On our last evening in Pingelap, a huge crimson sunset shot with purples and yellows and a touch of green hung over the ocean and filled half the sky. Even Knut exclaimed 'Unbelievable!' and said he had never seen such a sunset before. As we came down to the shore, we saw dozens of people almost submerged in the water – only their heads were visible above the reef. This happened every evening, James had told us – it was the only way to cool off. Looking around, we saw others lying, sitting, standing and chatting in small clusters – it looked as if most of the island's population was here. The cooling hour, the social hour, the hour of immersion, had begun.

As it got darker, Knut and the achromatopic islanders moved more easily. It is common knowledge among the Pingelapese that those with the maskun manage better at scotopic times – dusk and dawn, and moonlit nights – and for this reason, they are often employed as night fishers. And in this the achromatopes are preeminent; they seem able to see the fish in their dim course underwater, the glint of moonlight on their outstretched fins as they leap – as well as, or perhaps better than, anyone else.

Our last night was an ideal one for the night fishers. I had hoped we might go in one of the enormous hollow-log canoes with outriggers, which we had seen earlier, but we were led instead toward a boat with a small outboard motor. The air was still very warm and still, so it was sweet to feel a slight breeze as we moved out. As we glided into deeper waters, the shoreline of Pingelap vanished from sight, and we moved on a vast lightless swell with only the stars and the great arc of the Milky Way overhead.

Our helmsman knew all the major stars and constellations, seemed completely at home with the heavens – Knut, indeed, was the only one equally knowledgeable, and the two of them exchanged their knowledge in whispers: Knut with all modern astronomy at his fingertips, the helmsman with an ancient practical knowledge such as had enabled the Micronesians and Polynesians, a thousand years ago, to sail across the immensities of the Pacific, by celestial navigation alone, in voyages comparable to interplanetary travel, until, at last, they discovered islands, homes, as rare and far apart as planets in the cosmos.

About eight o'clock the moon rose, almost full, and so brilliant that it seemed to eclipse the stars. We heard the splash of flying fish as they arced out of the water, dozens at a time, and the plopping sound as they plummeted back to the surface.

The waters of the Pacific are full of a tiny protozoan, *Noctiluca*, a bioluminescent creature able to generate light, like a firefly. It was Knut who first noticed their phosphorescence in the water – a phosphorescence most evident when the water was disturbed. Sometimes when the flying fish leapt out of the water, they would leave a luminous disturbance, a glowing wake, as they did so – and another splash of light as they landed.[23]

Night fishing used to be done with a flaming torch; now it is done with the help of a flashlight, the light serving to dazzle as well as spot the fish. As the beautiful creatures were illuminated in a blinding flashlight beam, I was reminded how, as a child, I would see German planes transfixed by roving searchlights as they flew in the darkened skies over London. One by one we pursued the fish; we followed their careerings relentlessly, this way and that, until we could draw close enough for the fisher to shoot out the great hoop of his net, and catch them as they returned to the water. They accumulated in the bottom of the boat, silvery, squirming, until they were hit on the head (though one, actually, in its frenzy, managed to leap out of the boat, and we so admired this that we did not try to catch it again).

After an hour we had enough, and it was time to go after deeper-water fish. There were two teenage boys with us, one achromatopic, and they now donned scuba gear and masks and, clutching spears and flashlights, went over the side of the boat. We could see them, two hundred yards or more from the boat, like luminous fish, the phosphorescent waters outlining their bodies as they moved. After ten minutes they returned, loaded with the fish they had speared, and climbed back into the boat, their wet scuba gear gleaming blackly in the moonlight.

The long, slow trip back was very peaceful – we lay back in the boat; the fishers murmured softly among themselves. We had enough, more than enough, fish for all. Fires would be lit on the long sandy beach, and we would have a grand, final feast on Pingelap before flying back to Pohnpei the next morning. We reached the shore and waded back onto the beach, pulling the boat up behind us. The sand itself, broader with the tide's retreat, was still wet with the phosphorescent sea, and now, as we walked upon it, our footsteps left a luminous spoor.

Pohnpei

In the 1830s, when Darwin was sailing on the *Beagle*, exploring the Galapagos and Tahiti, and the youthful Melville was dreaming of South Seas travels to come, James O'Connell, a sailor from Ireland, was marooned on the high volcanic island of Pohnpei. The circumstances of his arrival are unclear – he claimed, in his memoirs, to have been shipwrecked in the *John Bull* near Pleasant Island, eight hundred miles away; and then, improbably, to have sailed from Pleasant Island in an open boat to Pohnpei in a mere four days. Once he arrived, O'Connell wrote, he and his companions were seized by 'cannibals', and narrowly escaped being eaten for dinner (so they thought) by diverting the natives with a rousing Irish jig. His adventures continued: he was submitted to a tattooing ritual by a young Pohnpeian girl who turned out to be the daughter of a chief; he then married the daughter, and became a chief himself.[24]

Whatever his exaggerations (sailors tend to tall tales, and some scholars regard him as a mythomaniac), O'Connell had another side, as a curious and careful observer. He was the first European to call Pohnpei, or Ponape, by its native name (in his orthography, 'Bonabee'); the first to give accurate descriptions of many Pohnpeian customs and rites; the first to provide a glossary of the Pohnpeian language; and the first to see the ruins of Nan Madol, the remnant of a monumental culture going back more than a thousand years, to the mythological *keilahn aio*, 'the other side of yesterday'.

His exploration of Nan Madol formed the climax and the consummation of his Pohnpeian adventure; he described the 'stupendous ruins' in meticulous detail – their uncanny desertion, their investment with taboo. Their size, their muteness, frightened him, and at one point, overwhelmed by their alienness, he suddenly 'longed for home'. He did not refer to, and probably did not know of, the other megalithic cultures which dot Micronesia – the giant basalt ruins in Kosrae, the immense taga stones in Tinian, the ancient terraces in Palau, the five-ton stones of Babeldaop bearing Easter Island-like faces. But he realized what neither Cook nor Bougainville nor any of the great explorers had – that these primitive oceanic islands, with their apparently simple, palm-tree cultures, were once the seat of monumental civilizations.

*

We set out for Nan Madol on our first full day in Pohnpei. Located off the far side of Pohnpei, it was easiest to approach by boat. Not sure exactly what we would encounter, we took gear of every kind – storm gear, scuba gear, sun gear. Moving slowly – we had an open boat with a powerful outboard – we left the harbour at Kolonia and passed the mangrove swamps which fringe the main island; I could pick out their aerial roots with my binoculars, and Robin, our boatman, told us about the mangrove crabs which scuttle among them and are considered a delicacy on the island. As we moved into open water, we picked up speed, our boat throwing a huge foaming wake behind it, a great scythe of water which glittered in the sun. A sense of exhilaration seized us as we sped along, almost on the surface, like a giant water ski. Bob, who has a catamaran and a windsurfer, was excited by seeing canoes with brilliantly coloured sails here and there, tacking sharply in the wind, but absolutely stable with their outriggers. 'You could cross an ocean,' he said, 'with a proa like that.'

Rather suddenly, about half an hour out, the weather changed. We saw a grey funnel of cloud barrelling rapidly toward us – another few seconds, and we were in the thick of it, being tossed to and fro. (Bob, with great self-possession, managed to get a superb photo of the cloud before it hit us.) Our visibility down to a few yards, we bncould no longer get our bearings. Then, just as abruptly, we were out of the cloud and wind, but in the midst of torrential and absolutely vertical rain – at this point, absurdly, we unfurled the bright red umbrellas our hotel had provided, no longer heroes in the eye of the storm, but parasoled picnickers in a Seurat painting. Though the rain still poured down, the sun came out once again, and a spectacular rainbow appeared between sky and sea. Knut saw this as a luminous arc in the sky, and started to tell us of other rainbows he had seen: double rainbows, inverted rainbows, and, once, a complete rainbow circle.

Stephen Wiltshire

Listening to him now, as so often before, we had the sense that his vision, his visual world, if impoverished in some ways, was in others quite as rich as our own.

There is nothing on the planet quite like Nan Madol, this ancient deserted megalithic construct of nearly a hundred artificial islands, connected by innumerable canals. As we approached – going very slowly now, because the water was shallow, and the waterways narrow – we started to see the details of the walls, huge hexagonal columns of black basalt, so finely interlocking and adjusted to each other as to have largely survived the storms and seas, the depredations of many centuries. We glided silently between the islets, and finally landed on the fortress island of Nan Douwas, which still has its immense basalt walls, twenty-five feet in height, its great central burial vault, and its nooks and places for meditation and prayer.

Stiff from the boat, eager to explore, we scrambled out and stood beneath the giant wall, marvelling how the great prismatic blocks – some, surely, weighing many tons – had been quarried and brought from Sokehs on the other side of Pohnpei (the only place on the island where such columnar basalt is naturally extruded) and levered so precisely into place. The sense of might, of solemnity, was very strong – we felt puny, overwhelmed, standing next to the silent wall. But we had a sense too of the folly, the megalomania, which goes with the monumental – the 'wilde enormities of ancient magnanimity' – and all its attendant cruelties and sufferings; our boatman, Robin, had told us about the vicious overlords, the Saudeleurs, who had conquered Pohnpei and reigned in Nan Madol for many centuries, exacting an ever more murderous tribute of food and labour. When one looked at the walls with this knowledge, they took on a different aspect, and seemed to sweat with the blood and pain of generations. And yet, like the Pyramids or the Colosseum, they were noble as well.

Nan Madol is still virtually unknown to the outside, almost as unknown as when O'Connell stumbled upon it 160 years ago. It was surveyed by German archaeologists at the beginning of the twentieth century, but it is only in the past few years that a detailed knowledge of the site and its history has been achieved, with radiocarbon dating human habitation to 200 BC. The Pohnpeians, of course, have always known about Nan Madol, a knowledge embedded in myth and oral history, but because the place itself is still invested with a sense of sacredness and taboo, they hesitate to approach it – their tradition is full of tales of those who met untimely deaths after offending the spirits of the place.

It was an uncanny feeling, as Robin gave us vivid details of life as it once was in the city around us – I began to feel the place breathing, coming to life. Here are the old canoe docks, Robin said, gesturing at Pahnwi; there is the boulder where pregnant women went to rub their stomachs to ensure an easy birth; there (he pointed to the island of Idehd) is where an annual ceremony of atonement was held, culminating in the offering of a turtle to Nan Samwohl, the great salt-water eel who served as a medium between the people and their god. There, on

Peikapw, the magical pool where the ruling Saudeleurs could see all that was taking place on Pohnpei. There, the great hero Isohkelekel, who had finally vanquished the Saudeleurs, shocked at seeing his aged face reflected in the waters, threw himself into the pool and drowned, a Narcissus in reverse.

It is the emptiness, the desertedness, finally, of Nan Madol which makes it so uncanny. No one now knows when it was deserted, or why. Did the bureaucracy collapse under its own weight? Did the coming of Isohkelekel put an end to the old order? Were the last inhabitants wiped out by disease, or plague, or climatic change, or starvation? Did the sea rise, inexorably, and engulf the low islands? (Many of them, now, are under water.) Was there a feeling of some ancient curse, a panicked and superstitious flight from this place of the old gods? When O'Connell visited a hundred and sixty years ago, it had already been deserted for a century or more. The sense of this mystery, the rise and fall of cultures, the unpredictable twists of fate, made us contemplative, silent, as we returned to the mainland.[25]

The return journey, indeed, was difficult, and frightening, as night fell. It started to rain again, and this time the rain was driven violently, slantingly, by a strong wind. In a few minutes we were utterly soaked, and began to shiver in the chill. A dense, drizzling mist settled over the water as we inched in, with extreme circumspection, fearing every moment to be grounded on the reef. After an hour in this thick, soupy, blinding fog, our other senses had adapted, sharpened – but it was Knut who picked out the new sound: an intricate, syncopated drumming, which gradually grew louder as, still blinded, we approached the shore. Knut's auditory acuteness is quite remarkable – this was not unusual in achromatopes, he told us, perhaps a compensation for the visual impairment. He picked up the drumming when we were still half a mile or more from shore, even before Robin, who, expecting it, was listening intently.

This beautiful, mysterious, complex drumming came, we were to discover, from a trio of men pounding sakau on a large stone by the dock. We watched them briefly when we landed. I was eagerly curious about sakau, especially as Robin had expatiated on its virtues as we returned from Nan Madol. He drank it every night, he said, and with this the tension of the day drained out, a peaceful calm came upon him, and he slept deeply and dreamlessly (he could not sleep otherwise). Later that evening Robin came along to the hotel with his Pohnpeian wife, bearing a bottle of slimy greyish liquid; it looked, to my eyes, like old motor oil. I sniffed it gingerly – it smelled of licorice or anise – and tasted a little, uncouthly, in a tooth glass from the bathroom. But sakau is supposed to be drunk with due protocol, from coconut shells, and I looked forward to drinking it in the proper way, at a traditional sakau ceremony.

*

Pohnpei was one of the first of the Carolines to be colonized by humans – Nan Madol is much older than anything to be found on any of the outlying atolls – and with its high terrain, its size, and rich natural resources, it is still the ultimate refuge when disaster strikes the smaller islands. The atolls, smaller, more fragile, are intensely vulnerable to typhoons, droughts, and famines – Oroluk, according to legend, was once a thriving atoll, until most of it washed away in a typhoon; it now consists of a fifth of a square mile.[26] Moreover, all of these islands, with their limited size and resources, are liable sooner or later to reach a Malthusian crisis of overpopulation, which must lead to disaster, unless there can be emigration. Throughout the Pacific, as O'Connell observed, islanders are periodically forced to emigrate, setting out in their canoes, as their ancestors did centuries before, not knowing what they will find, or where they will go, and hoping against hope that they may find a new and benign island to resettle.[27]

But Pohnpei's satellite atolls are able to turn to the mother island in such times, and thus there are separate enclaves in the town of Kolonia, Pohnpei's capital, of refugees from other islands – Sapwuahfik, Mwoakil, Oroluk, and even the Mortlock Islands, in the neighbouring state of Chuuk. There are two sizeable Pingelapese enclaves on Pohnpei, one in Sokehs province, the other in Kolonia, first established when Pingelap was devastated by the 1905 typhoon, and enlarged by subsequent emigrations. In the 1950s there came yet another emigration from Pingelap, this time in consequence of extreme overcrowding, and a new enclave was established by six hundred Pingelapese in the remote Pohnpeian mountain valley of Mand. Since then the village has burgeoned to a population of more than two thousand Pingelapese – three times the population of Pingelap itself.

Mand is isolated geographically, but even more ethnically and culturally – so that forty years after the original settlers migrated here from Pingelap, their descendants have avoided, largely, any contact or marriage with those outside the village, and have maintained, in effect, an island on an island, as homogenous genetically and culturally as Pingelap itself – and the maskun is, if anything, even more prevalent here than on Pingelap.

The road to Mand is very rough – we had to travel in a jeep, often slowing down to little more than a walking rate – and the journey took more than two hours. Outside Kolonia, we saw occasional houses and thatched sakau pubs, but as we climbed, all signs of habitation disappeared. A separate trail – traversable only by foot or by four-wheel drive – led off from the main road, climbing steeply up to the village itself. As we got higher, the temperature and humidity diminished, a delightful change after the heat of the lowlands.

Though isolated, Mand is a good deal more sophisticated than Pingelap, with electricity, telephones, and access to university-trained teachers. We stopped first at the community centre, a spacious, airy building with a large central hall used for village meetings, parties, dances. Here we could spread out our equipment and meet some of the achromatopes of the community, and distribute sunglasses and visors. Here, as on Pingelap, there was a certain amount of formal testing, and we explored the details of daily life in this very different environment, and how much this might be helped with proper visual aids. But, as in Pingelap, it was Knut, quietly open about himself, who could do the deepest, most sympathetic probing and counselling. He spent a good deal of time with the mother of two achromatopic children, five years and eighteen months old, who was deeply anxious that they might go completely blind – fearful too that their eye condition might have been her fault, that it was something she had done during pregnancy. Knut did his best to explain to her the mechanisms of heredity, to reassure her that her daughters would not go blind, that there was nothing wrong with her as a wife or a mother, that the maskun was not necessarily a barrier to receiving an education and holding a job, and that with the proper optical aids and eye protection, the proper understanding, her daughters could do as well as any other child. But it was only when he made clear that he himself had the maskun – she suddenly stared at him in a new way at this point – that his words seemed to take on a solid reality for her.[28]

*

We moved on to the school, where a busy day was in progress. There were twenty or thirty children in each class, and, in each, two or three were colour-blind. There were a number of excellent, well-trained teachers here, and the level of education, sophistication, was clearly far better than on Pingelap; some of the classes were in English, others in Pohnpeian or Pingelapese. In one class of teenagers, we sat in on a lesson in astronomy – this included pictures of earthrise from the moon and close-ups of the planets from the Hubble space telescope. But admixed with the latest astronomy and geology, the secular history of the world, a mythical or sacred history was given equal force. If the students were taught about shuttle flights, plate tectonics and submarine volcanoes, they were also immersed in the traditional myths of their culture – the ancient story, for example, of how the island of Pohnpei had been built under the direction of a mystical octopus, Lidakika. (I was fascinated by this, for it was the only cephalopod creation myth I had ever heard.)

Watching two little achromatopic girls doing their arithmetic lessons with their noses virtually touching the pages of the book, Knut was reminded powerfully of his own school days, before he had any optical aids. He pulled out his pocket magnifying loupe to show them – but it is not easy, unpractised, to use a high-power magnifying glass to read with.

We stayed longest in a class of five- and six-year-olds, who were just learning to read. There were three achromatopic children in this class – they had not been placed, as they should have been, in the front row; and it was immediately apparent that they could not see the letters on the blackboard where the teacher was printing, which the other children could see easily. 'What's this word?' the teacher would ask – everyone's hands would shoot up, including the achromatopes', and when another child gave the answer, they echoed it in unison. If they were asked first, though, they could not answer – they were just imitating the other children, pretending to know. But the achromatopic children seemed to have developed very acute auditory and factual memories, precisely as Knut had developed in his own childhood:

> Since I could not actually discern the individual letters even in ordinary book print ... I had developed a very keen memory. It was usually enough if a class-mate or someone in the household read my home-assignment to me once or twice, in order for me to remember and reproduce it, and to perform a rather convincing reading behaviour in class.

The achromatopic children were oddly knowledgeable too about the colours of people's clothing, and various objects around them – and often seemed to know what colours 'went' with what. Here again Knut was reminded of his own childhood strategies:

> A constantly recurring harassment throughout my child-hood, and later on too, was having to name colours on scarves, ties, plaid skirts, tartans, and all kinds of multi-coloured pieces of clothing, for people who found my inability to do so rather amusing and quite entertaining. As a small child I could not easily escape these situations. As a pure defence measure, I always memorized the colours of my own clothes and of other things around me, and eventually I learned some of the 'rules' for 'correct' use of colours and the most probable colours of various things.

Thus we could already observe in these achromatopic children in Mand how a sort of theoretical knowledge and know-how, a compensatory hypertrophy of curiosity and memory, were rapidly developing in reaction to their perceptual problems. They were learning to compensate cognitively for what they could not directly perceive or comprehend.[29]

*

'I know that colours carry importance for other people,' Knut said later. 'So I will use colour names when necessary to communicate with them. But the colours as such carry no meaning for me. As a kid, I used to think that it would be nice to see colours, because then I would be able to have a driver's licence and to do things that people with normal colour vision can do. And if there were some way of *acquiring* colour vision, I suppose it might open a new world, as if one were tone deaf and suddenly became able to hear melodies. It would probably be a very interesting thing, but it would also be very confusing. Colour is something you have to grow up with, to mature with – your brain, the whole system, the way you react to the world. Bringing in colour as a sort of add-on later in life would be overwhelming, a lot of information I might not be able to cope with. It would give new qualities to everything that might throw me off completely. Or maybe colour would be disappointing, not what I expected – who knows?'[30]

We met Jacob Robert, an achromatope who works at the school, in charge of ordering books and supplies. He was born in Pingelap, but emigrated to Mand in 1958 to finish high school. In 1969, he told us, he had been flown, with Entis Edward and a few others, to the National

Institutes of Health in Washington for special genetic studies associated with achromatopsia – this was his first glimpse of life outside Micronesia. He was particularly intrigued, when he was there, to hear about the island of Fuur, in Denmark. He had not known there were any other islands of the colour-blind in the world, and when he returned to Pohnpei, his fellow achromatopes were fascinated too. 'It made us feel less alone,' he said. 'It made us feel we had brothers somewhere in the big world. It also started a new myth, that there was a place in Finland, which gave us the achromatopsia.' When we had heard this myth in Pingelap, we had assumed it was a new one, generated by Knut's presence; now, as we listened to Jacob, and how he had brought back news of a place in the far north with the maskun, it became evident that the myth had arisen twenty-five years earlier and, perhaps now half forgotten, had been reanimated, given a new form and force, with Knut's arrival.

He was intrigued to hear the story of Knut's own childhood in Norway, so similar in many ways to his – and yet different, too. Jacob had grown up surrounded by others with the maskun and by a culture which recognized this; most achromatopes around the world grow up in complete isolation, never knowing (or even knowing of) another of their kind. Yet Knut and his brother and sister, by a rare genetic chance, had each other – they lived on an island, a colour-blind island, of three.

The three of them, as adults, all achromatopic, all highly gifted, have reacted and adapted to their achromatopsia in very different ways. Knut was the firstborn, and his

achromatopsia was diagnosed before he started school –
but it was felt that he would never be able to see well
enough to learn to read, and recommended that he (and
his siblings, later) be sent to the local school for the blind.
Knut rebelled at being regarded as disabled, and refused
to learn Braille by touch, instead using his sight to read
the raised dots, which cast tiny shadows on the page. He
was severely punished for this and forced to wear a
blindfold in classes. Soon after, Knut ran away from the
school, but, determined to read normal print, taught
himself to read at home. Finally, having convinced the
school administrators that he would never make a willing
student, Knut was allowed to return to regular school.

Knut's sister, Britt, dealt with her loneliness and isolation as a child by identifying with, becoming a member
of, the blind community. She flourished at the school for
the blind as much as Knut hated it, becoming fluent in
Braille; and she has spent her professional life as an
intermediary between the blind and sighted worlds, super-
vising the transcription and production of books into
Braille at the Norwegian Library for the Blind. Like Knut,
Britt is intensely musical and auditory and loves to close
her eyes and surrender herself to the non-visual domain of
music; but equally, she relaxes by doing needlework, using
a jeweller's loupe attached to her glasses, to keep her
hands free.

*

It was now three in the afternoon – time to set back for
Kolonia – and despite our altitude, burningly hot. While

Knut sat under a shade tree to cool off, Bob and I decided to dive into the beautifully clear stream which ran nearby. Finding a flat rock under the surface, shaded by ferns, I clung onto this and let the cool waters stream over me. Downstream, a quarter of a mile or so, some of the women were washing dark, heavy clothes – the formal Sunday wear of Mand.

Refreshed by our swim, Bob and I decided to walk down the trail from the village; the others would meet us at the road below in the jeep. In the afternoon light, we were dazzled by the brilliance of oranges hanging in the trees – they seemed almost alight in the dark green foliage, like Marvell's oranges in his poem 'Bermudas':

> He hangs in shades the Orange bright,
> Like golden Lamps in a green Night.

I felt a sudden sadness that Knut, that the achromatopes around us, could not share this startling Marvellian vision.

We had gone a couple of hundred yards when we were overtaken by a twelve-year-old boy running at top speed, fearlessly, looking like a young knight with his new sun visor. He had been squinting, looking down, avoiding the light when we saw him earlier, but now he was running in broad daylight, confidently making his way down the steep trail. He pointed to the dark visor and gave a big smile. 'I can see, I can see!' and then he added, 'Come back soon!'

*

Dusk descended as we drove back slowly to Kolonia, and we began to see occasional bats, then great numbers of them, rising from the trees, taking off on their night-time forays, emitting shrill cries (and doubtless sonar too). Bats are often the only mammals that manage to make it to distant islands (they were the only mammals in Pohnpei and Guam, until rats and others were introduced from sailing ships), and one feels they ought to be more respected, more loved, than they are. They are considered fancy eating on Guam, and exported by the thousand to the Marianas. But they are an essential part of the island's ecology, eating many types of fruit and distributing the seeds, and one hopes their delicious taste does not lead to their extinction.

*

Greg Dever, director of the Pacific Basin Medical Officers Training Program in Kolonia, has a brusque surface, but underneath this is deeply romantic and dedicated to his work. He had gone to Palau as a young man in the Peace Corps, and had been shocked at what he saw – a fearful incidence of treatable diseases, combined with a drastic shortage of doctors – and this decided him on a career in medicine, so that he could return to Micronesia as a doctor. He trained as a paediatrician at the University of Hawaii and moved to the Carolines fifteen years ago. Here on Pohnpei he has established a small hospital, a clinic and out-reach service stretching to the outlying atolls, and a medical programme aimed at training indigenous students from all the archipelagoes, in the hope that when they graduate as doctors they will stay and practise and teach in the islands (although some, now that their degrees are accepted in the States, have gone on to more lucrative careers on the mainland).[31]

He had asked us, as visiting scientists, to give a presentation on the maskun. We felt odd, as visitors, talking to these doctors, mostly native, about problems they themselves presumably had lived with and knew intimately. But we thought that our very naïveté, coming at the subject from another angle, might have some value for the audience – and we hoped we might learn more from them as well. But it became increasingly clear – as Bob spoke about the genetics and retinal basis of the maskun; I about adapting neurologically to such a condition; and Knut about the challenges of actually living with it – that many of those in the audience had never actually encountered the maskun. We found this extraordinary. Even though there are half a dozen papers in the scientific literature on the maskun, here in the capital of achromatopsia there was almost no local medical awareness of the problem.

One reason for this, perhaps, had to do with the simple act of recognizing and naming the phenomenon. Everyone with the maskun has behaviours and strategies which are obvious once one is attuned to them: the squinting, the blinking, the avoidance of bright light. It was these which allowed an instant mutual recognition between Knut and the affected children the moment he landed on Pingelap. But before one has assigned a meaning to these behaviours, categorized them, one may just overlook them.

And there is also a medical attitude, enforced by necessity, which militates against proper recognition of the maskun. Greg and many others have worked incessantly to train good doctors in under-doctored Micronesia. But their hands are constantly full with critical conditions demanding immediate attention. Amoebiasis and other parasitic infections are rife (there were four patients with amoebic liver abscesses in the hospital while we were there). There are constant outbreaks of measles and other infectious diseases, partly because there are not enough resources to vaccinate the children. Tuberculosis is endemic in the islands, as leprosy once was.[32] Widespread chronic vitamin-A deficiency, probably linked to the shift to a Western diet, can cause severe ear and eye problems (including night blindness), lower resistance to infection, and lead to potentially fatal malabsorption syndromes. Though almost every form of venereal disease is seen, AIDS has not yet appeared in this remote place, but Greg worries about the inevitable: 'All hell will break loose when we get AIDS,' he said. 'We just don't have the manpower or the resources to deal with it.'

This is the stuff of medicine, the acute medicine which must be the first priority in the islands. There is little time or energy left over for something like the maskun, a congenital, non-progressive condition which one can live with. There is no time for an existential medicine which enquires into what it might *mean* to be blind or colour-blind or deaf, how those affected might react and adapt, how they might be helped – technologically, psychologically, culturally – to lead fuller lives. 'You are lucky,' said

Greg. 'You have the time. We're too harried here, we don't have the time.'

But the unawareness of achromatopsia is not limited to medical professionals. The Pingelapese of Pohnpei tend to stay among their own, and the achromatopes among them – who often stay inside, out of the bright light and out of sight, for much of the day – form an inconspicuous and almost invisible enclave within the Pingelapese enclave itself, a minority within a minority. Many people on Pohnpei do not know of their existence.

*

Kolonia is the only major town on Pohnpei, situated on the north coast next to a wide harbour. It has a charming, indolent, run-down feel. There are no traffic lights in Kolonia, no neon signs, no cinemas – only a shop or two, and, everywhere, sakau bars. As we walked along the middle of the main street, almost deserted at noontime, looking in at the sleepy souvenir shops and scuba shops on either side, we were struck by its nonchalant, dilapidated air. The main street has no name, none of the streets now have names; Kolonians no longer remember, or are anxious to forget, the street names imposed by successive occupations and have gone back to talking of them, as in precolonial days, as 'the street by the waterfront' or 'the road to Sokehs'. The town seemed to have no centre, and what with this, and the nameless streets, we kept getting lost. There were a few cars on the road, but they moved extraordinarily slowly, at a walking pace or slower, stopping every few yards for dogs which were lying in the road. It was difficult to believe that this lethargic place was in fact the capital not only of Pohnpei, but of the Federated States of Micronesia.

And yet, here and there, rising incongruously above tin-roofed shanties, were the bulky cinder-block buildings of the government and the hospital, and a satellite dish so vast that it brought to mind the huge radio telescopes in Arecibo. I was amazed to see this – were the Pohnpeians searching for life in outer space? The explanation, more mundane, was still in its way rather astonishing. The satellite dish is part of a modern telecommunications system: the mountainous terrain and bad roads had prevented the installation of a telephone system until a few years ago; now the satellite system allows instant, crystal-clear conversations between the most isolated parts of the island, and gives Pohnpei access to the Internet as well, a page on the World Wide Web. In this sense, Kolonia has skipped the twentieth century and moved direct, without the usual intermediate stages, to the twenty-first.

As we explored further, we also got the feeling of Kolonia as an archaeological site or palimpsest composed of many strata, many cultures superimposed one upon another. There were signs of American influence everywhere (perhaps one saw this most in the Ambrose supermarket, where tins of cuttlefish in their own ink sat next to entire aisles devoted to Spam and other tinned meats); but beneath this, more faintly, those of the Japanese, the German, and the Spanish occupations, all superimposed upon the original harbour and village, which the

Pohnpeians, in O'Connell's day, had called Mesenieng, 'the eye of the wind', a magical and sacred place.

We tried to imagine what the town had been like in the 1850s, a couple of decades after O'Connell landed here. Then too it had been a roistering town, for Pohnpei had become a favourite stopping place for British vessels plying the trade routes to China and Australia and, a little later, for American whalers. The attractions of Pohnpei, allied to the brutalities and hardships of shipboard life (which had caused Melville to jump ship in the 1840s), incited frequent desertions, and the island rapidly acquired a colourful assortment of 'beachcombers', to use the contemporary term.[33] The beachcombers brought with them tobacco, alcohol, and firearms; and fights, inflamed by liquor, would end, as often as not, in gunfire. Thus the atmosphere, by the 1850s, was that of a frontier town, not unlike Copperopolis or Amarillo, full of high living and adventure (for the beachcombers, not the Pohnpeians), but also of violence, prostitution, exploitation, crime. With these outsiders descending on an immunologically naive population, disaster, in the form of infectious disease, could not be long in coming. Half the population was wiped out by smallpox in 1854 following the arrival of the American whaler *Delta*, which landed six infected men on the island; and this was soon followed by epidemics of influenza and measles.[34] Barely a seventh of the population was left by the 1880s, and they might not have survived had it not been for the Scottish, English, and American missionaries who had started to come thirty years earlier, determined to bring morality to Pohnpei, turf out the beachcombers, stop sex and crime, and bring medical and spiritual aid to the beleaguered people of the island.

If the missionaries succeeded in saving Pohnpei physically (it was not totally destroyed, like Melville's valley of the Typee), it may have been at another, spiritual cost. The traders and beachcombers had seen Pohnpei as a rich prize to plunder and exploit; the missionaries saw it as a prize too: an island of simple heathen souls waiting to be converted and claimed for Christ and country. By 1880 there were fourteen churches on Pohnpei, dispensing an alien mythology, morality, and set of beliefs to hundreds of converts, including several of the local chiefs; missionaries had been sent to Pingelap and Mwoakil as well. And yet, as with the Marranos in Spain, the old religion was not so easily denied; and beneath the veneer of an almost universal conversion, many of the old rites, the old beliefs, remained.

While beachcombers and missionaries were fighting it out, Germany had been quietly building an empire in the Carolines, based especially on the marketing of coconut meat, copra; and in 1885 she laid claim to Pohnpei and all the Carolines – a claim which was immediately contested by Spain. When papal arbitration awarded the Carolines to Spain, Germany withdrew, and a brief period of Spanish hegemony began. The Spanish presence was passionately resented, and there were periodic rebellions, quickly suppressed. The colonists fortified their district of Mesenieng (now renamed La Colonia), surrounding themselves with a high stone wall, which by 1890 encircled much of the town. A good part of the old wall survives today (though much of it was destroyed by later colonists and by Allied bombing in 1944); this, along with the bell tower of the old Catholic church, gave us some sense of La Colonia as it must have been a century ago.

Spanish rule in the Carolines was ended by the Spanish–American War, and the whole of Micronesia was sold to Germany for four million dollars (apart from Guam, which remained in American hands). Determined to mould Pohnpei into a profitable colony, the Germans instituted large agricultural schemes, uprooting acres of native flora to plant coconut trees and employing forced labour to build roads and public works. German administrators moved into the town, which they now renamed Kolonia.

A blow-up finally occurred in 1910, when the resentful people of Sokehs province gunned down the tyrannical new German district administrator and his assistant, along with two of their overseers. Reprisals were swift in coming: the entire population of Sokehs had its land confiscated, many were killed or exiled to other islands, the young men being sent to labour in the phosphate mines of Nauru, from which they returned, if at all, broken and destitute, a decade later. We were intensely conscious, wherever we walked, of Sokehs Rock – it looms massively to the northwest and forces itself upon the eye at every point in Kolonia – a reminder of the brutal German occupation and the hopeless uprising of the rebels, whose mass grave, we were told, lay just outside town.

We found oddly few reminders of the Japanese occupation, though of all the occupations, this most transformed Kolonia. It was difficult to visualize, as we wandered through the run-down, slow-paced town, the bustling place it had been in the 1930s, in the heyday of the Japanese occupation. Its population then had been swelled by ten thousand Japanese immigrants, and it was a thriving business and cultural centre, full of commerce and recreation (including, I read, some twenty restaurants, fifteen dispensers of Japanese medicines, and nine brothels). The Pohnpeians themselves enjoyed little of these riches, and indeed were strictly segregated, with contact between Pohnpeian men and Japanese women totally prohibited.

The mark of occupation, of desecration, of conversion and exploitation, has been imprinted not only on the place, but on the identities of those who live here. There is another Colonia a few hundred miles away, on the island of Yap – there are Colonias and Kolonias all over Micronesia – and one elderly citizen there, when questioned by E. J. Kahn some years ago, said: 'You know, we've learned in our day to be Spanish, and we've learned to be German, and we've learned to be Japanese, and now we're learning to be American – what should we be preparing to learn to be next?'

*

The following day we set off for the rain forest with a botanist friend of Greg's, Bill Raynor, and he brought along two Pohnpeian colleagues: Joakim, a medicine man, deeply knowledgeable about the native plants and their traditional uses, and Valentine, an expert on location, who seemed to know every inch of the island, where every plant was to be found, its favourite conditions, its relationship to all the other inhabitants of the ecosystem. Both men seemed to be born naturalists; in the West, they might have become doctors or botanists.[35] But here their powers had been moulded by a different tradition – more concrete, less theoretical than ours, so that their knowledge was intimately bound up with the bodily and mental and spiritual balance of their people, with magic and myth, the sense that man and his environment were not separable, were one.

Bill himself came to Pohnpei as a volunteer Jesuit missionary, prepared to teach the natives about agricultural management and plant conservation. He had arrived with a sort of arrogance, he told me, flushed with the hubris of Western science, and then had been astonished, humbled, by finding in the local medicine men a vastly detailed and systematic knowledge of the plants on the island – they recognized dozens of different ecosystems, from the mangrove swamps and seagrass beds to the dwarf forests at the summit. Every plant on the island, Bill said, was considered significant and sacred; the vast majority were seen as therapeutic. Much of this he had discounted as mere superstition when he came to Pohnpei, but now he was more inclined to think in anthropological terms, and to see what he had first called 'superstition' as a highly developed 'concrete science' (in Lévi-Strauss's term), an immense system of knowledge and principles wholly different from his own.

Having come to teach, he found himself instead listening and learning, and after a while started to form fraternal or collegial relationships with the medicine men, so that their complementary knowledge and skills and attitudes could be joined. Such a working together is essential, he feels, the more so as Pohnpei is still formally owned by the nahnmwarkis, and without their willing cooperation, nothing can be done. In particular, he believes, a comprehensive investigation of all the plants in Pohnpei is needed to see whether any have unique pharmacological properties – and it is urgent to do so now, before the plants themselves, and knowledge about them, become extinct.

It has been similar, in a way, in the matter of religion. Arriving as a missionary with a firm conviction of the primacy of Christianity, Bill was struck (as many of his fellow missionaries have been) by the moral clarity of those he came to convert. He fell in love with and married a Pohnpeian woman, and has a whole clan now of Pohnpeian in-laws, as well as a fluent command of the language. He has lived here for sixteen years, and plans to remain for the rest of his life.[36]

*

Islands were thought, in the eighteenth century, to be broken-off pieces of continent, or perhaps the peaks of submerged continents (and thus, in a sense, not islands at all but continuous with the main). The realization that for oceanic islands, at least, no such continuity existed – that they had risen as volcanoes from the depths of the ocean floor, and had never been part of the main, that they were *insulae*, insulated, in the most literal sense – was largely due to Darwin and Wallace and their observations of island fauna and flora. Volcanic islands, they made clear, had to start from scratch; every living creature on them had to make its way or be transported to them.[37] Thus, as Darwin noted, they often lacked entire classes of animals, such as mammals and amphibians; this was certainly true of Pohnpei, where there were no native mammals, other than a few species of bats.[38] The flora of oceanic islands was also quite restricted, compared to that of continents – though, because of the relatively ready dispersal of seeds and spores, not nearly to such a degree. Thus a considerable range of plants had made it to Pohnpei, and settled and survived, in the five million years that it had existed, and though the rain forest was not as rich as the Amazon's, it was, none the less, quite remarkable – and no less sublime. But it was a rain forest of a peculiar sort, because many of the plants here occurred nowhere else in the world.

Bill brought this out, as we made our way through the dense vegetation: 'Pohnpeians recognize and name about seven hundred different native plants, and, interestingly, these are the same seven hundred that a Western botanist would pick out as separate species.' Of these, he said, about a hundred species were endemic – they had evolved on Pohnpei, and were unique to the island.[39] This was often stressed in the species names: thus there were *Garcinia ponapensis*, *Clinostigma ponapensis*, *Freycinetia ponapensis*, and *Astronidium ponapense*, as well as *Galeola ponapensis*, a native orchid.

94

Pohnpei's sister island, Kosrae, is a very beautiful and geologically similar high volcanic island, little more than three hundred miles away. You might expect Kosrae to have much the same flora as Pohnpei, said Bill, and many species are of course common to both. But Kosrae has its own endemic plants, unique to it, like Pohnpei. Though both islands are young in geological terms – Pohnpei is perhaps five million years old and Kosrae, much steeper, only two million – their flora have already diverged quite widely. The same roles, the same eco-niches, are filled with different species. Darwin had been 'struck with wonder', in the Galapagos, at the occurrence of unique yet analogous forms of life on contiguous islands; indeed this seemed to him, when he looked back on his voyage, the most central of all his observations, a clue to 'that great fact – that mystery of mysteries – the first appearance of new beings on this earth'.

Bill pointed out a tree fern, *Cyathea nigricans*, with its massive trunk, twice my height, and a crown of long fronds overhead, some of them still unfurling in hairy croziers or fiddleheads. Another tree fern, *Cyathea ponapeana*, was now rather rare and grew only in the cloud forest, he added, but despite its name it was not completely endemic, for it had also been found on Kosrae (*Cyathea nigricans*, similarly, had been found on both Pohnpei and Palau). The tree fern's wood is prized for its strength, Joakim said, and used to build houses. Another giant fern, *Angiopteris evecta*, spread low to the ground, with twelve-foot fronds arching, tentlike, from its short stubby base; and there were bird's-nest ferns four feet or more in diameter, clinging high up to the tops of trees – a sight which reminded me of the magical forests of Australia. 'People take these bird's-nest ferns from the forest,' Valentine interjected, 'and reattach them so they can grow, epiphytically, on pepper plants, sakau – the two of them together, tehlik and sakau, are a most prized gift.'

At the other extreme, Bill pointed out delicate club mosses sprouting on the base of a bird's-nest fern – an epiphyte growing upon an epiphyte. These too, Joakim said, were traditional medicine (in my medical student days we used their spores, lycopodium powder, on rubber gloves – though it was subsequently found to be an irritant and carcinogen). But the strangest, perhaps – Bill had to search hard to find one – was a most delicate, iridescent, bluish-green filmy fern, *Trichomanes*. 'It is said to be fluorescent,' he added. 'It grows chiefly near the summit of the island, on the trunks of the moss-covered trees in the dwarf forest. The same name, didimwerek, is used for luminous fish.'[40]

Here is a native palm, *Clinostigma ponapensis*, Bill said – not so common here, but plentiful in the upland palm forests, where it is the dominant plant. Valentine told us the ancient story of how this palm, the kotop, had protected Pohnpei from invading warriors from Kosrae – seeing the hundreds of palms with their light-coloured flowering stalks on the mountainside, the invaders had mistaken these for men's skirts made from hibiscus bark. Thinking the island must be heavily defended, they withdrew. So the kotop saved Pohnpei, as the geese saved Rome.

Bill pointed out a dozen different trees used in making

canoes. 'This is the traditional one; the Pohnpeians call it dohng ... but if lightness and size are desired, they use this one, sadak.' The sadak tree he pointed out was more than a hundred feet high. There were many wonderful smells in the forest, from cinnamon trees with their aromatic bark, to native koahnpwil trees with their powerful, resinous sap – these were unique to the island and useful, Joakim said, for stopping menstrual bleeding or dysentery and also to kindle fires.

The drizzling rain in which we had started had steadily mounted in intensity, and our path was rapidly becoming a stream of mud, so, reluctantly, we had to return. Bill commented on the many streams which traced down through the forest to the gully. 'They used to be absolutely clear and transparent,' he said. 'Now look at them – turbid and brown.' This was due, he said, to people clearing forest on the steep hills – illicitly, as this is a state preserve – to grow their own sakau. Once the trees and vines are cleared, the soil on the hills begins to crumble, and washes down into the streams. 'I am all for sakau,' said Bill. 'I revere it ... you could call it one of the moral vines which hold us together – but it is madness to uproot the forest to grow it.'

*

There is no sakau in Pingelap; like alcohol, it is forbidden by the Congregationalist Church. But in Pohnpei, the drinking of sakau, once reserved only for those of royal blood, has now become virtually universal (indeed I wondered whether it was partly responsible for the lethargic pace of life here); the Catholic Church, more accommodating than the Congregationalist, accepts it as a legitimate form of sacrament.[41] We had seen sakau bars in town and thatched, open-air bars all over the countryside – circular, or semicircular, with a great metate, or grinding stone (which the Pohnpeians call a peitehl) in the centre, and we remained eager to try some ourselves.

We had been invited by a local physician and colleague of Greg's, May Okahiro, to experience a traditional sakau ceremony that evening. It was a cloudless evening, and we got to her house at sunset, and settled into chairs on her deck, overlooking the Pacific. Three Pohnpeian men, wiry and muscular, arrived, carrying pepper roots and a sheaf of slimy inner bark from a hibiscus plant – a large peitehl awaited them in the courtyard. They chopped the roots into little pieces, and then started pounding those with heavy stones, in an intricate, syncopated rhythm like the one we heard across the water on our return from Nan Madol, a sound at once attention holding and hypnotic, because, like a river, it was both monotonous and ever changing. Then one man got up, went to get fresh water, and poured this in, a little at a time, to wet the pulpy mass in the metate, while his companions continued their complex, iridescent rhythm.

The roots were all macerated now, their lactones emulsified; the pulp was placed on the sinewy, glistening hibiscus bark, which was twisted around it to form a long, closely wound roll. The roll was wrung tighter and tighter, and the sakau exuded, viscous, reluctant, at its margins. This liquid was collected carefully in a coconut shell, and

I was offered the first cup. Its appearance was nauseating – grey, slimy, turbid – but thinking of its spiritual effects, I emptied the cup. It went down easily, like an oyster, numbing my lips slightly as it did so.

More sakau was squeezed out of the hibiscus sheath, and a second cup of fluid obtained – it was offered to Knut, who took it in the proper way, hands crossed, palms up, and then quaffed it down. The cup, emptied and refilled half a dozen times, went to each person, according to a strict order of precedence. By the time it came back to me, the sakau was thinner. I was not wholly sorry, for a sense of such ease, such relaxation, had come on me that I felt I could not stand, I had to sink into a chair. Similar symptoms seemed to have seized my companions – but such effects were expected, and there were chairs for us all.

The evening star was high above the horizon, brilliant against the near-violet backdrop of the night. Knut, next to me, was looking upward as well, and pointed out the pole star, Vega, Arcturus overhead. 'These are the stars the Polynesians used,' said Bob, 'when they sailed in their proas across the firmament of space.' A sense of their voyages, five thousand years of voyaging, rose up like a vision as he talked. I felt a sense of their history, all history, converging on us now, as we sat facing the ocean under the night sky. Pohnpei itself felt like a ship – May's house looked like a giant lantern, and the rocky prominence we were on like the prow of the ship. 'What good chaps they are!' I thought, eyeing the others. 'God's in his heaven and all's well with the world!'

Startled at this unctuous, mellifluous flow of thought –
so far from my usual anxious, querulous frame of mind –
I realized my face was set in a mild, vapid smile; and
looking at my companions, I could see the same smile had
them too. Only then did I realize that we were all stoned;
but sweetly, mildly, so that one felt, so to speak, more
nearly oneself.

I gazed at the sky once again, and suddenly a strange
reversal or illusion occurred, so that instead of seeing the
stars in the sky, I saw the sky, the night sky, hanging on
the stars, and felt I was actually seeing Joyce's vision of
'the heaventree of stars hung with humid nightblue fruit'.[42]
And then, a second later, it was 'normal' again. Something
odd was going on in my visual cortex, I decided, a
perceptual shift, a reversal of foreground and background
– or was this a shift at a higher level, a conceptual or
metaphoric one? Now the sky seemed full of shooting
stars – this, I assumed, was an effervescence in my cortex,
and then Bob said, 'Look – shooting stars!' Reality,
metaphor, illusion, hallucination, seemed to be dissolving,
merging into one another.

I tried to get up, but found I could not. There had been
a gradually deepening numbness in my body, starting as a
tingling and numbness in my mouth and lips, and now I
no longer knew where my limbs were, or how I could get
them to move. After a momentary alarm, I yielded to the
feeling – a feeling which, uncomprehended, was frightening uncontrol, but which, now accepted, was delicious,
floating, levitation. 'Excellent!' I thought, the neurologist
in me aroused. 'I have read of this, and now I'm experi-

encing it. Lack of light touch, lack of proprioception – this must be what de-afferentation feels like.' My companions, I saw, were all lying motionless in their chairs, levitating too, or perhaps asleep.

All of us, indeed, slept deeply and dreamlessly that night, and the next morning awoke crystal clear, refreshed. Clear, at least, cognitively and emotionally – though my eyes were still playing tricks, lingering effects, I presumed, of the sakau. I got up early and recorded these in my notebook:

Floating over coral-heads. Lips of giant clams, perseverating, filling whole visual field. Suddenly a blue blaze. Luminous blobs fall from it. I hear the falling blobs distinctly; amplifying, they fill my auditory sensorium. I realize it is my heartbeats, transformed, that I am hearing.

There is a certain motor and graphic facilitation, perseveration too. Extracting myself from the sea bottom, the clam lips, the blue falling blobs, I continue writing. Words speak themselves aloud in my mind. Not my usual writing, but a rapid perseverative scrawl which at times more resembles cuneiform than English. The pen seems to have an impetus of its own – it is an effort to stop it once it has started.

These effects continue at breakfast, which I share with Knut.[43] A plate of bread, but the bread is pale grey. Stiff, shining, as if smeared with paint, or the thick, shiny, grey sludge of the sakau. Then, deliciously, liqueur chocolates – pentagonal, hexagonal, like the columns at Nan Madol. Ghost petals ray out from a flower on our table, like a halo around it; when it is moved, I observe, it leaves a slight train, a visual smear, reddish, in its wake. Watching a palm waving, I see a succession of stills, like a film run too slow, its continuity no longer maintained. And now, isolated images, scenes, project themselves on the table before me: our first moment on Pingelap, with dozens of laughing children running out of the forest; the great floodlit hoop of the fisherman's net, with a flying fish struggling, iridescent, inside it; the boy from Mand, running down the hill, visored, like a young knight, shouting 'I can see, I can see.' And then, silhouetted against the heaventree of stars, three men round a peitehl, pounding sakau.

*

That evening we all packed up, sad to be leaving these islands. Bob would be returning directly to New York, and Knut heading back, by stages, to Norway. Bob and I had seen Knut at first as a charming, scholarly, slightly reserved colleague – an expert on, and exemplar of, a rare visual condition. Now, after our few weeks together, we saw all sorts of other dimensions: his omnivorous curiosity and sometimes unexpected passions (he was an expert on trams and narrow-gauge railways and was full of recondite knowledge on these), his sense of humour and adventure, his cheerful adaptability. Having seen the difficulties which attend achromatopsia, especially in this climate – above all the painful sensitivity to light and inability to see fine detail – we had a renewed appreciation of Knut's determination, his boldness in making his way around new places, his openness to every situation despite his poor sight (perhaps indeed his resourcefulness and unerring sense of direction had been heightened in compensation for this). Reluctant to say goodbye, the three of us stayed up half the night, finishing off a bottle of gin which Greg had given us. Knut took out the cowrie necklace which Emma Edward had given him on Pingelap and, turning it over and over in his hands, started to reminisce about the trip. 'To see an entire community of achromats has changed my entire perspective,' he said. 'I am still reeling from all of these experiences. This has been the most exciting and interesting journey I will ever make in my life.'

When I asked him what stayed in his mind above all, he said, 'The night-fishing in Pingelap . . . that was fantastic.' And then, in a sort of dreamlike litany, 'The cloudscapes on the horizon, the clear sky, the decreasing light and deepening darkness, the nearly luminous surf at the coral reefs, the spectacular stars and Milky Way, and the shining flying fishes soaring over the water in the light from the torches.' With an effort he pulled himself back from the night fishing, though not before adding, 'I would have no trouble at all tracking and netting the fish – maybe I'm a born night fisher myself!'

But *was* Pingelap an island of the colour-blind after all, an island of the Wellsian sort I had fantasized or hoped for? Such a place, in the full sense, would have to consist of achromatopes only, and to have been cut off from the rest of the world for generations. This was manifestly not the case with the island of Pingelap or the Pingelapese ghetto of Mand, where the achromatopes were diffused amid a larger population of colour-normals.[44]

Yet there was an obvious kinship – not just familial, but perceptual, cognitive – among the achromatopes we met on Pingelap and Pohnpei. There was an immediate understanding and sharing between them, a commonality of language and perception, which instantly extended to Knut as well. And everyone on Pingelap, colour-blind or colour-normal, knows about the maskun, knows that it is not only colour-blindness that those affected must live with, but a painful intolerance of bright light and inability to see fine detail. When a Pingelapese baby starts to squint and turn away from the light, there is at least a cultural knowledge of his perceptual world, his special needs and strengths, even a mythology to explain it. In this sense, then, Pingelap is an island of the colour-blind. No one born here with the maskun finds himself wholly isolated or misunderstood, which is the almost universal lot of people with congenital achromatopsia elsewhere in the world.

*

Knut and I each stopped in Berkeley, separately, on our way back from Pohnpei, to visit our achromatopic correspondent, Frances Futterman, and tell her what we had found on the island of the colour-blind. She and Knut were especially excited to meet one another finally; Knut told me later that it was 'an unforgettable and very stimulating experience – we had so much to talk about and so much to share with each other that we talked incessantly like excited children for several hours'.

Like many achromatopes in our society, Frances grew up with a severe degree of disability, for although her condition was diagnosed relatively early, good visual aids were not available to her, and she was forced to remain indoors as much as possible, avoiding any situation with bright light. She had to contend with a great deal of misunderstanding, and isolation, from her peers. And perhaps most importantly, she had no contact with others of her kind, with anyone who could share and understand her experience of the world.

Did such isolation have to exist? Could there not be a sort of community of achromatopes who (even though geographically separated) were bound together by commonalities of experience, of knowledge, of sensibility, of perspective? Was it possible that even if there was no actual island of the colour-blind, there might be a conceptual or metaphoric one? This was the vision which haunted Frances Futterman and inspired her, in 1993, to start an Achromatopsia Network, publishing monthly newsletters so that achromatopes all over the country – and potentially all over the world – could find each other, communicate, share their thoughts and experiences.

Her network and newsletter – and now a Web site on the Internet – have indeed been very successful, have done much to annul geographical distance and apartness. There are hundreds of members spread around the world – in New Zealand, Wales, Saudi Arabia, Canada, and now in Pohnpei too – and Frances is in contact with them all, by phone, fax, mail, Internet. Perhaps this new network, this island in cyberspace, is the true Island of the Colour-blind.

Book Two

Cycad Island

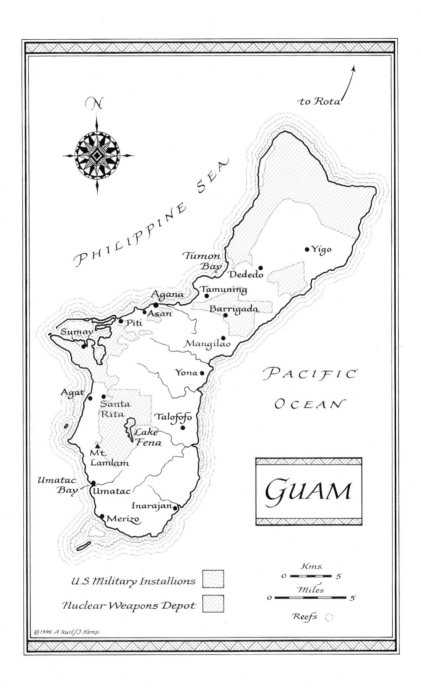

N

to Rota

PHILIPPINE SEA

Tumon
Bay
• Yigo
• Dededo
Agana • Tamuning
• Asan • Barrigada
Sumay • Piti
• Mangilao
Agat • Yona
Santa
Rita
• Talofofo
Lake
Fena
▲ Mt.
Lamlam
Umatac
Bay • Umatac
• Inarajan
• Merizo

PACIFIC

OCEAN

GUAM

U.S Military Installions

Nuclear Weapons Depot

Kms.
0   5
Miles
0   5
Reefs

©1996 A Karl/J Kemp

Guam

It all started with a phone call, at the beginning of 1993. 'It's a Dr Steele,' Kate said. 'John Steele, from Guam.' I had had some contact with a John Steele, a neurologist in Toronto, many years before – could this possibly be the same one? And if so, I wondered, why should he be calling me now, calling from Guam? I picked up the phone, hesitantly. My caller introduced himself; he was indeed the John Steele I had known, and he told me that he now lived in Guam, had lived and worked there for a dozen years.

Guam had a special resonance for neurologists in the 1950s and '60s, for it was then that many descriptions were published of an extraordinary disease endemic on the island, a disease the people of Guam, the Chamorros, called lytico-bodig. The disease, seemingly, could present itself in different ways – sometimes as 'lytico', a progressive paralysis which resembled amyotrophic lateral sclerosis (ALS or motor neurone disease), sometimes as 'bodig', a condition resembling parkinsonism, occasionally with dementia. Ambitious researchers converged on Guam from all over the world, eager to crack this mysterious disease. But, strangely, the disease defeated all comers, and, with repeated failures, the excitement died down. I had not heard anyone mention the lytico-bodig for twenty years, and presumed it had died out quietly, unexplained.

This was far from the case, John now told me. He still had hundreds of patients with lytico-bodig; the disease was still very active – and still unexplained. Researchers had come and gone, he said, few stayed too long. But what had especially struck him, after twelve years on the island, and seeing hundreds of these patients, was the lack of uniformity, the variability and richness, the strangeness of its presentations, which seemed to him more akin to the range of post-encephalitic syndromes seen in vast numbers after the encephalitis lethargica epidemic in the First World War.

The clinical picture of bodig, for example, was often one of a profound motionlessness, almost catatonia, with relatively little tremor or rigidity – a motionlessness which might suddenly dissolve or switch explosively into its opposite when these patients were given the smallest dose of L-DOPA – this, he thought, seemed extremely similar to what I had described with my post-encephalitic patients, in *Awakenings*.

These post-encephalitic disorders have all but disappeared now, and since I had worked with a large and unique population of (mostly elderly) post-encephalitic patients in New York during the 1960s and '70s, I was among the very few contemporary neurologists who had actually seen them.[45] So John was most eager that I come to see his patients in Guam, so that I could make direct comparisons and contrasts between them and my own.

The parkinsonism which affected my post-encephalitic

patients had been caused by a virus; other forms of parkinsonism are hereditary, as in the Philippines; and yet others have been linked to poisons, as with the parkinsonian manganese miners in Chile or the 'frozen addicts' who destroyed their midbrains with the designer drug MPTP. In the 1960s, it had been suggested that the lytico-bodig was also caused by a poison, acquired through eating the seeds of the cycad trees which grew on the island. This exotic hypothesis was all the rage in the mid-sixties when I was a neurology resident – and I was especially taken by it because I had a passion for these primitive plants, a passion which went back to childhood. Indeed, I have three small cycads in my office – a *Cycas*, a *Dioön*, and a *Zamia*, all clustered around my desk (Kate has a *Stangeria* beside hers) – and I mentioned this to John.

'Cycads – this is the place for them, Oliver!' he boomed. 'We have them all over the island; the Chamorros love to eat the flour made from their seeds – they call it fadang or federico. . . . Whether this has anything to do with lytico-bodig is another matter. And on Rota, north of here, a short hop in a plane, you can see absolutely untouched cycad jungles, so thick, so wild, you'd think you were in the Jurassic.

'You'll love it, Oliver, whichever hat you wear. We'll go around the island seeing cycads and patients. You can call yourself a neurological cycadologist, or a cycadological neurologist – either way, it will be a first for us on Guam!'

✳

As the plane began its descent, circling the airport, I got my first glimpse of the island – it was far bigger than Pohnpei, and elongated, like a giant foot. As we skimmed over the southern end of the island, I could see the small villages of Umatac and Merizo nestled in their hilly terrain. One could see, from a height, how the entire north-eastern part of the island had been turned into a military base; and the skyscrapers and superhighways of central Agana rapidly loomed as we descended.

The terminal was teeming with people of a dozen nations, scurrying in all directions – not only Chamorros, Hawaiians, Palauans, Pohnpeians, Marshallese, Chuukese, and Yapese, but Filipinos, Koreans, and, in vast numbers, Japanese. John was waiting at the barrier, an easy figure to pick out among the bustling crowds, for he was tall and fair, with very pale hair and a ruddy complexion. He was the only person in the entire airport, as far as I could see, wearing a suit and tie (most were dressed in brightly coloured T-shirts and shorts). 'Oliver!' he boomed. 'Welcome to Guam! So good to see you! You survived the Island Hopper, eh?'

We walked through the steaming airport and out through the parking lot to John's car, a battered white convertible. We skirted Agana, and started toward the southern part of the island, to the village of Umatac, where John lives. I had been somewhat taken aback by the airport, but now as we drove south, the hotels, the supermarkets, the Western bustle, died away, and we were soon in gentle, undulating country. The air grew cooler as the road climbed higher and wound along the slopes of

Mount Lamlam, the highest point on the island. We stopped at a lookout point, got out, and stretched. There were grassy slopes all around us, but higher, on the mountain, a thick cloak of trees. 'You see those bright green dots, standing out against the darker foliage?' John asked me. 'Those are the cycads, with their new foliage. You're probably used to *Cycas revoluta*, the bristly, low Japanese cycad, which one sees everywhere,' he added. 'But what we have here is a much larger, indigenous species, *circinalis* – they look almost like palms from a distance.' Pulling out my binoculars, I scanned them with delight, glad I had made the long journey to this island of cycads.

*

We got back into the car, drove a few minutes more, and then John stopped again at a final ridge. There, spread out below us, glinting in the sun, was the Bay of Umatac, the bay where Magellan had anchored his ships in the spring of 1521. The village clustered around a white church by the water, with its spire rising above the surrounding buildings; the hillside sloping down to the bay was dotted with houses. 'I've seen this a thousand times,' said John, 'but I never get tired of it. It is always as beautiful as the first time I saw it.' John had been rather formal, in manner as well as dress, when we met at the airport, but now, as he looked down at Umatac, a different aspect of him appeared. 'I have always loved islands,' he said, 'and when I read Arthur Grimble's book, *A Pattern of Islands* – do you know it? – anyhow, when I read it, I

knew I would never be happy unless I lived on a Pacific island.'

We got back into the car and started the winding descent to the bay. At one point, John stopped the car again, and pointed to a graveyard on a hilly slope. 'Umatac has the highest incidence of lytico on the entire island,' he said. 'That's how it ends.'

There was a large cantilevered bridge – ornate, gaudy, startling – spanning a gulch as the main road entered town. I had no idea of its history or function; it was as absurd, in its way, as the transplanted London Bridge in Arizona – but it looked festive, fun, as it leapt into the air, a pure effervescence of high spirits. As we entered the village, and drove slowly through, people waved or called out greetings to John as we passed, and with this, it seemed to me, the remaining reserve fell away – suddenly he looked completely at ease, at home.

John has a low, comfortable house, a little to one side of the main village, sheltered by palms, banana trees, and cycads. He can retreat to his study and immure himself among his books – or, in a minute, be with his friends and patients. He has a new passion, beekeeping; hives, in wooden hutches, stood by the side of the house, and I could hear the murmur of bees as we pulled up.

While John went to make tea, I waited in his study and glanced at his books. I had seen a Gauguin reproduction in the living room above the sofa, and now my eye was instantly caught by seeing Gauguin's *Intimate Journal*, wedged between copies of the *Annals of Neurology*. The juxtaposition was striking: Did John see himself as a neurological Gauguin? There were hundreds of books and leaflets and old prints of Guam, especially relating to the original Spanish occupation – all mixed, higgledy-piggledy, with his neurology books and papers. John returned as I was looking at these, with a large pot of tea and a strange, phosphorescent purple confection.

'It's called Ube,' he said. 'Very popular here. Made from the local purple yams.' I had never had an ice cream so mealy, so mashed potato-like, nor one of so extraordinary a colour; but it was cool and sweet, and grew on me as I ate it. Now that we were in his library, relaxing over tea and Ube, John started to tell me more of himself. He had spent his formative years in Toronto (indeed we had exchanged letters when he was there, more than twenty years earlier, on the subject of children's migraines and the visual hallucinations which sometimes accompany them). When John was a resident, in his twenties, he and his colleagues had discovered an important neurological condition (progressive supranuclear palsy, now called Steele-Richardson-Olszewski syndrome). He did further postgraduate work in England and France and a brilliant academic career seemed to be opening for him. But he also felt obscurely conscious of wanting something quite different and had a strong desire to care for patients as a general physician, as his father and grandfather had before him. He taught and practised in Toronto for another few years, and then in 1972 he moved to the Pacific.

Arthur Grimble, whose book had so excited John, had been a district officer in the Gilbert and Ellice Islands before the First World War, and the picture he gave of life in these islands determined John to go to Micronesia. Had he been able to, he would have gone to the Gilberts, like Grimble – for though these islands had changed their name (to Kiribati), they remained otherwise unchanged, hardly contaminated by commerce or modernization. But there were no medical postings available there, so John went instead to the Marshall Islands, to Majuro. In 1978, he moved to Pohnpei, his first experience of a high volcanic island (and it was here that he learned of the maskun, the hereditary colour-blindness among the Pingelapese, several of whom he saw in his practice at this time). Finally, in 1983, having sampled the Marshalls and the Carolines, he went to the Marianas and to Guam. He hoped he might settle here, and live the quiet life of a country doctor, an island practitioner, surrounded by community and relationship – though also, at the back of his mind, there was always the riddle of the Guam disease, and the thought that he, perhaps, might be the one to solve it.

He had lived first in noisy, Westernized Agana, but soon felt an overwhelming need to move to Umatac. If he was to work with the Chamorros and their disease, he wished to be among them, surrounded by Chamorro food, Chamorro customs, Chamorro lives. And Umatac was the epicentre of the disease, the place where it had always been most prevalent: the Chamorros sometimes referred to the lytico-bodig as 'chetnut Humatac', the disease of Umatac. Here in this village, within the span of a few hundred acres, the secret of lytico-bodig must lie. And with it, perhaps, the secret of Alzheimer's disease, Parkinson's disease, ALS, whose varied characteristics it seemed to bring together. Here in Umatac is the answer, John said, if we can find it: Umatac is the Rosetta Stone of neurodegenerative disease, Umatac is the key to them all.

*

John had sunk into a sort of reverie as he recounted the story of his wandering, lifelong passion for islands, and his finally coming to Guam, but now he suddenly jumped to his feet, exclaiming, 'Time to go! Estella and her family are expecting us!' He seized his black bag, donned a floppy hat, and made for the car. I too had sunk into a sort of trance, but was precipitated out of this by the urgent tone of his voice.

Soon we were whizzing down the road to Agat – a drive which made me slightly nervous, for John was now launching into another reminiscence, a very personal history of his own encounter with the Guam disease, the vicissitudes of his thought, his work, and his life on Guam. He spoke with passion, and with vehement, darting gestures, and I feared his attention was not fully on the road.

'It's an extraordinary story, Oliver,' he started, 'whatever way you look at it – in terms of the disease itself, and its impact on the people here on the island, the tantalizing, round-and-round search for its cause.' Harry Zimmerman, he said, had first seen it in 1945, as a young navy doctor arriving after the war; he had been the first to observe the extraordinary incidence of ALS here, and when two patients died he was able to confirm the diagnosis at autopsy.[46] Other physicians stationed on Guam provided further, richer documentation of this puzzling disease. But it required perhaps a different sort of mind, the mind of an epidemiologist, to see the greater significance of all this. For epidemiologists are fascinated by geographic pathology, so to speak – the special vicissitudes of constitution or culture or environment which predispose a population to a specific disease. Leonard Kurland, a young epidemiologist at the National Institutes of Health in Washington, realized at once when he read these initial reports that Guam was that rare phenomenon, an epidemiologist's dream: a geographic isolate.

'These isolates,' Kurland was later to write, 'are sought constantly, because they stimulate our curiosity and because the study of disease in such an isolate may demonstrate genetic or ecological associations that otherwise might not be appreciated.' The study of geographic isolates – islands of disease – plays a crucial role in medicine, often leading to the identification of a specific agent of disease, or genetic mutation, or environmental factor that is linked to the disease. Just as Darwin and Wallace found islands to be unique laboratories, hothouses of nature which might show evolutionary processes in an intensified and dramatic form, so isolates of disease excite the epidemiological mind with the promise of understandings to be obtained in no other way. Kurland felt that Guam was such a place. He shared his excitement with his colleague Donald Mulder, at the Mayo Clinic, and they decided to go to Guam right away, to launch a major investigation there, with all the resources of the NIH and the Mayo.

This was not, John suspected, just an intellectual moment for Kurland, but an event which changed his life. His initial visit, in 1953, opened intoxicating horizons for him – a love affair, a mission, which was never to stop. 'He is *still* writing and thinking about it, and coming here,' John added, 'forty years later – once it gets to you, it never lets you go.'

When Kurland and Mulder arrived they found more than forty cases of lytico on the island, and these, they felt, were only the most severely affected, milder cases probably having escaped medical attention. A tenth of all the adult Chamorro deaths on Guam were due to the disease, and its prevalence was at least a hundred times greater than on the mainland (in some villages, like Umatac, it was over four hundred times greater). Kurland and Mulder were so struck by this concentration of the disease in Umatac that they wondered whether it might have originated here and then spread to the rest of the island. Umatac, John pointed out, had always been the most isolated, least modernized village on Guam. There was no access by road in the nineteenth century, and even in 1953, the road was often impassable. Sanitary and health conditions were poorer than anywhere else on the island at that time, and traditional customs remained very strong.

Kurland was also struck by the way in which certain families seemed predisposed to get lytico: he mentioned one patient who had two brothers, a paternal uncle and aunt, four paternal cousins, and a nephew with the disease (and he observed that health records back to 1904 showed this family to have been singled out even then). Many of the family, John said, were now his patients. And there were other families, like the one we were on our way to see, who seemed particularly vulnerable to the disease.

'But you know,' said John, gesturing violently, and causing the car to lurch to one side, 'there was something else very interesting which Len described then, but which he first regarded as unconnected. He found not only forty-odd people with lytico, but no less than twenty-two with parkinsonism – far more than one would expect to see in a community of this size. And it was parkinsonism of an unusual sort: it would often begin with a change in sleeping habits, with somnolence, and go on to profound mental and physical slowing, profound immobility. Some had tremor and rigidity, many had excessive sweating and salivation. He thought at first that it might be a form of

post-encephalitic parkinsonism – there had been an out-
break of Japanese B encephalitis a few years earlier – but
he could find no direct evidence for this.'

Kurland started to wonder about these patients, the
more so as he found another twenty-one cases of parkinsonism (some with dementia as well) in the following
three years. By 1960 it seemed clear that these could not
be post-encephalitic in origin, but were cases of what the
Chamorros called bodig, a disease, like lytico, endemic for
at least a century in Guam. Now, when the patients were
examined more closely, many of them seemed to have
signs of both bodig *and* lytico; and Kurland wondered if
the two might in some way be allied.

Finally, when Asao Hirano, a young neuropathologist
(and student of Zimmerman's), came to Guam in 1960 to
do a post-mortem study of the brains of those who had
died from lytico and from bodig, he was able to show that
both diseases involved essentially the same changes in the
nervous system, though with varying distributions and
severity. So pathologically it seemed that lytico and bodig
might not be separate diseases, but a single disease which
could present in very different ways.[47]

This again was reminiscent of the encephalitis lethargica: when this first broke out in Europe, there seemed to
be half a dozen separate diseases rampaging – so-called
epidemic polio, epidemic parkinsonism, epidemic schizo-
phrenia, etc. – and it was not realized until pathological
studies were done that all of these were in fact manifesta-
tions of the same disease.

'There is no standard form of lytico-bodig,' John said,

as we pulled up in front of a house in the little village of Agat. 'I could show you a dozen, two dozen patients, and no two would be the same. It is a disease which is polymorphous in the extreme, which can take three, or six, or twenty different forms – you'll see with Estella and her family.'

We were welcomed by a young woman, who shyly motioned us to come in. 'Hello, Claudia,' said John. 'It's nice to see you. How is your mother today?' He introduced me to the family: José and Estella, Claudia and her two brothers, in their twenties, and José's sister, Antonia. I was struck by Estella as soon as we entered the house, because she looked so much like one of my post-encephalitic patients as she stood, statuelike, with one arm outstretched, her head tilted back, and an entranced look on her face. One could put her arms in any position, and they would be maintained like this, apparently effortlessly, for hours. Left alone, she would stand motionless, as if spellbound, staring blankly into space, drooling. But the moment I spoke to her, she answered – appropriately, with wit; she was perfectly capable of lucid thought and speech, provided somebody started her going. Similarly, she could, if she was with someone, go shopping, or to church, always pleasant and alert, but with a sort of detached, preoccupied, sleepwalking air, a strange immurement in herself. I wondered how she might react to L-DOPA – it had not yet been tried with her – for such catatonic patients, in my experience, could show the most dramatic reactions to the drug, bursting out of their catatonia with projectile-like force, and sometimes, with the continuation of the drug, developing multiple tics. Perhaps the family had some inkling of this, I am not sure; when I asked them, they said only that she did not seem to be suffering, that she never complained of her catatonia, that she seemed to be perfectly serene inside.

I found myself in two minds at this. Part of me wanted to say: 'But she is ill, catatonic, she can't fully respond – don't you want to bring her back? She has a right to be medicated, we have a duty to medicate her.' But I hesitated to say anything, feeling an outsider. Later, when I asked John about this, he said, 'Yes – that would have been my reaction, when I came here in '83. But the attitude to illness is different here.' In particular, he said, the Chamorros seem to have a certain stoicism or fatalism – he hardly knew which word to use – about illness, and the lytico-bodig in particular.

With Estella, specifically, there was the sense of calm, of her being in her own world, the sense of an achieved equilibrium both within her, and in relation to her family and community – and the fear that medication might 'stir her up' and imperil this.

But it was very different for José, her husband: physiologically different, as a start – for he had the most intense jamming, clenching, locking parkinsonism, where muscle groups, rigid, fought against each other and jammed each movement at its inception. If he wished to straighten his arm, activation of the triceps was at once opposed by an activation of its antagonist, the biceps (which normally relaxes to allow the arm's extension), and vice versa – so that the arm got locked, perpetually, in strange positions, and he could neither bend nor straighten it. Similar jams, similar binds, affected all his muscle groups – the whole innervation of the body was perverse. He would go red in the face with the intensity of his effort to get through the block, and sometimes it would give way suddenly, and then the force of his effort would make him jerk violently or fall.

In this sort of parkinsonism, the 'explosive-obstructive' sort, the whole body, so to speak, is set against itself, locked in irresoluble inner conflict. It is a state full of tension, effort, and frustration, a tormenting condition which one of my patients once called 'the goad and halter'. José's state was wholly different from the strange muscular compliance, the waxy flexibility, which went with Estella's catatonia. One could see, in this one couple, the extremes of furious resistance and total surrender – the antipodes of the subcortical will. After José and Estella, I examined Claudia and her two brothers briefly, but none of them, it was clear, had any sign of the disease. Nor did they seem to have any fear of getting it, despite the fact that both their parents, and many older relatives, were affected. John contrasted their confidence with the great anxiety often felt by members of the older generation, who often feared – especially if they had relatives with the disease – that they might have it already latent in their bodies. These folk attitudes, John pointed out, were entirely appropriate, given the fact that no one born after 1952 had been known to contract the disease.

José's sister, who lives with them, showed yet another form of the disease, one marked by a severe and progressive dementia. She was at first frightened by our presence – she had lunged at me, and tried to scratch me, when we first entered the house. She became angry, and perhaps jealous, as we talked to the others, and now she came across the room, pointing to herself, saying 'Me, me, me – ME.' She was also quite aphasic, and very restless, given to bursts of screaming and giggling – but music calmed and cohered her to an amazing extent. This too had been discovered by the family; the traditional knowledge of these disorders, and ways of dealing with them, is very considerable. To calm her, the family started to sing an old folk song, and the old lady, so demented, so fragmented most of the time, joined in, singing fluently along with the others. She seemed to get all the words, all the feeling, of the song, and to be composed, restored to herself, as long as she sang. John and I slipped out quietly while they were singing, suddenly feeling, at this point, that neurology was irrelevant.

*

'You can't see a family like this,' said John as we set out the next morning, 'without wondering what causes so many of them to be affected. You see José and his sister, and you think, this must be hereditary. You see Estella and her husband, who are not blood relatives, though their lives are intertwined: is the lytico-bodig due to something in the environment they share, or has one passed the disease to the other? You look at their children, born in the 1960s, free of the disease, like all their contemporaries, and infer that the cause of the disease, whatever it was, vanished or became inoperative in the late forties or fifties.'

These were some of the clues and contradictions, John continued, which faced Kurland and Mulder when they came here in the 1950s – and which are so difficult to reconcile by any single theory. Kurland was at first inclined to think in terms of a genetic origin. He looked at the early history of the island, and how a near genocide reduced the population from 100,000 to a few hundred – the sort of situation which disposes to the spread of an abnormal trait or gene (as with the achromatopsia on Pingelap) – yet there was no simple Mendelian pattern linking those with the disease. He wondered, in the absence of such a pattern, whether this was a gene with 'incomplete penetrance'. (He wondered too if a genetic predisposition to lytico-bodig might also have a paradoxical selective advantage – perhaps increasing fertility or conferring immunity to other diseases.) But he had to wonder whether there might not be some environmental factor, in addition to a genetic susceptibility, a 'necessary adjunct', as he put it, to developing the disease.

In the late 1950s he extended his studies to the very large population of Chamorros who had migrated to California. They had, he observed, the same incidence of lytico-bodig as the Chamorros in Guam, but the disease might only develop ten or twenty years after they had left Guam. There were, on the other hand, a few non-Chamorro immigrants who seemed to have developed the disease a decade or two after moving to Guam and adopting a Chamorro lifestyle.

Could the environmental factor, if there was one, be an infectious agent, a virus, perhaps? The disease did not appear to be contagious or transmissible in any of the usual ways, and no infectious agent could be found in the tissues of those affected. And if there was such an agent, it would have to be one of a very unusual sort, one which might act as a 'slow fuse' – John repeated the phrase for emphasis – a slow fuse in the body, setting off a cascade of events which only later might manifest as clinical disease. As John said this, I thought of various post-viral neurodegenerative syndromes, and especially again of my post-encephalitic patients, who in some cases only started to show symptoms decades after the initial encephalitis lethargica – sometimes as much as forty-five years later.

*

At this point in the story, John started pointing emphatically through the window. 'Look!' he said. 'Look! Look! Cycads!' Indeed I saw cycads all round, some growing wild but many, I now saw, cultivated in gardens, as we drove to Talafofo to visit another patient of John's, a former mayor of the village, whom everyone called the Commissioner.

Cycads only grow in tropical or semi-tropical regions and were new, alien, to the early European explorers when they first saw them. At first glance, cycads bring to mind palms – indeed the cycad is sometimes called a sago palm – but the resemblance is superficial. Cycads are a much more ancient form of life, which arose a hundred million years or more before there were palms or any other flowering plants.

There was a huge native cycad, at least a century old, growing in the Commissioner's yard, and I stopped to gaze at this splendid tree, fondled a stiff, glossy frond, then caught up with John at the front door. He knocked on the door, and it was opened by the Commissioner's wife, who ushered us into the main room where her husband sat. Sitting in a massive chair – rigid, immobile, and parkinsonian, but with a sort of monumental quality, the Commissioner looked younger than his seventy-eight years and still exuded a sense of authority and power. Besides his wife, there were his two daughters and a grandchild – he was still, for all his parkinsonism, very much the patriarch of the house.

In a deep musical voice, as yet scarcely touched by parkinsonism, the Commissioner told us of his life in the village. He had at first been a cattle rancher, and the village strongman, able to bend horseshoes with his bare hands (his hands, gnarled now, and slightly tremulous, still looked powerful enough to crush stones). Later he had been a teacher in the village school; and then, after the war, he had been drawn more and more into village affairs – very complex and unsettled after the Japanese occupation, and with all the new pressures of Americanization on the island, trying (without being 'backward') to preserve the traditional Chamorro ways and myths and customs – finally becoming mayor. His symptoms had begun eighteen months ago, at first with a strange immobility, a loss of initiative and spontaneity; he found he had to make a huge effort to walk, to stand, to make the least movement – his body was disobedient, seemed disconnected from his will. His family and friends, who had known him as a driving, energetic man, first took this as ageing, a natural slowing down after a life of intense activity. Only by degrees did it become clear to them, and him, that this was an organic malady, an all-too-familiar one, the bodig. This fearful, thick immobility advanced with frightening speed: within a year he had become unable to get up alone; once up, unable to sense or control the posture of his body, he might fall suddenly and heavily, without warning, to either side. He now had to have a son-in-law, a daughter, with him all the while, at least if he wanted to get up and go anywhere. He must have found this humiliating in a way, I thought, but he seemed to have no sense of being a burden, imposing on them at all. On the contrary, it seemed natural that his family should come to his aid; when he was younger he too had had to help others – his uncle, his grandfather, two neighbours in his village who had also contracted the strange disease he himself now had. I saw no resentment in his children's faces or their behaviour; their helping seemed entirely spontaneous and natural.

I asked, a little diffidently, if I might examine him. I still thought of him as a powerful authority figure, not someone to lay hands on. And I was still not quite certain of local customs: would he see a neurological examination as an indignity? Something to be done, if at all, behind closed doors, out of sight of the family? The Commissioner seemed to read my mind, and nodded. 'You can examine me here,' he said, 'with my family.'

When I examined him, testing his muscle tone and balance, I found fairly advanced parkinsonism, despite the fact that his first symptoms had begun little more than a year before. He had little tremor or rigidity, but an overwhelming akinesia – an insuperable difficulty in initiating movement; greatly increased salivation, and profound impairment of his postural sense and reflexes. It was a picture somewhat unlike that of 'ordinary' Parkinson's disease, but more suggestive of the much rarer post-encephalitic form.

When I asked the Commissioner his thoughts on what might have caused his illness, he shrugged. 'They say it is fadang,' he said. 'Our own people sometimes thought this, and then the doctors too.'

'Do you eat much of it?' I asked.

'Well, I liked it when I was young, but when they announced it was the cause of lytico-bodig I quit, we all did.' Despite concerns about the eating of fadang as far back as the 1850s (which Kurland had reiterated in the 1960s), the notion that it might be dangerous was only widely publicized in the late 1980s, so this quitting, for the Commissioner, must have been relatively recent – and he was evidently nostalgic for the stuff. 'It has a special taste,' he said, 'strong, pungent. Ordinary flour has no taste at all.' Then he motioned to his wife, and she brought out a huge bottle of cycad chips – obviously the family supply, and one which they had not thrown away, but were still at pains to keep, despite the decision to 'quit'.

They looked delicious – like thick corn chips – and I was strongly tempted to nibble them, but refrained.

The old man suggested we all go outside for a photograph before we left, and we lined up – his wife, himself, and me in the middle – in front of the giant cycad. Then he walked slowly back to the house, a regal figure, a parkinsonian Lear, on the arm of his youngest daughter – not merely dignified in spite of his parkinsonism, but somehow gaining a strange dignity from it.

*

There had been some controversy about the local cycads for two centuries or more. John was interested in the history of Guam and had copies of documents from the early missionaries and explorers, including a Spanish document from 1793, which praised fadang or federico as 'a divine providence', and Freycinet's 1819 *Voyage Autour du Monde*, in which he described seeing this harvested on a large scale in Guam.[48] He described the elaborate process of soaking and washing the seeds, and drying and grinding them to make a thick flour ideal for tortillas and tamales and a soup or porridge called atole – all this is illustrated in his account. It was well known, Freycinet remarked, that if the seeds were not washed sufficiently, they might still be highly poisonous:

> A bird, goat, sheep or hog that drinks from the first water in which the federico has been soaked is apt to die. This does not happen with the second, much less the third, which can be consumed without danger.

Although this washing of the seeds was supposed to be effective in leaching out their poisons, several governors of Guam were to express reservations, especially when federico became the main article of the diet (as happened, typically, after typhoons, when all the vegetation was destroyed except for the tough cycads).

Thus Governor Pablo Perez wrote, in the famine of 1848, that

> not having sweet potatoes, yams and taro, food staples destroyed by the storm, [the Chamorros] have to betake themselves to the woods to seek there the few fruits which are left, which, though noxious, they use as a last resource. . . . This is now their chief staple of food; and notwithstanding the precautions with which they prepare it, all believe that it is injurious to health.

This was echoed by his successor, Don Felipe de la Corte, seven years later, who singled out federico as the most dangerous of all the 'fruits . . . of the forest'.[49]

Kurland, a century later, having found no clear evidence for an infectious or genetic origin for the lytico-bodig, now wondered whether fadang or another element of the Chamorro diet might be the pathogen he sought; and he invited Marjorie Whiting, a nutritionist working on Pohnpei, to come to Guam to investigate this. Whiting had a special interest in indigenous plants and cultures of the Pacific islands, and as soon as Kurland outlined the problem to her, she was fascinated and agreed to come. On her first visit to Guam, in 1954, she spent time in two very different communities – Yigo, which is close to

132

Agana, and part of the Westernized, administrative centre of the island; and Umatac, where she lived in a traditional Chamorro household. She became very close to the Chamorro family, the Quinatas, with whom she lived, and often joined Mrs Quinata and the women of the village in preparing foods for Umatac's frequent fiestas. Often one of the village women would invite her to their ranch or home for the preparation of some special dish.

Cycads had never particularly attracted her attention before (there are no cycads on Pohnpei) – but now everything she encountered seemed to direct her attention to the local species, so common on Guam and the neighbouring island of Rota. *Cycas circinalis* was indigenous, it grew wild, it was free, it required only the labour of collection and preparation.

I had met Marjorie in Hawaii, on my way to Micronesia, and she had told me some vividly personal anecdotes from her time on Guam. She had gone out to do field studies each day for six months, coming back each evening to her Chamorro family – she only discovered later, somewhat to her chagrin, that the rich soups she had been served every day had all been thickened with fadang. People were well aware of its toxic properties and the need for very elaborate washing, but enjoyed the taste of fadang, and especially prized it for making tortillas and thickening soup, 'because of its peculiar mucilaginous quality'. The Chamorros sometimes chewed the green outer seed husks to relieve thirst; when dried, the husks were considered a tasty sweet.

Whiting's experience in Guam initiated an entire decade

Cycas circinalis: male plant with cone (*left*), from Rumphius' 1741 *Herbarium Ambionense* and developing female megasporophylls, first with ovules (*right*) and then with large seeds and new leaves (*below*), from Rheede's 1682 *Hortus Indicus Malabaricus*.

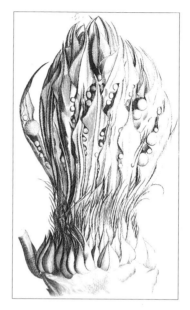

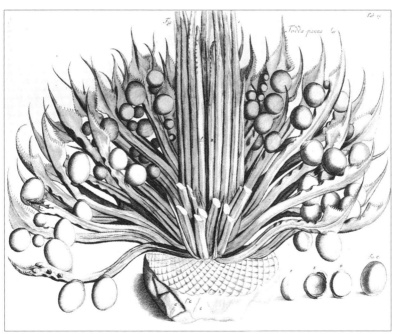

of research in which, collaborating at times with the botanist F. R. Fosberg, she made an encyclopaedic investigation of cycads around the world, and their use by dozens of different cultures as foods, medicines, and poisons.[50] She undertook historical research, exhuming incidents of cycad poisoning among explorers as far back as the eighteenth century. She put together the scattered but voluminous evidence on the neurotoxic effects of cycads in various animals. Finally, in 1963, she published a detailed monograph on her work in the journal *Economic Botany*.

There were approximately a hundred species of cycad around the world, and nine genera,[51] she noted, and most of these had been used as sources of food, containing as they did large quantities of edible starch (sago), which could be extracted variously from the root, stem, or nut.[52] Cycads were eaten not merely, Whiting noted, as a reserve during times of shortage, but as a food with 'a special prestige and popularity'. They were used on Melville Island for first-fruit rites; among the Karawa in Australia for initiation ceremonies; and in Fiji, where they were a special food reserved only for the use of chiefs. The kernels were often roasted in Australia, where settlers referred to them as 'blackfellows' potatoes'. Every part of the cycad had been used for food: the leaves could be eaten as tender young shoots; the seeds, when green, could be 'boiled to edible softness; the white meat has a flavour and texture . . . compared to that of a roasted chestnut'.

Like Freycinet, Whiting described the lengthy process of detoxification: slicing the seeds, soaking them for days or weeks, drying and then pounding them, and, in some cultures, fermenting them too. ('Westerners have compared the flavour of fermented cycad seeds with that of some of the best-known European cheeses.') Stems of *Encephalartos septimus* had been used in parts of Africa to make a delicious cycad beer, she wrote, while the seeds of *Cycas revoluta* were used, in the Ryukyu Islands, to prepare a form of sake.[53] Fermented *Zamia* starch was regarded as a delicacy throughout the Caribbean, where it was consumed in the form of large alcoholic balls.

Every culture which uses cycads has recognized their toxic potential, and this was implied, she added, by some of the native names given to them, like 'devil's coconut' and 'ricket fern'. In some cultures, they were deliberately used as poisons. Rumphius (the Dutch naturalist whose name is now attached to the widespread Pacific species *Cycas rumphii*) recorded that in the Celebes 'the sap from the kernels . . . was given to children to drink in order to kill them so that the parents would not be hampered when they went to follow their roving life in the wilderness of the forest'.[54] Other accounts, from Honduras and Costa Rica, suggested that *Zamia* root might be used to dispose of criminals or political enemies.

None the less many cultures also regarded cycads as having healing or medicinal properties; Whiting instanced the Chamorro use of grated fresh seeds of *Cycas circinalis* as a poultice for tropical leg ulcers.

The use of cycads as food had been independently discovered in many cultures; and each had devised their own ways of detoxifying them. There had been, of course, innumerable individual accidents, especially among explorers and their crews without this cultural knowledge. Members of Cook's crew became violently ill after eating unprepared cycad seeds at the Endeavour River in Australia, and in 1788 members of the La Pérouse expedition became ill after merely nibbling the seeds of *Macrozamia communis* at Botany Bay – the attractive, fleshy sarcotesta of these are loaded with toxic macrozamin.[55] But there had never been, Whiting thought, a cultural accident, where an entire culture had hurt itself by cycad eating.

There were, however, examples of animals poisoning themselves *en masse*, unprotected by any 'instinctive' knowedge. Cattle which browse on bracken may come down with a neurological disorder which resembles beriberi or thiamine deficiency – this is caused by an enzyme in bracken which destroys the body's thiamine. Horses in the Central Valley of California have come down with parkinsonism after eating the toxic star thistle. But the example which Whiting especially remarks is that of sheep and cattle, which are extremely fond of cycads; indeed, the term 'addiction' has been used in Australia, where some animals will travel great distances for the plants. Outbreaks of neurocycadism, she noted, had been recorded in Australian cattle since the mid-nineteenth century. Some animals, browsing on the fresh young cycad shoots (this would especially occur in dry seasons, when other plants had died off, or after fires, when cycads would be the first plants to reshoot new leaves) would get a brief, acute gastrointestinal illness, with vomiting and diarrhoea – this, if not fatal, would be followed by complete recovery, as with acute cycad poisoning in man. But with continued browsing on the plants, neurocycadism would develop; this would begin as a staggering or weaving gait (hence the colloquial name 'zamia staggers'), a tendency to cross the hind legs while walking, and finally complete and permanent paralysis of the hind limbs. Removing the animals from the cycads at this stage was of no use; once the staggers had set in, the damage was irreversible.

Could this, Whiting and Kurland wondered, be a model for lytico? The idea was intriguing: fadang had been a common food before the war and, during the Japanese occupation, was used in much larger quantities, as other crops were requisitioned or destroyed. After the war, fadang consumption declined sharply because of the greater availability of imported wheat and corn flour – this, it seemed to them, could provide a very plausible scenario for the disease, why it had peaked immediately following the war, and steadily declined thereafter, an incidence which ran parallel to the use of fadang.

But the cycad theory was problematic on several grounds. First, there were no other known examples, outside Guam, of a chronic human illness ascribable to the use of cycads, despite their very wide and long use throughout the world. It was, of course, possible that there was something special about the Guam cycad, or some special vulnerability to it among the Chamorros. Second, the period of decades which might elapse between exposure to the cycads and the onset of lytico-bodig, if indeed the two were connected, was something which had no precedent in poisonings of the nervous system. All known neurotoxins acted immediately or within a few weeks, the time needed to accumulate to toxic levels in the body or for neurological damage to reach critical, symptomatic levels – this was so with heavy metal poisoning, as had occurred in the notorious Minamata Bay paralysis, with the neurolathyrism in India caused by eating the toxic chickling pea, and with the neurocycadism in cattle.[56] But these seemed quite different from a poison which, while causing no immediate effects, might lead to a progressive degeneration of particular nerve cells starting many years later. No such delayed toxic effect had ever been described – the very concept strained belief.

*

We set off again, to return to Umatac; John had more patients he wanted me to meet. He loved showing me patients, he said, taking me on house calls with him – I also loved this, seeing his energy, his neurological skill, and, even more, the delicate feeling, the caring, he showed for his patients. It took me back to my own growing up, when I would go out on house calls with my father, a general practitioner – I had always been fascinated by his technical skills, his elicitation of subtle symptoms and signs, his knack for making diagnoses, but also by the warm feeling which manifestly flowed between him and his patients. It was similar, I felt, with John; he too is a sort of GP – a neurological GP, an island GP – for his hundreds of patients with lytico-bodig. He is not just a physician to a group of individuals, but physician to a whole community – the community of the afflicted Chamorros and their relatives who live in Umatac, Merizo, Yona, Talofofo, Agat, Dededo, in the nineteen villages which are scattered over Guam.

Juan, another of John's patients, has a very unusual form of the disease, John had told me. 'Not like ALS, not like parkinsonism, not like any of the typical forms of lytico-bodig. What he does have is a peculiar tremor which I have never seen before in lytico-bodig – but I am sure this is the beginning of the disease in him.' Juan was fifty-eight, very powerfully built, deeply sunburned, looked much younger than his years. His own symptoms had come on a couple of years ago, and he noticed them first when he was writing a letter. The act of writing brought on a shaking, and within a year it was no longer possible to write, at least with his right hand. But he had no other symptoms at all.

I examined him and was puzzled by the tremor. It looked nothing like the resting ('pill-rolling') tremor one usually sees in parkinsonism, for it came on with action or intention (which suppress the resting tremor). Nor did it resemble the 'intention tremor' which one may see (with incoordination and other cerebellar signs) if there is damage in the cerebellum or its connections. It resembled instead what neurologists gaily call essential or benign tremor. 'Essential' because it seems to arise without any demonstrable lesion in the brain, and 'benign' because it is usually self-limiting, responds well to medication, and does not interfere with life too much.

Usually this is the case. But there are a certain number of people who go on from such a 'benign' tremor to develop full-blown parkinsonism or other neurodegenerative disease. I thought of one patient of mine, an elderly woman in New York, who, when she developed such a tremor, in her seventies, was severely incommoded by it. She burst into tremor whatever she did, and could only prevent this by sitting stock-still. 'They call it benign,' she said, 'what's so benign about it?' In her case, it was intensely malignant, not only in the way it interfered with her life, but in the fact that it proved to be the first symptom of a rare corticobasal degeneration, going on to rigidity, spasticity, and dementia, and, within two years, death.

There was no reason to suppose that Juan had anything like this. What he probably had, John felt – and I trusted his intuition – was an extremely mild form of bodig, so mild that he would probably be able to work and live independently for the rest of his life. Progressive and disabling as the lytico-bodig usually is, there are some, like Juan, who are only touched by it lightly, and who, after a sometimes rapid development of symptoms over a year or two, seem to show little further advance of the disease (though I have recently heard from John that Juan has developed some parkinsonian rigidity now).[57]

Had I let him, John would have driven straight on to the next patient, and the next. He was eager to show me everything in the few days I would be on Guam, and his energy and enthusiasm seemed to know no limits. But I had had enough for one day, and needed a break, needed a swim. 'Yes, you're right, Oliver,' said John. 'Let's take a break – let's go snorkelling with Alma!'

*

Alma van der Velde has a charming, sloping house, covered by vines, perhaps held together by them, surrounded by ferns and cycads, right by the water's edge in Merizo. She herself is a water creature, who spends half her days swimming in the reef – badly arthritic, she moves painfully on land, but she is a graceful, strong, and tireless swimmer. She came to Micronesia as a young woman, fell in love with it, has never left. She has swum among these reefs daily for thirty years; she knows where to find the best chitons, cowries, and top shells, she knows the caves where octopuses hide, the underhangs of the reef where the rarest corals are found. When she is not swimming, she sits on her verandah, painting the sea, the clouds, the rocky outcroppings by the reef – or reading, or writing, completely self-sufficient. She and John are close friends, so close they hardly need to talk when they are together; they sit, they watch the waves thundering on the reef, and John is able, briefly, to forget the lytico-bodig.

Alma greeted us, and smiled when she saw I had brought my own fins and snorkel. John wanted to stay on the verandah and read; Alma and I would go to the reef together. She gave me a stick to walk over the shallow coral shelf with its razor-sharp branches, and then led the way – following a path which I could not have discerned, but which she clearly knew intimately, out to the clear waters beyond. As soon as the water was more than a couple of feet deep, Alma dived in, and, following her, I dived in too.

We moved past great coral canyons, with their endless forms and colours and their gnarled branches – some shaped like mushrooms, some like trees, being nibbled at by tetrodons and filefish. Clouds of tiny zebra fish and fish of an iridescent blue swam through them, and around me, between my arms, between my legs, unstartled by my movements.

We swam through shoals of wrasse and parrot fish and damsels, and saw turkey fish, with rusty feather fans, hovering beneath us. I reached out my hand to touch one as it hovered, but Alma shook her head violently (later she told me the 'feathers' were quite poisonous to touch). We saw flatworms waving like tiny scarves in the water and plump polychaetes with iridescent bristles. Large starfish, startlingly blue, crawled slowly on the bottom, and spiny sea urchins made me glad my feet were protected by fins.

Another few yards and we were suddenly in a deep channel, the bottom forty feet below us, but the water so clear and transparent that we could see every detail as if it were at arm's length. Alma made some gesture I could not understand as we swam in this channel; and then we turned back, to the shallower waters of the reef. I saw hundreds of sea cucumbers, some nearly a yard long, making their cylindrical way slowly across the ocean floor, and found these enchanting – but Alma, to my surprise, made a grimace, shook her head.

'They're bad news,' she said, after we had come in and showered and were eating fresh tuna and a salad with

John on the porch. 'Bottom feeders! They go with pollution – you saw how pale the reef was today.' Indeed, the corals were varied and beautiful, but not quite as brilliant as I had hoped, not as brilliant as they had been when I snorkelled off Pohnpei. 'Each year it gets paler,' Alma continued, 'and the sea cucumbers multiply. Unless they do something, it'll be the end of the reef.'[58]

'Why did you gesture when we were in the channel?' I asked.

'That means it's a shark channel – that is *their* highway. They have their own schedules and times, times I would never dream of going near it. But it was a safe time today.'

*

We decided to rest and read for a while, in companionable silence on the verandah. Wandering inside to Alma's comfortable living room, I spotted a large book on her shelf entitled *The Useful Plants of the Island of Guam*, by W. E. Safford. I pulled it out – gingerly, as it was starting to fall apart. I had thought, from the title, that it was going to be a narrow, rather technical book on rice and yams, though I hoped it would have some interesting drawings of cycads as well. But its title was deceptively modest, for it seemed to contain, in its four hundred densely packed pages, a detailed account not only of the plants, the animals, the geology of Guam, but a deeply sympathetic account of Chamorro life and culture, from their foods, their crafts, their boats, their houses, to their language, their myths and rituals, their philosophical and religious beliefs.

Safford quoted detailed accounts of the island and its people from various explorers – Pigafetta, Magellan's historian, writing in 1521; Legazpi in 1565; Garcia in 1683; and half a dozen others.[59] These all concurred in portraying the Chamorros as exceptionally vigorous, healthy, and long-lived. In the first year of the Spanish mission, Garcia recorded, there were more than 120 centenarians baptized – a longevity he ascribed to the ruggedness of their constitutions, the naturalness of their food, and the absence of vice or worries. All of the Chamorros, noted Legazpi, were excellent swimmers and could catch fish in their bare hands; indeed, he remarked, they sometimes seemed to him 'more like fish than human beings'. The Chamorros were skilled as well in navigation and agriculture, maintained an active trade with other islands, and had a vital society and culture. Romantic exaggeration is not absent in these early accounts, which sometimes seem to portray Guam as an earthly paradise; but there is no doubt that the island was able to support a very large community – the estimates all fall between 60,000 and 100,000 – in conditions of cultural and ecological stability.

Though there were occasional visitors in the century and a half that followed Magellan's landing, there was to be no massive change until the arrival of Spanish missionaries in 1668, in a concerted effort to Christianize the population. Resistance to this – to forced baptism, in the first place – led to savage retaliation, in which whole villages would be punished for the act of a single man, and from this to a horrifying war of extermination.

On top of this, there now came a series of epidemics introduced by the colonists – above all smallpox, measles, and tuberculosis, with leprosy as a special, slowly smouldering gift.[60] And in addition to actual extermination and disease, there were the moral effects of a forced colonization and Christianization – the attempted soul murder, in effect, of an entire culture.

> This ... weighed so heavily upon [them] ... that some even sacrified their lives in despair; and some women either purposely sterilized themselves or cast into the waters their new-born infants, believing them happy to die thus early, saved from the toils of a life gloomy, painful, and miserable ... they judge that subjection is the worst misery in the world.

By 1710, there were virtually no Chamorro men left on Guam, and only about a thousand women and children remained. In the space of forty years, ninety-nine per cent of the population had been wiped out. Now that the resistance was over, the missionaries sought to help the all-but-exterminated Chamorros to survive – to survive, that is, on their own, Christian and Western, terms – to adopt clothing, to learn the catechism, to give up their own myths and gods and habits. As time passed, new generations were increasingly hybridized, as mestizo children were born to women who were married to, or raped by, the soldiers who had come to subdue their nation. Antoine-Alfred Marche, who travelled the Marianas between 1887 and 1889, felt there were no longer any pure-blooded Chamorros in Guam – or at most a few families on the neighbouring island of Rota, where they had fled two centuries before. Their bold seafaring skills, once renowned throughout the Pacific, were lost. The Chamorro language became creolized, admixed with much Spanish.

As the nineteenth century progressed, Guam, once a prized Spanish colony on the galleon route, fell into deepening neglect and oblivion; Spain herself was in decline, had problems at home, other interests, and all but forgot her colonies in the Western Pacific. This period, for the Chamorros, was a mixed one: if they were less persecuted, less actively under the heel of their conquerors, their land, their diet, their economy, had become more and more impoverished. Trade and shipping continued to decline, and the island became a distant backwater, whose governors had neither the money nor the influence to change things.

The final sign of this decline was the farcical way in which Spanish rule was officially ended, by a single American gunboat, the USS *Charleston*, in 1898. There had been no ships for two months, and when the *Charleston* and its three companion vessels appeared off Guam, a pleasurable excitement swept the island. What news, what novelties, the ships might bring! When the *Charleston* fired, Juan Marina, the governor, was pleased – this must be, he assumed, a formal salute. He was stunned to discover that it was not a greeting, but war – he had no idea that there *was* a war going on between America and Spain – and he now found himself led in chains aboard the *Charleston*, a prisoner of war. Thus ended three centuries of Spanish rule.

It was at this point that Safford himself entered the history of Guam. He was a navy lieutenant at the time, an aide to Captain Richard Leary, the first American governor – but Leary, for reasons of his own, elected not to leave his ship, which was moored in the harbour, and sent Safford to act in his stead. Safford soon gained a working knowledge of the Chamorro language and customs, and his respect for the people, his courtesy, his curiosity, made him an essential bridgehead between the islanders and their new masters.[61] The new American administration, though not quite as out of touch as the Spanish one it replaced, did not institute too many changes in Guam. It did, however, open schools and English classes – the first of which were conducted by Safford in 1899 – and greatly improved medical observation and care. The first medical reports of 'hereditary paralysis' and its unusual incidence date from 1900; the more specific term, 'ALS', was used as early as 1904.

Life in Guam remained much the same as it had been for the past two centuries. The population had gradually increased since the genocide of 1670–1700; a census in 1901 found 9,676 people, of whom all but forty-six considered themselves to be Chamorros. Nearly 7,000 of them lived in the capital of Agana or its adjacent villages. Roads were very poor, and the villages in the south, like Umatac, were almost inaccessible in the rainy parts of the year, and could only reliably be reached by sea.

Nevertheless, Guam was deemed important from a military point of view, because of its size and crucial position in the Pacific. During the First World War, Japan was one of America's allies, and Guam was not drawn into the conflict. But there was great tension on 8 December 1941, as Guam got news of the attack on Pearl Harbor; within hours, it too found itself under attack as Mitsubishis from Saipan, just a hundred miles to the north, suddenly appeared in the sky above Agana, spitting machine-gun fire. Two days later, Japanese infantry, which had been massing on Rota, landed, and Guam could offer little resistance.

The Japanese occupation was a time of great cruelty and hardship, reminiscent of the conquistadores. Many Chamorros were killed, many were tortured or enslaved for war work, and others fled their villages and farms to live out the occupation, as best they could, in the hills and jungle. Families and villages were broken up, fields and food supplies were taken over, and famine ensued. Cycad seeds had been an important part of their diet for two hundred years at least; now they became a near-exclusive diet for some. Many more Chamorros were brutally murdered near the end of the war, especially when it became clear that the Japanese days were numbered, and that the island would soon be 'liberated' by the Americans. The Chamorros had suffered appallingly during the war, and welcomed the American soldiers, when they came, with jubilation.

The real Americanization of Guam came after 1945. Agana, which had housed half of Guam's population before the war, had been levelled in the recapture of the island and had to be totally rebuilt; the rebuilding transformed it from a small town of low, traditional houses to an American city with concrete roads, gas stations, super-markets, and ever-higher high-rise apartments. There was massive immigration, mostly of servicemen and their dependents, and the population of the island swelled from its pre-war 22,000 to more than 200,000.

Guam remained closed to visitors and immigrants, under military restriction, until 1960. The entire north and north-eastern portions, which contained the best beaches on the island, and the beautiful and ancient village of Sumay (taken over by the Japanese in 1941, and finally flattened by the Americans in 1944), were appropriated for new military bases, and closed even to the Chamorros who had once lived there. Since the 1960s, huge numbers of tourists and immigrants have arrived – Filipino workers by the tens of thousands, and Japanese tourists by the million, requiring ever vaster golf courses and luxury hotels.

The traditional Chamorro ways of life are dwindling and vanishing, receding to pockets in the remotest southern villages, like Umatac.[62]

*

John normally goes on his rounds with Phil Roberto, a young Chamorro man who has had some medical training, and who acts also as his interpreter and assistant. Like Greg Dever in Pohnpei, John feels strongly that Micronesia has been far too dominated by America and Ameri-can doctors, imposing their own attitudes and values, and that it is crucial to train indigenous people – doctors,

151

nurses, paramedics, technicians – to have an autonomous health-care system. John hopes that Phil will succeed him, completing his medical degree and taking over his practice when John retires, for Phil, as a Chamorro himself, will be an integral part of the community in a way that John can never fully be.

Over the years there has been increasing resentment among the Chamorros in regard to Western doctors. The Chamorros have given their stories, their time, their blood, and finally their brains – often feeling that they themselves are no more than specimens or subjects, and that the doctors who visit and test them are not concerned with *them*. 'For people to admit that their family has this disease is a big step,' Phil said. 'And then to let medical people come into their homes is another big step. Yet in terms of treatment or care, health care, home care, they're really not given enough assistance. Visiting doctors come and go, with their forms and research protocols, but they don't know the people. John and I go into people's houses regularly, and we come to know the families, their histories, and how they've come to this point in their lives. John has known many of his patients for ten or twelve years. We have videotaped hundreds of hours of interviews with patients. They have come to trust us, and are more open in terms of calling for assistance – saying, "So-and-so is looking rather pale, what should I do?" They know we are here for them.

'We are the ones who go back to their homes weeks after the researchers have been here and taken their samples back to the States. The patients ask us, "So what happened to those tests performed on us?" But we have no answers for them, because they're not our tests.'

*

The next morning John and Phil picked me up early. 'You saw a little of the parkinsonism and dementia – the bodig – yesterday,' he said. 'Kurland felt this form of the disease was replacing ALS in the 1970s – but you must not imagine the ALS is extinct. I have lytico patients I have been following for years, and new cases as well – we'll see some today.' He paused, and added, 'There is something unbearable about ALS; I'm sure you have felt it, Oliver – every neurologist does. To see the strength go and the muscles wasting, people unable to move their mouths to speak, people who choke to death because they can't swallow . . . to see all this and feel you can do nothing, absolutely nothing, to help them. Sometimes it seems especially horrible because their minds remain absolutely clear until the end – they know what is happening to them.'

We were on our way to see Tomasa, whom John has known ever since he came to Guam. She had already had lytico for fifteen years when he met her; it has advanced steadily since, paralysing not only her limbs but the muscles of breathing, speech, and swallowing. She is now near the end, but has continued to bear it with fortitude, to tolerate a nasogastric tube, frequent choking and aspiration, total dependence, with a calm, unfrightened fatalism. Indeed a fatality hangs over her entire family – her father suffered from lytico, as did two of her sisters, while two of her brothers have parkinsonism and dementia. Out of eight children in her generation, five have been afflicted by the lytico-bodig.

When we entered her room, Tomasa looked wasted, paralysed, but alert. With a cheery 'Hello, Tomasa, how is everything today?' John walked over to the couch where she was lying. He leaned over and touched her shoulder, and she followed his hand with her eyes, which were bright and attentive. She followed everything, with an occasional (perhaps sometimes reflexive, pseudobulbar) smile, and a slight groaning as she exhaled. She was dying in full consciousness, after twenty-five years of an implacable disease, in a bright sunlit room. John introduced me to Tomasa and to her daugher, Angie, who was with her. When I asked her date of birth, Tomasa produced a string of (to me) unintelligible sounds, but her daughter interpreted this as 12 April 1933. Tomasa could open her mouth on request, and put out her tongue. It was fearfully wasted, fissured, fasciculating, like a bag of worms. She made another unintelligible sound. 'She wants me to bring you and Dr Steele something to drink,' Angie said. Tomasa's manners had not deserted her, even at this point. 'She has taught countless people about the disease on Guam,' said John; Tomasa smiled. 'Don't worry, Tomasa – Angie will not get the lytico. No one in the younger generation gets this, thank God,' he added softly.

Family, friends, neighbours, come in at all hours, read the papers to her, tell her the news, give her all the local gossip. At Christmas, the Christmas tree is put by her couch; if there are local fiestas or picnics, people gather in her room. She may scarcely be able to move or speak, but she is still, in their eyes, a total person, still part of the family and community. She will remain at home, in the bosom of her family and community, in total consciousness and dignity and personhood, up to the day of her death, a death which cannot, now, be too far off.

Seeing Tomasa surrounded by her large family made me think of a 1602 description of the Chamorros by an early missionary, Fray Juan Pobre, which I had seen while browsing in John's office:

> They are naturally very compassionate people. . . . The day when the master of the house, or his wife, or a child falls ill, all the relatives in the village will take dinner and supper to them, which will be prepared from the best food they have in the house. This is continued until the patient dies or recovers.

This acceptance of the sick person *as* a person, a living part of the community, extends to those with chronic and incurable illness, who may, like Tomasa, have years of invalidism. I thought of my own patients with advanced ALS in New York, all in hospitals or nursing homes, with nasogastric tubes, suction apparatus, sometimes respirators, every sort of technical support – but very much alone, deliberately or unconsciously avoided by their relatives, who cannot bear to see them in this state, and almost prefer to think of them (as the hospital does) not as human beings, but as terminal medical cases on full 'life support', getting the best of modern medical care. Such patients are often avoided by doctors too, written, even by them, out of the book of life. But John has stayed close to Tomasa, and will be with her, with the family, the day she finally dies.

*

From Tomasa's house, we drove north across the island, up through the cycad-dappled hills, and past placid Lake Fena, Guam's only reservoir of fresh water.[63] Everything looked very dry on the plateau; at one point, John pointed out the charred trees and large areas of blackened ground which were the legacy of a great forest fire the previous summer. And yet here, even in these blackened areas, were new shoots of green – shoots which came from the stumps of cycads.

Dededo is a more modern village, now the largest on Guam after Agana. It has a somewhat suburban look, with each house set at a little distance from the others, so there is more sense of 'privacy' (though this seems to be more a Western concept than a Chamorro one). It is in one of these houses that Roque lives. He is a strong, muscular man in his early fifties – robust, covered with tattoos from his tour of duty in the army – in perfect health, apparently, until fourteen months ago, when he started to complain of something blocking his throat. He soon noticed symptoms in his voice, his face, his hands, and it became clear that he had a rapidly progressive, almost fulminating, form of lytico. While he is not too disabled at this point, he knows he will be dead in a few months. 'You can talk to me about it,' he said, seeing my reluctance. 'I have no secrets from myself.' Part of the problem, he said, was the mealy mouthed doctors in Agana, who were evasive, who wished to convey hope and reassurance – an optimistic, false view of the lytico, which might prevent him from coming to terms with it, with his rapidly narrowing life and the certainty of death. But his body told him the truth – and John did too.

'I was a very athletic man, and now the disease has pulled me down,' he told us. 'I accept it, but sometimes I feel so depressed that I feel like doing something drastic. . . . To commit suicide is no good. It's not right. But I wish the Lord would take me rather than wait for no result or no cure. If there's no cure, I would have the Lord take me.'

Roque was deeply sad, he said, that he would not see his children grow up, and that his youngest son (just two now) might not retain any memories of him; he was sad that he would be leaving his wife a widow, and his old parents, still in good health, bereaved.

What will happen with him, I asked John – will he die at home, like Tomasa, or will he go to a hospital? 'That depends,' said John, 'on what he wants, what the family wants, the course of the illness. If you have complete bulbar paralysis, and respiration is affected, you have to have assisted breathing, a respirator, or you die. Some people want this, some do not. I have a couple of patients on respirators at St Dominic's – we'll see them tomorrow.'

*

Later in the afternoon, Phil and I had planned to go down to the beach at Sumay, said to be the finest for snorkelling in Guam. This was on the military base, so Phil had arranged permission for us to go. We arrived around four, and presented our papers. But our reception at the gate was surly and suspicious, especially when the guards saw that Phil was a Chamorro. When I tried to put a good-natured, genial spin on things, I was met by a blank, faceless stare – I was reminded, unavoidably, of the hateful episode on Kwajalein, the helplessness of civilians, civility, in the face of military bureaucracy. Phil had warned me that I had best say nothing, that we both had to behave in the most deferential, abject manner, or they would find reason to deny us entrance at all. I had thought, at the time, that his advice was a little overstated – but now I saw that it was not. In the event, we were kept waiting at the gate for an hour, while the guards phoned for various permissions and confirmations. At five o'clock, we were told that our admittance had been approved – but also that it was too late, because the base was now closed. At this point, fortunately (for I was about to explode with rage), a senior officer came along; we could override the regulations this time, he said – we could enter and have our swim, but we would have to be accompanied by military police as long as we were on the base.

Phil choked at this, and the feeling of supervision made me furious, but having come this far, we decided to go ahead and have our swim. Changing into our swimming gear in full sight of a jeep with four police was slightly unnerving, and an antinomian part of me wanted to do something outrageous – but I controlled myself, with some regret, tried to put the police out of mind, and surrendered to the water.

It was, indeed, exquisite. There are more than three hundred species of coral native to Guam, and the colours of these at Sumay seemed far richer than those at Alma's, or even those of the glorious corals off Pohnpei. A little farther from shore, we could see the outlines of the wreck of a Japanese warship, richly and strangely meta-morphosed by a crust of barnacles and corals – but it would take more time, and scuba gear, to examine it properly. As we swam back in, I could see the shape of the waiting jeep shivering through the transparent waters, and the stiff figures of the MPs, distorted by their shifting refraction. As we dried ourselves in the gloaming, I seethed to think that this perfect reef was denied to the people of Guam, hoarded and locked up by institutional order.

But Phil's anger had a deeper layer. This was the site of the old village of Sumay, he said as we drove back to the entrance of the base. 'It was the most beautiful village in the whole of Guam. It was bombed by the Japanese, the first day they attacked Guam; then all the inhabitants were evicted or killed. When the Allies came, the Japanese retreated to those caves in the cliffs you can see, and trying to get them out, the Americans bombed the whole place into dust. That fragment of the church and the graveyard – that's the only thing left. My grandparents were born here,' he added, 'and they are buried here too. Many of us have ancestors in the graveyard here, and we want to visit the graves, pay our respects – but then we have to go through the bureaucratic process you've seen. It is a great indignity.'

*

The next day, John and I set out for St Dominic's, a beautiful new hospital, or, as the nuns prefer to call it, Home, with gardens, patios, a tranquil chapel, perched on Mount Barrigada, overlooking Agana. Here were two more patients of John's – both, like Roque, still in their fifties, and stricken by lytico in its most virulent form. Both had been in perfect health, seemingly, eighteen months before; both had now reached a point where the muscles of respiration were paralysed, and mechanical ventilation was needed to help them breathe. As we approached their rooms, I heard the heavy, animal-like breathing of their respirators, and the unpleasant sucking sounds made as their throats were suctioned dry (for they could no longer swallow their own secretions and had to have these sucked out mechanically, lest they be aspirated into the trachea and lungs). I could not help wondering whether life was worth it under these conditions, but both patients had children with them – an adult son in one case, an adult daughter in the other – with whom some contact and simple communication was still possible; they could still be read to, watch television, listen to the radio. Their minds were still alive and active, even if their muscles were not, and both had indicated that they wanted to go on, to stay alive as long as they could, even if this meant being maintained on a machine. Both were surrounded by religious pictures and icons, which they gazed at with unblinking eyes. Their faces, I wanted to think, seemed to be at peace, despite the heaving, gurgling bodies below.

Many patients with very advanced bodig come to St Dominic's too, in some cases suffering not only from parkinsonism, but from a severe dementia and spasticity as well. In such patients, in the final stages, the mouth hangs open, drooling with saliva; the palate hangs motionless, so that speech and swallowing are impossible; and the arms and legs, severely spastic, become bent in immovable flexion contractures. Patients in this state can hardly be looked after at home by even the most devoted families, and are usually brought to St Dominic's, where the nuns are devoted to their care. I was deeply moved by the dedication of the nuns who undertook this care; they reminded me of the Little Sisters of the Poor, an order of nuns I work with in New York. Unlike what one sees in most hospitals, the Sisters' first care, and continuing concern, is with the dignity and state of mind of each patient. There is always a sense of the patient as a total individual, not just a medical problem, a body, a 'case'. And here, where family and communal ties are so close, the patients' rooms, the corridors, the patios, the gardens of St Dominic's, are always thronged with family and neighbours – the family, the village, the community, of each patient is reconstituted here in miniature. Going to Saint Dominic's does not mean a removal from all that is dear and familiar, but rather a translocation of all this, as much as is possible, into the medical milieu of the hospital.

I felt drained by seeing these patients with lytico and bodig in their final, terrible stages, and I wanted desperately to get away, to lie down and collapse on my bed, or swim again in a pristine reef. I am not sure why I was so overwhelmed; much of my practice in New York involves working amid the incurable and disabled, but ALS is rare – I may see only one case every two or three years.

I wondered how John, who has forty or more patients with advanced lytico-bodig, dealt with his feelings. When he was with patients, I noted, he often adopted his booming, professional voice, and an optimistic, bracing, cheery manner – but this was only a surface, behind which he remained intensely sensitive and vulnerable. Phil later told me that when John is alone, or thinks he is alone, he may weep at the plight of his patients, and at his impotence, our impotence, to do anything about it.

*

After lunch we visited a different part of St Dominic's – a pleasant, open room looking on to a garden, where some of the day patients had collected for their afternoon session. St Dominic's is not just a chronic-care hospital, but also has an active day programme for ambulatory patients who come from all over the island. It is a place where they can meet, enjoy meals together, walk in the gardens, or work in a workshop, and receive therapy of all sorts – physiotherapy, speech therapy, arts and music therapy. It was here that John brought me to see Euphrasia, another patient of his. She is seventy, but looks much younger, and has had a parkinsonian form of bodig for twenty-four years, though not the least memory impairment or dementia. She had moved to California as a young bride soon after the war, and did not revisit Guam for many years. Nevertheless, she came down with bodig in 1969, despite having lived out of Guam for twenty-two years.

Seeing Euphrasia brought home to me the immense lag which might exist between exposure to whatever it is (or was) on Guam, and the subsequent development of lytico-bodig. John told me, indeed, that he had heard of one patient in whom the gap between leaving Guam and developing the disease was more than forty years – and that there might be similar lags in those who came *to* Guam. No Caucasian, as far as he knew, had ever contracted the disease, but he knew of a few Japanese and Filipino patients who had come to Guam, married Chamorros, entered the culture completely, and then come down with apparent lytico or bodig many years later.[64]

This, for him, was the most convincing clinical evidence of the extraordinary 'silent' period in which the lytico-bodig must, in some sense, be present – but subclinical or latent. Was it burning away slowly beneath the surface, all through these years? Or did there have to be a new event, which might ignite a previously harmless, perhaps arrested, process and turn it into an active one? Sometimes he favoured the first thought, John said; sometimes the second – though seeing a patient such as Roque, in whom there had been so explosive an onset of disease, erupting in the midst of seemingly perfect health, one had less sense of a steady, ongoing process finally surfacing than of a sudden, lethal transformation.

I thought of how von Economo, the physician who had first identified the encephalitis lethargica, had spoken of post-encephalitic patients as 'extinct volcanoes'. This seemed an apt comparison until L-DOPA came along, when I began to think of them as *sleeping* volcanoes, which might suddenly (sometimes dangerously) erupt with this new drug. But these patients were already manifestly ill – frozen, catatonic; whereas the lytico-bodig patients, seemingly, were perfectly well and active before their symptoms began. 'But you can't be sure of that on purely clinical grounds,' said John. 'You have no way of judging what may be going on at the cellular level.' What had been going on, we wondered, in Euphrasia during those twenty-two years after she had left Guam?

Euphrasia was started on L-DOPA by her doctor in California in 1969 (this intrigued me, as it was the same year I had started my own post-encephalitic patients on L-DOPA). In ordinary Parkinson's disease, the initial effects of the drug are smooth and steady and last for many hours, though sooner or later, its effects may become unstable, giving patients a brief period of fluidity, some-times accompanied by chorea and other involuntary movements, followed in an hour or so by an intense immobility – a so-called on-off effect. Such on-off effects, I had found, tended to set in much earlier with my post-encephalitic patients – sometimes, indeed, from the very start, and Euphrasia too, John said, had shown reactions which were extreme and hyperbolic from the beginning.

And yet despite its ups and downs, she continued to get a crucial benefit from L-DOPA, for it allowed her a few hours of relatively good function each day.

She had not had any medication for several hours when we stopped by, and she was in an 'off' state, sitting completely motionless in a chair, her head bent, almost jammed, on her chest, only her eyes still capable of any movement. There was extreme rigidity in all her limbs. Her voice was very soft, flat, almost inaudible, and devoid of any animation or expression. She drooled constantly.

John introduced us, and I took her hand and squeezed it gently. She could not speak, but she smiled back, her eyes crinkling, and I could feel a faint squeeze in response.

With a conspiratorial wink to Euphrasia, I said to John, 'I'll show you something – or Euphrasia will.' I managed, with some difficulty, to get her to her feet. Walking backward in front of her, holding her gnarled hands, cueing her all the time, I was able to guide her, with tiny, tottering steps, to the garden just outside. There was a rock garden in the form of a little hill, with irregular ledges and slopes. 'OK,' I said to Euphrasia, pointing to a rock, 'climb over this, you're on your own – go!' To John's horror, and the nuns', I took my hands off her, and let her go. But Euphrasia, who had been almost incapable of movement on the flat, featureless floor of the dayroom, lifted her leg high, and stepped boldly over the rock, and then over another one, and another, up to the top of the rock garden, without difficulty. She smiled, and climbed down again, as surefootedly as she had gone up. As soon as she reached the level ground, she was as helpless as before. John looked rather stunned at this, but Euphrasia still had a ghost of a smile on her lips – *she* was not in the least surprised at all. And had she been capable of speaking, she might have said, like so many of my post-encephalitic patients, 'If only the world consisted of stairs!'

It was two o'clock, the nun said, time for her medicine. She brought Euphrasia, now sitting in the dayroom once again, a tiny white pill with some water. Fourteen minutes after receiving her L-DOPA – we timed this, as if waiting for a chemical reaction, or explosion – she suddenly jumped to her feet with such energy her chair fell over backward, hurtled along the corridor, and burst into lively, even rambunctious, conversation, bursting with all the things she had wanted to say, but could not while she was frozen. This was not just a disappearance of her parkinsonism, her motor problems, but a transformation of her senses, her feelings, her whole demeanour. I had not seen anything like this in more than twenty years, and was both stunned (though I had half-expected her to show such a reaction) and a bit nostalgic – Euphrasia especially reminded me of my post-encephalitic patient Hester, in whom there was a similar, instantaneous transformation, with no intermediary state, no warming-up period whatever.

But it was not a wholly simple 'awakening' for Euphrasia, any more than it had been for hyperbolic Hester. For along with the motor animation, the liveliness, the playfulness, which suddenly came on her, there came a tendency to wisecrack, to tic, to sudden lookings and touchings, to tossing and darting, to jabbing and lunging – a dozen strange impulsions, a drivenness of body and mind. There was this tremendous rush of life, of extravagant activation, both healthy and pathological, and then, twenty minutes later, a re-descent into her original state, coupled with repeated yawning, a sudden complete lethargy.

'What do you think of that, eh?' asked John, at my side, eagerly. 'Remind you of anything?'

*

When he is not seeing patients, John teaches at the Guam Memorial Hospital in Mangilao and does research in his laboratory there. He has lobbied hard for more research funding to be put into local facilities, and would like to establish a complete centre on the island for investigating the lytico-bodig, with sophisticated neuropathology equipment and facilities for MRI scans and other brain imaging. At present, many of these studies have to be done on the mainland, while much of the epidemiological work – interviewing patients and piecing together extensive family trees – as well as basic clinical and lab work of various kinds, is done here on the island.

He showed me into his lab; he had something special he wanted me to see. 'Let me show you these slides, Oliver,' said John, waving me over to a microscope. I looked through the eyepiece, under low power first, and saw pigmented cells, symmetrically arranged in a V.

'Substantia nigra,' I said. 'Many of the cells are pale and depigmented. There's a lot of glial reaction, and bits of loose pigment.' I shifted to a higher power, and saw a huge number of neurofibrillary tangles, densely staining, convoluted masses, harshly evident within the destroyed nerve cells. 'Do you have samples of cortex, hypothalamus, spinal cord?' John handed these to me, I looked at them one after another – all were full of neurofibrillary tangles.

'So this is what lytico-bodig looks like,' I said, 'neurofibrillary degeneration everywhere!'

'Yes,' said John, 'that's very typical. Here's another case – have a look at this.' I went over it as before; the findings were very similar, and there was much the same distribution of tangles.

'All the lytico-bodig cases look like this?' I asked.

'Actually, Oliver' – John smiled broadly – 'what you're looking at now isn't lytico-bodig at all. It's *your* disease, it's post-encephalitic parkinsonism – these slides were sent to me by Sue Daniel in London.'

'I haven't done much pathology since I was a resident,' I said, 'and I'm no expert – but I can't tell them apart.'

John grinned, pleased. 'Here, I have some more slides for you.' I looked at this new series, starting with the substantia nigra, the midbrain, moving up and down from there.

'I give up,' I said, 'I can't tell whether it's lytico-bodig or post-encephalitic parkinsonism.'

'Neither,' said John. 'This is *my* disease, progressive supranuclear palsy. In fact, it's from one of the original cases we described in 1963 – even then we wondered about its similarity to post-encephalitic parkinsonism. And now we look at the Guam disease . . . and all three look virtually the same.

'Sue Daniel and Andrew Lees and their colleagues at the Parkinson's Brain Bank have wondered whether these diseases are, in fact, related – perhaps even the same disease, a viral one, which could take three different forms.

'These are very similar to the neurofibrillary tangles to be found in Alzheimer's disease,' John went on, 'though in Alzheimer's there are not as many, and they occur in a different distribution. So we have tangles – like little tombstones in the nervous system – in four major neuro-degenerative diseases. Perhaps the tangles contain vital clues to the process of neurodegeneration, or perhaps they are relatively nonspecific neural reactions to disease – we don't know.'

*

As we got back in his car to return to Umatac, John continued to sketch the history of the lytico-bodig. Another dimension was added to the problem as the 1960s advanced, and a curious change was observed in the natural history of the disease: cases of bodig, which had been much rarer than cases of lytico in the 1940s and early '50s, now came more and more to outnumber them. And the age of onset was also increasing – there were no more teenage cases (like the nineteen-year-old youth with lytico whom Kurland had seen), and almost no cases in their twenties.

But why should a single disease present itself chiefly as lytico in one decade, and then predominantly as bodig the next? Did this have something to do with age – bodig patients, by and large, were a decade older than those with lytico? Did it have something to do with dose – could it be that the most severely exposed patients had their motor neurons knocked out in the 1950s, producing an ALS-like syndrome; whereas those exposed to less of the agent (whatever it was) were then caught by the slower effects of this on the brain, which might cause parkinsonism or dementia? Would most patients with lytico, were they to survive long enough, go on to develop bodig years later? (This, of course, was an impossible question, because lytico in its acute form cuts short the course of life. But Tomasa, still alive after twenty-five years of lytico, showed not a trace of bodig.) All of these questions were posed – but none of them could be answered.

Kurland had always felt that the possibility of cycad toxicity, however odd it seemed, should be investigated as carefully as possible, and to this end, he had organized, with Whiting, a series of major conferences starting in 1963 and continuing for a decade. The first of these were full of excitement, hopes of a breakthrough, and brought together botanists, nutritionists, toxicologists, neurologists, pathologists, and anthropologists to present research from all over the world. One constituent of cycad seeds was cycasin, a glycoside which had been isolated in the 1950s, and this was now reported to have a remarkable range of toxic effects. Large doses caused death from acute liver failure; smaller doses might be tolerated by the liver, but later gave rise to a variety of cancers. While cycasin did not seem to be toxic to adult nerve cells, it was one of the most potent carcinogens known.

There was renewed excitement when another compound found in cycad seeds was isolated – an amino acid, beta-N-methylamino-laevoalanine (BMAA), very similar in structure to the neurotoxic amino acid beta-N-oxalylamino-laevoalanine (BOAA), which was known to cause the paralysis of neurolathyrism. Was BMAA, then, the cause of lytico-bodig? It had been administered in many animal experiments, John said, but none of the animals developed anything like lytico-bodig.

Meanwhile there were two further discoveries of an epidemiological sort. In 1962 Carleton Gajdusek, who had been working on the cause of kuru, a fatal neurological disease in eastern New Guinea (work for which he was later awarded a Nobel Prize), now found an endemic lytico-bodig-like condition among the Auyu and Jakai people on the southern coastal plain of Western New Guinea.[65] This proved indeed to be an extraordinarily 'hot' focus, for the incidence of disease here was more than 1300 per 100,000, and thirty per cent of those affected were under the age of thirty. At about the same time, in Japan, Kiyoshi Kimura and Yoshiro Yase discovered a third focus of a lytico-bodig-like disease on the Kii peninsula of the island of Honshu. But in neither of these places, it seemed, were cycads consumed as food.

With these new findings, and the inability to produce an animal model of the disease, the plausibility of the cycad hypothesis seemed to fade. 'The cycad proponents thought they had it,' said John, somewhat wistfully. 'They thought that they'd cracked the lytico-bodig, and it was a real loss to let the cycad hypothesis go. Especially as they had nothing to replace it; they were left with a sort of conceptual vacuum.' By 1972 only Kurland continued to consider it a possibility, but for most of the researchers, the cycad hypothesis had died, and attention turned elsewhere.

*

John had arranged to take me that evening to a Japanese restaurant in Agana. 'With our huge tourist trade,' he said, 'we get the best Japanese food in the world here, outside Japan.' As we sat down and studied the enormous, exotic menus before us, I was interested to see fugu, puffer fish, listed; it was ten times as expensive as anything else on the menu.

'Don't try it!' said John, adamantly. 'You have a one in two hundred chance of being poisoned – the chefs are highly trained, but sometimes they make a mistake, leave a trace of skin or viscera on the fish. People like to play Russian roulette with the stuff, but I think there are better ways to die. Tetrodotoxin – a ghastly way to go!'

On Guam, John continued, warming to his theme, the most common form of toxic seafood illness was ciguatera poisoning – 'It's so common here, we just call it fish poisoning.' Ciguatoxin is a powerful neurotoxin produced by a tiny organism, a dinoflagellate called *Gambierdiscus toxicus*, which lives among the algae that grow in channels on the coral reefs. Herbivorous fish feed on the algae, and carnivorous fish in turn feed on them, so the toxin accumulates in large, predatory fish like snapper, grouper, surgeon fish, and jack (all of which I saw on the menu). The ciguatoxin causes no illness in fish – they seem to thrive on it – but it is very dangerous to mammals, and to man. John is something of an expert on this. 'I first saw it when I was working in the Marshall Islands twenty years ago – a fourteen-year-old boy, who became totally paralysed, with respiratory paralysis as well, after eating a grouper. I saw hundreds of cases in those days. There were fifty-five different species of fish we found which could carry the ciguatoxin. There is no way a fisherman can tell whether a particular fish is toxic, and no way of preparing or cooking it that will deactivate the toxin.

'At one point,' he added, 'people wondered if the lytico might be caused by some similar kind of fish poisoning – but we've never found any evidence of this.'

Thinking of the delectable sushi I had looked forward to all day, I was conscious of a horripilation rippling up my spine. 'I'll have chicken teriyaki, maybe an avocado roll – no fish today,' I said.

'A wise choice, Oliver,' said John. 'I'll have the same.'

*

We had just started eating when the lights went out. A groan – 'Not again!' – went around the restaurant, and the waiters quickly produced candles, which they lit. 'They seem very well prepared for power outages,' I said.

'Sure,' said John, 'we have them all the time, Oliver. They're caused by the snakes.'

'What?' I said. Did I mishear? Was he mad? I was startled, and for an instant wondered if he had somehow eaten some poison fish after all, and was beginning to hallucinate.

'Sounds odd, doesn't it? We have millions of these brown, tree-climbing snakes everywhere – the whole island is overrun by them. They climb the telephone poles, get into the substations, through the ducts, into the transformers, and then, pfft! We have another outage. The blackouts can happen two or three times a day, and so everyone is prepared for them – we call them snakeouts. Of course, the actual times are quite unpredictable.

'How have you been sleeping?' he added, inconsequentially.

'Rather well,' I said. 'Better than usual. At home, I tend to be woken by the birds at dawn.'

'And here?' John prompted.

'Well, now you mention it, I haven't heard any birds at dawn. Or any other time. It's strange; I hadn't realized it until you asked.'

'There is no birdsong on Guam – the island is silent,' John said. 'We used to have many birds, but all of them are gone – there is not a single one left. All of them have been eaten by the tree-climbing snakes.' John had a prankish sense of humour, and I was not quite sure whether to believe this story. But when I got back to my hotel that evening, and pulled out my trusty *Micronesia Handbook*, I found confirmation of all that he had said. The tree-climbing snake had made its way to Guam in the hold of a navy ship toward the end of the Second World War and, finding little competition among the native fauna, had rapidly multiplied. The snakes were nocturnal, I read, and could reach six feet in length, 'but are no danger to adults as their fangs are far back in their jaws.' They did, however, feed on all manner of small mammals, birds, and eggs; it was this which had led to the extinction of all the birds on Guam, including a number of species unique to the island. The remaining Guam fruit bats are now in danger of vanishing. The electrical outages, I read, cost millions of dollars in damages each year.[66]

*

The next morning I had arranged to spend some time hunting for ferns in the Guamanian jungle. I had heard of Lynn Raulerson, a botanist, from my friends at the American Fern Society in New York. She and another colleague, Agnes Rinehart, both work at the herbarium at the University of Guam and had published, among other things, a delightful book on *Ferns and Orchids of the Mariana Islands* (its frontispiece, a representation of the life cycle of a fern, was drawn by Alma). I met Lynn at the university, and we set off for the jungle, accompanied by one of her students, Alex, who was equipped with a machete. Alex remarked on the denseness of the forest in places. 'You can still get completely lost, even with a good sense of direction,' he said. 'You go five yards in, and it's so thick, you're already dislocated.'

The road itself was soon surrounded by an ocean of very large, bright-green sword ferns. Hundreds, thousands, of them pointed straight up into the air, almost as far as we could see. *Nephrolepis biserrata*, at least the variety we saw, is not your ordinary, humble sword-fern, but a species indigenous to the Marianas, with huge fronds sometimes as much as ten feet long. Once we had waded through these, we were into the jungle, with its great pandanus and ficus trees, and a canopy so dense it closed over our heads. It was a jungle as rich, as green, as any I had ever seen, the trunks of every tree blanketed with a dozen epiphytes, every available inch crowded with plants. Alex walked a few yards ahead of us, clearing a path with his machete. We saw huge bird's-nest ferns – the Chamorros, Alex told us, call them galak – and a smaller 'bird's-nest' fern which looked like a close relative, but was actually, Lynn told me, a different genus, a *Polypodium* indigenous to the Marianas.

I was delighted to see ferns of all shapes and sizes, from the lacy, triangular fronds of *Davallia*, and bristly *Pyrrosia* sheathing the trunks of the pandanus, to the gleaming shoestring fern, *Vittaria*, which seemed to hang everywhere. In moist, protected areas we saw a filmy fern, *Trichomanes*, which excited me, not just because of its delicacy and beauty, but because Safford, in an uncharacteristic error, had written that there were no filmy ferns on Guam (there are actually three species, said Lynn). We came upon the rare *Ophioglossum pendulum*, an immense ribbon fern with great succulent fronds, rippling and forking as they descended from the crotch of a tree.[67] I had never seen this species before, and even Lynn was excited to find it. We took pictures of it, with ourselves standing by – as one might photograph oneself with a marlin one had caught, or a tiger. But we were careful not to disturb the plant – and glad to think that our path to it would close itself up within days.

'There is one more fern, over here,' said Lynn, 'you'll want to see. Take a look at this fellow, with its two different types of leaves. The divided fronds are the fertile ones; the spearlike ones are sterile. Its name is *Humata heterophylla*, and it is named after Umatac (or Humátag) where it was found in the 1790s, by the first botanical expedition to Guam – you might call it the national fern of Guam.'

*

John and I made some more housecalls in the afternoon. We drove to the village of Yona, and stopped at the first house, where John's patient, Jesus, was sitting on the porch; now that he had become almost petrified with the bodig, this was where he loved, above all, to sit all day. I was told he had 'man-man' – the Chamorro word for staring blankly into space – though this was not a blank staring, a staring at nothing, but an almost painfully engrossed, wistful staring, staring out at the children who played in the road, staring at the occasional passing cars and carts, staring at the neighbours leaving for work each morning, and returning late in the day. Jesus sat on his porch, unblinking, unmoving, motionless as a tortoise, from sunrise till midnight (except on the rare days when high winds or rain lashed across it), forever gazing at a constantly varying spectacle of life before him, an enraptured spectator, no longer able to take part.[68] I was reminded of a description of the aged Ibsen after his stroke, aphasic, partly paralysed, no longer able to go out or write or talk – but insistent, always, that he be allowed to stand by the tall windows in his room, looking out on the harbour, the streets, the vivid spectacle of the city. 'I see everything,' he had once murmured, years before, to a young colleague; and there was still this passion to see, to be an observer, when all else was gone. So it was, it seemed to me, with old Jesus on his porch.

When John and I greeted Jesus, he answered in a small, flat voice, devoid of inflection or intonation, but his answers were precise and full of detail. He spoke of Agana, where he had been born in 1913, and how pleasant and tranquil it was then ('Not like now – it's completely changed since the war'), of coming to Umatac with his parents when he was eight, and of a long life devoted to fishing and farming. He spoke of his wife, who had been half Japanese and half Chamorro; she had died of bodig fifteen years ago. Many people in her family had lytico or bodig; but his own children and grandchildren, fortunately, seemed free of it.

We had been told that Jesus might pass the whole day with scarcely a word. And yet he spoke well, even volubly, when we engaged him in conversation; though, it soon became apparent, he waited for our questions. He could respond quite readily, but could not initiate a sentence. Nor, it seemed, a movement either – he might sit totally motionless for hours, unless something or someone *called* him to move. I was again strongly reminded of my post-encephalitic patients and how they were crucially depend-ent on the initiative of others, calling them to speech or action. I tore a page out of my notebook, balled it up, and threw the balled paper at Jesus. He had been sitting, seemingly incapable of movement, but now his arm shot up in a flash, and he caught the paper ball precisely. One of his little grandsons was standing by, and his eyes widened with astonishment when he saw this. I continued playing ball, and then asked Jesus to throw the ball at his grandson, and then to another child, and another. Soon we had the entire family playing ball, and akinetic Jesus, no longer akinetic, kept it going between us all. The children had not realized that their 'paralysed' grandfather could move by himself at all, much less that he could catch a ball, aim it accurately, bluff, throw it in different styles and directions, and improvise a fast ball game among them.

For his grandchildren it was a discovery, and one, I thought, which might transform his relationship with them – but this calling-into-action was well known to his old friends in the community. Once a week, he would go to the senior centre – he would have to be picked up and lifted ('like a corpse', he said) into the car; but once there, and seated at a card table, he could play a fast and hard game of gin rummy. He could not start the play – someone else had to do this – but once the first card was slapped down, he would suddenly come to life, respond, pick up another card, and continue the game. The people of Umatac, Merizo, Dededo, and Santa Rita may have little scientific knowledge of parkinsonism, but they have a great deal of informal knowledge, a folk neurology based on decades of close observation of the bodig in their midst.

They know well how to unfreeze or unlock patients if they get frozen, by initiating speech or action for them – this may require another person walking with the patient or the rhythmic pulse of music. They know how patterns on the floor or the ground can help the parkinsonian to organize his walking; how patients scarcely able to walk on a flat surface can negotiate complex obstacles, rough terrain, easily (and indeed, fare oddly well with these); how the mute and motionless parkinsonian can respond beautifully to music, singing and dancing, when speech and motion had previously seemed impossible.

*

But what was it that had caused the lytico-bodig, what was it that had come and gone? There had been a sort of conceptual vacuum, John said, when the cycad hypothesis had collapsed in the early seventies. The disease continued to claim more Chamorros, and patients were treated, when possible, for their symptoms – but there was a marked lull in research for a while, at least in Guam.

And yet in the 1970s there was a discovery of great importance. Two pathologists, Frank Andersen and Leung Chen, performed autopsies on two hundred Chamorros, many of whom had died suddenly in traffic accidents. (Agana had been a small, slow-moving town before the war, and transport was leisurely – usually by carts pulled by the big-horned carabao, along the rutted and frequently flooded roads. But following the war, there was a sudden increase in population, especially American military, who brought along with them fast roads and cars; this caused a sudden rise in traffic fatalities among the Chamorros, who were wholly unused to this rapid pace.) None of these people had ever shown any neurological symptoms; yet seventy per cent of those born before 1940 showed clear pathological changes in the nervous system similar to the neurofibrillary tangles which Hirano had found in patients with lytico-bodig. The occurrence of these neuro-fibrillary tangles fell off sharply in those born in the 1940s, and they were not seen at all in anyone born after 1952. This extraordinary finding suggested that the lytico-bodig might have been almost universal among the Chamorros at one time – even though only a small proportion went on to develop overt neurological symptoms. It suggested, moreover, that the risk of contracting the disease was now very much reduced – and that even though cases continued to occur, these had probably been contracted many years before, and were only now becoming symptomatic. 'What we are now seeing, Oliver,' said John, pounding the steering wheel for emphasis, 'are the late effects of something that happened long ago.'[69]

*

When Yoshiro Yase, an ardent sport-fisherman as well as a neurologist, went to study the newly identified disease focus on the Kii peninsula, he was told there were scarcely any fish in the local rivers, and this prompted him – memories of the Minamata tragedy still being vivid – to analyse their waters. Though these were free of infectious agents or toxins, they were oddly low in calcium and magnesium. Could this, he wondered, be the cause of the disease?

Gajdusek was fascinated by Yase's findings, the more so as he had been struck by the red soil, rich in iron and bauxite, in the swamp lands around the Auyu and Jakai villages. When he was able to return in 1974 – Western New Guinea having become Irian Jaya in the intervening upheavals – he now tested the water from the shallow wells which the villagers dug in the red soil, and found unusually low levels of calcium and magnesium, as well as elevated levels of iron, aluminium, and other metals.

At this point, Kurland moved to the Mayo Clinic to pursue other research, feeling that the cycad hypothesis, though valid, could not be proven. His place at the NIH was taken by Gajdusek, who was now intrigued and excited at the notion of a mineral aetiology of the Western Pacific disease. Gajdusek enlisted Yase, and together they examined well water from Guam and found that this too was low in calcium and magnesium. This triple coincidence seemed definitive:

> Comparison of the Western New Guinea focus with the foci of ALS and Parkinson's disease on Guam and the Kii Peninsula of Japan is inescapable [Gajdusek wrote], and the close association of parkinsonism and motor neuron symptoms in yet another non-Chamorro population group should not only dispel most doubts about the probably close relationship between the two syndromes, but also point to an aetiologic role of some unknown environmental factor.

The unknown environmental factor, it seemed likely, had to do with low calcium and magnesium levels in the drinking water, and the consequences of these on the nervous system. Such low levels, he speculated, might trigger a compensatory reaction in the parathyroid glands, leading in turn to excessive absorption of calcium, aluminium, and manganese ions. The deposition of these in the nervous system, he felt, might result in the premature neuronal ageing and death seen with the lytico-bodig.

It was John's hope, in 1983, that he might join Gajdusek's team and help crack the disease at last. But Gajdusek told him he was too late – the cause of the lytico-bodig had now been established, and in any case the disease had almost vanished, because of the shift to a Western diet, which was high in calcium – there was not much left to do, and his team would be pulling out of there soon. John was surprised to hear Gajdusek express himself so forcefully, he told me, and disappointed, because he had hoped to work with him. But he decided to come to Guam none the less, if only to take care of patients as a physician, and not as an investigator.

But the very day after John arrived on Guam, he had an experience comparable to Zimmerman's nearly forty years before: working in the naval hospital in Agana, he saw a dozen patients with the lytico-bodig in his first clinic. And one of them also had a supranuclear palsy – a complex disturbance of gaze, in which the patient can look sideways, but not up or down. This had never previously been reported in lytico-bodig, but it was the hallmark of the syndrome John and his Toronto colleagues had delineated nearly twenty years before. This convinced him that lytico-bodig was neither extinct nor comprehensively described, and that there was still time and opportunity for its further investigation.

Guam had superb medical facilities on the naval base, but in the outlying villages, basic medical care was very inadequate, and neurological care scarce – there was only one overworked neurologist, Dr Kwang-Ming Chen, to care for 50,000 Chamorros, and 100,000 other residents of the island as well. Not only were there still many hundreds of Chamorro people with lytico-bodig, Chen told John, but new cases kept appearing – several dozen a year, he thought, and these new cases sometimes took forms different from either the classical lytico or bodig; the man with supranuclear palsy was a case in point.

In particular, John observed, he began to see increasing numbers of elderly people, women especially, who had severe memory disturbances, amnesiac syndromes, without any dementia; catatonia without parkinsonism (like Estella); dementia without parkinsonism (like her sister-in-law); arousal-disorders (like Euphrasia); or unclassifiable syndromes (like Juan's), novel forms of the disease never described before.

John was still excited by the mineral hypothesis, and he wanted to pursue it, to gather more conclusive evidence. He invited an old friend and colleague from Toronto, Donald Crapper McLachlan (a neurologist and chemist who had shown elevated levels of aluminium in Alzheimer's brains as far back as 1973), to join him on Guam, and working with colleagues from the University of Guam, they compared soil samples from Umatac with soil from fifty-five other sites on Guam and re-examined mineral levels in samples of well water all over the island.

Their results, to their surprise, differed greatly from Gajdusek and Yase's – indeed it seemed that the one water source in Umatac, the Piga spring, which the early investigators had found to have low calcium, was quite atypical. Every other water source and all the soils they sampled had *high* levels of calcium, as might be expected on a limestone island. Further analysis of the soils and of vegetables grown in them found adequate levels of calcium and magnesium and normal levels of aluminium, which seemed to shake the notion of a mineral deficiency or aluminium excess as the cause of lytico-bodig (without, however, excluding it completely).

John is of a passionate disposition and tends to get strongly invested in theories and ideas. He had a huge respect for Gajdusek's intuition, and was greatly taken by the mineral hypothesis; John had hoped to confirm, and perhaps elucidate, this with his own investigations. He had been elated by these hopes, and the promise of Gajdusek and Yase's hypothesis – and now, suddenly, all this had collapsed. He was back to where Kurland had been a decade earlier, in a conceptual void.

*

Then, in 1986, his eye was caught by a letter in the *Lancet* which, intriguingly, resurrected the cycad hypothesis. Peter Spencer, a neurotoxicologist, using a purified form of the amino acid BMAA from cycad seeds, found that it could induce a neurological syndrome in monkeys, conceivably analogous to human lytico.

Spencer's work in this realm went back to the 1970s, when, with his colleague Herb Schaumburg, he had travelled to India to investigate the neurolathyrism there. It had been known for centuries that a spastic paralysis of the legs could follow continued eating of the chickling pea; that this was due to the neurotoxic amino acid BOAA, which damaged the cortical motor cells and their descending connections in the spinal cord, had been known since the 1960s. Spencer's new studies made clear how BOAA heightened sensitivity to glutamate, one of the neurotransmitters involved in the motor system, and simulated its action as well. BOAA intoxication could push the glutamate receptor cells into a sort of overdrive, until they literally died of overexcitation and exhaustion. BOAA was an excitotoxin – this was the new term. Could BMAA, he wondered, so similar in structure to BOAA, also act as an excitotoxin and produce a disorder like lytico?

There had been attempts to induce such disorders in animal experiments during the 1960s, but the results were inconclusive, and this line of research had been dropped. Now, using cynomolgus monkeys and repeated administrations of BMAA, Spencer succeeded, after eight weeks, in inducing 'a degenerative motor system disease' associated with damage to the motor cells in the cerebral cortex and spinal cord.[70] He further observed that BMAA might have two distinct effects: given in high doses, it caused an

ALS-like condition to develop rapidly; but smaller doses seemed to cause, after a considerably longer period, a parkinsonian condition – a double action reminiscent of the Guam disease.

These results seemed to refute the first criticism made in the 1960s of the cycad hypothesis – that there existed no animal model. Now Spencer, with a characteristic burst of energy, set about refuting the other, seemingly lethal criticism of the cycad hypothesis – that there was no significant use of unprocessed cycads in the Kii Peninsula or Irian Jaya. Like Gajdusek before him, he trekked into the jungles of Irian Jaya to investigate the local use of cycads. What he discovered was that there were cycads here (though they seemed to be a different species from the Guam one), and they were indeed treated as veritable medicine cabinets by the local people. Likewise, on the Kii peninsula, he found, cycads were also used medicinally, the raw seeds sometimes used in poultices on open wounds. With these two discoveries, in the lab and the field, the cycad hypothesis, discarded fifteen years earlier, was now revivified.

John could not contain his excitement at these new thoughts and findings – everything seemed to fit together perfectly. He would phone Spencer in Oregon, and the two would have excited conversations for hours, sometimes nightly, discussing clinical data and bringing out more and more coincidences of cycads and disease in the Marianas. With his colleague Tamara Guzman, John now embarked on re-examining the whole question of cycad distribution and use in the Marianas. They observed that while lytico-bodig was common among the Chamorros on Guam and Rota, where cycads were plentiful, there was no lytico-bodig reported on the island of Saipan (at least none in the previous seventy years – it remained uncertain whether the Saipanese Chamorros had been prone to it before this).[71] But they pointed out that the cycad forests of Saipan had been cut down by the Japanese in 1914, to clear land for sugar cane, and that the use of fadang had ceased soon after this. And that on lytico-bodig-free Tinian, where there were forests of cycads, the Chamorros had never made use of them. They proposed that the family clusters of disease found on Guam, which did not follow any known genetic distribution, could be related to differences in the way each family prepared their fadang – some family recipes involved soaking the seeds overnight, some for three weeks; some would use seawater, some fresh; some would shorten the washing process so that the flour would have a stronger taste. Steele and Guzman ended their paper with some striking accounts of people who had developed lytico-bodig as long as twenty years after a single exposure to fadang.

But many researchers felt, after the first flush of enthusiasm, that the amounts of BMAA Spencer was feeding his monkeys were completely unphysiological – more than the most devoted fadang eater could consume in a lifetime. Indeed, Gajdusek calculated, to reproduce Spencer's experiment in a human being, the subject would have to eat a ton and a half of unprocessed cycad seeds in twelve weeks. This in itself was not an annihilating criticism – experimental toxicology often uses massive doses of materials in its initial experiments in order to increase the chance of getting consistent results. But now John, knowing how meticulously the seeds were detoxified before the production of fadang, set about measuring the amount of BMAA the flour actually contained; he started sending samples out for analysis, and was surprised to find that some of these seemed to have almost no BMAA at all.

Gajdusek and his group, meanwhile, had also been trying to produce an animal model for lytico-bodig and had been maintaining a number of macaques on a low-calcium, high-aluminium diet. The monkeys developed no clinical symptoms in the four years of the trial, but autopsies showed many neurofibrillary tangles, as well as degenerative changes in the motor neurons, throughout the neuraxis. These changes seemed to resemble those of lytico-bodig or the pre-symptomatic changes described by Andersen and Chen, and it was speculated that a longer period of calcium deficiency, or higher doses of toxic metals, might have led to overt clinical disease. And though Gajdusek had told John in 1983 that he thought the lytico-bodig was dying out in Guam, he has continued to investigate it in Irian Jaya, where in 1993 he found it still had a remarkably high incidence. He and his colleagues continue to see aluminium neurotoxicity as the cause of lytico-bodig and indeed of a wide range of other conditions.

While Spencer, for his part, was greatly excited by his own success in inducing neurological disorders with BMAA, he soon developed reservations. The disorders shown by his monkeys were dose-related, came on promptly, and were acute and non-progressive (they resembled, in this way, the neurocycadism of cattle); whereas human lytico-bodig, it was abundantly clear, had a very long latency or incubation period, but once it had become symptomatic, was almost invariably progressive. Was it possible, Spencer speculated, that another factor was involved besides the BMAA, which might not predispose to overt disorder for many years? Slow viruses had been described by Gajdusek; could there not be, analogously, a slow toxin? Spencer did not have any clear idea, at this stage, of how such a toxin might work, or any way of validating the concept.

Though Gajdusek might have been expected to be sympathetic to the idea of a slow toxin, he argued passionately against it in a sternly titled paper, 'Cycad toxicity not the cause of high-incidence amyotrophic lateral sclerosis/parkinsonism-dementia on Guam, Kii peninsula of Japan, or in West New Guinea', asserting that such a hypothesis was, first, redundant; second, without precedent; third, without support; and fourth, impossible:

> No neurotoxin has been demonstrated to give rise to fatal central nervous system disease, neurological signs and symptoms of which first start to be detectable years after exposure to the neurotoxin has ceased. In fact, we have *no* example of *any* toxin producing progressive damage to *any* organ years after last exposure to the substance. . . . Only hypersensitivity disorders, slow infections, and genetically timed disorders have given rise to this pattern of long delay.

Spencer, undeterred, saw Gajdusek's words as a challenge (indeed he has cited them in several of his own papers), and continued to see his task as the search for a new kind of toxin, a new kind of toxic mechanism, hitherto unrecognized in medicine. A great deal of attention was focused, in the sixties and seventies, on carcinogenesis, the appearance of cancers, in some cases, years after an initial exposure to the carcinogen, whether radioactivity, a toxin, or a virus. It had been established, in Kurland's original cycad conferences, what a potent carcinogen *cycasin* was, capable of inducing liver cancers and colon and kidney malformations. It had been observed, moreover, that if infant rats were fed cycasin-high diets, the still-dividing Purkinje cells of the cerebellum might develop bizarre multinucleated forms and ectopic 'nests', and such findings had also been reported, on occasion, in cases of human lytico-bodig.

What then might be the effect of cycasin, Spencer wondered, on adult nerve cells, which are no longer capable of dividing? He has postulated recently that cycasin (or its component, MAM, or methazoxymethanol) may be able to form stable compounds with the DNA in nerve cells (such adduct formation is believed to underlie the overt carcinogenic and teratogenic effects of cycasin elsewhere in the body). This aberrant DNA in the nerve cells, he thinks, could lead to subtly but persistently altered metabolic functions, the nerve cells finally becoming oversensitive to their own neurotransmitters, their own glutamate, so that this itself could act as an excitotoxin. No external agent would be needed to provoke a neurological disaster at this point, for in this pathologically sensitized state, even normal neural functioning would now overexcite neurotransmitter receptor cells and push them toward their own destruction.

The notion of such a gene toxin is not as outlandish as it seemed a decade ago, and Spencer has now observed DNA changes in tissue cultures of cells exposed to cycasin which suggest that such a mechanism may be at work in lytico-bodig. Such a gene toxin would actually alter the genetic character of the nerve cells it affected, producing, in effect, a genetically-based form of hypersensitivity disorder.

Now that Spencer was pondering the possible effects of cycasin on adult nerve cells, he had new analyses made of traditionally prepared cycad flours and found (contrary to what John had reported earlier) that the Guam samples in fact contained significant levels of BMAA and cycasin. The highest levels of cycasin, indeed, were found in samples from villages with the greatest prevalence of lytico-bodig, lending strong circumstantial support to the hypothesis of cycasin toxicity.[72]

*

While Gajdusek and Spencer have continued to think in terms of external causes, aluminium or cycad, John's focus has turned inward again. In the early 1990s, he had been very taken by the clinical and pathological similarities (which he had shown me in his lab) between lytico-bodig, progressive supranuclear palsy, and post-encephalitic syndromes and thought seriously in terms of a viral aetiology. But recently he has again returned to what first struck him when he came to Guam in 1983, the extraordinary tendency of certain families to develop the Guam disease. Had a genetic theory been thrown out prematurely? Much had changed since Kurland and Mulder first considered, then rejected, this in the 1950s. The classic Mendelian patterns of inheritance had now been joined by concepts of complex inheritance involving the presence of several genetic abnormalities and their interactions with each other and with environmental factors. Further, it was now possible to directly examine the genetic material with molecular biology, using technologies and concepts not available to the early investigators.

Working with Verena Keck, an anthropologist, John started to collect pedigrees of every patient he had seen – pedigrees of unprecedented accuracy and detail, including medical histories going back fifty years. The more pedigrees he obtained, the more he became convinced that there had to be some genetic predisposition, or perhaps several predispositions – for it looked as though the lytico and the bodig had different patterns in different families. Sometimes one saw a family in whom the affected members had only the lytico, sometimes a family in which the clinical expression was always bodig, and sometimes, more rarely, a family with both. The similarity of the pathological pictures in lytico and bodig, he started to feel, might have been misleading them all; genealogically, they seemed to be two separate diseases.

Recently John has embarked on a new series of studies, collecting DNA samples from all of his patients and sending them out for genetic analysis. He has been very excited by preliminary results indicating the presence of a genetic marker in several cases of bodig – a marker which seems to be absent in lytico and normal controls. His immediate reaction has been one of exuberance: 'I feel the excitement coming again, and it's a feeling I have not had since '86, when I was captivated by Spencer's hypothesis.' But it is an exuberance tempered by considerable caution ('I don't quite know what it means.') The search for genetic markers is extraordinarily laborious and difficult – it took more than a decade of incessant work to find a marker for Huntington's chorea – and John is not sure whether these preliminary results will be borne out.

It is now a third of a century since he and his colleagues delineated progressive supranuclear palsy in the early 1960s and perceived it as a unique yet exemplary disease which might shed some light on neurodegenerative disease in general. The similarity of the clinical picture of lytico-bodig and post-encephalitic parkinsonism to PSP continues to intrigue him. He had been struck from the start by the fact that supranuclear palsies could also be observed in some patients with lytico-bodig, and on occasion in those with post-encephalitic syndromes too (on a recent trip to New York, he was intrigued to meet one of my post-encephalitic patients who has had a supranuclear palsy for more than thirty years). But he is not yet sure how to interpret these affinities.

He has been fascinated, as well, by the similarities of the neurofibrillary tangles which are so characteristic of lytico-bodig, post-encephalitic parkinsonism, and PSP with those of classical Alzheimer's disease and has been investigating this with Patrick McGeer, a neuropathologist in Vancouver. The tangles themselves are virtually identical, as are the areas of inflammatory reaction about them (though there are other features of Alzheimer's, most notably the presence of so-called 'plaques', which one does not see in the other three diseases). At an immediate and practical level, the presence of these inflammatory reactions around the tangles makes him wonder whether anti-inflammatory agents can be helpful in lytico-bodig. Their use in Alzheimer's disease is under study, and John is eager to see if they can help his own patients, if only to retard the course of a fatal disease. This is one of the few thoughts which gives him a brief sense of therapeutic optimism or hope, as he does his daily rounds among chronically ill and ever-deteriorating patients. And he is concerned by the steadily rising incidence of classical Alzheimer's and Parkinson's disease – which rarely if ever occurred on Guam before the Second World War – even as the native disease, lytico-bodig, declines.

*

After forty years of research, then, we have four (or more) seemingly divergent lines of thought and research – genetic, cycadic, mineral, viral (Alma's money is on prions) – each with some support, but with no overwhelming evidence for any of them. The answer will not be a simple one, John now feels, but a complex interaction of a variety of genetic and environmental factors, as seems to be the case in many diseases.[73]

Or perhaps it is something else, as Ulla Craig, one of John's research colleagues, muses. 'I'm not sure what we are looking for – though, like John, I have the feeling of some sort of virus that came and went. Some mutant virus, perhaps, with no immediate effect, but affecting people later, as their immune systems responded. But I am not sure. I am afraid we are missing something – this is the value of a fresh mind, seeing things in a new way, someone who may ask the question we have not asked. We are looking now for something complex, but it could be something we have overlooked, something very simple.'

'Back in the 1940s and '50s,' John mused, 'there was a sense that we would find the cause of lytico-bodig in a matter of months. When Donald Mulder came here in '53, he thought he might have the problem solved by the time Kurland arrived six weeks later – but after forty-five years, it remains a complete enigma. Sometimes I wonder if we will ever decipher it. But time is running out: the disease may vanish before we can understand it. . . . This disease has become my passion, Oliver, and my identity.' If it is John's passion and identity, it is Kurland's, and Spencer's, and many others' as well. A colleague of mine, who knows and respects them all, says, 'Guam has been a tar baby for all of them – once they get stuck, they can never let go.'

The disease is indeed dying out at last, and as time goes on, the researchers who seek its cause grow more press- ured, more vexed, by the day. Will the quarry, hotly pursued for forty years now, with all the resources that science can bring, elude them finally, tantalizingly, by disappearing at the moment they are about to grasp it?

*

'We're on our way to see Felipe,' John said as we climbed into his car once more. 'You'll like him, he's a very sweet man. And he's been touched by at least four different forms of lytico-bodig.' He shook his head slowly.

Felipe was sitting on the patio at the back of his house, as he does most days, staring out, with a faint fixed smile, at his garden. It was a lovely garden, full of native plants, and the patio itself was shaded by banana trees. He has spent most of his life in Umatac, fishing and farming. He raises cockerels, and has a dozen of them, gorgeously coloured, and all very tame. My neurological examination of Felipe was punctuated by the crowings of cockerels, a sound which he imitated, very loudly, to perfection (this was in striking contrast to his poor vocal volume when talking); by their perching on both of us during the exam, and by the affectionate nuzzling and occasional barking of his black dog. This was all delightful, I thought – rustic neurology, rural neurology, in the backwoods of Guam.

Felipe spoke movingly of his life and the past. He enjoyed fadang occasionally ('we all did'), but he was not, like many other Chamorros, forced to subsist on it during the war. On the contrary, he spent the war as a sailor with the US Navy, stationed part of the time in Portsmouth, Virginia (hence his excellent English), and he was part of the navy force which retook Guam. He himself had to take part in the bombardment of Agana, a heartbreaking business, for it was the destruction of his native town. He spoke movingly of friends and family with lytico-bodig. 'And now,' he said, 'I have it too.' He said this quietly, simply, without a hint of self-pity or drama. He is fifty-nine.

His memory, intact for the past, has become severely eroded for recent events. We had in fact passed his house, and stopped to say hello the previous day – but he had no memory of this, showed no recognition now we had come to visit again. When John told him the Chamorran version of his name (John Steele translates as 'Juan Lulac'), he would laugh, repeat it, and forget it within a minute.

Though Felipe had an inability to register current events, to transfer them from short-term to permanent memory, he had no other cognitive deficits – his use of language, his perceptual powers, his powers of judgement, were all fine. His memory problem had worsened, very slowly, for about ten years. Then he had developed some muscular wasting – the thinning of his once thick and powerful farmer's hands was striking when we examined him. Finally, a couple of years ago, he had developed parkinsonism. It was this, finally, which had so slowed him down, taken him out of active life, made him a retiree in his garden. When John had examined him last, a few months before, the parkinsonism was entirely confined to one side, but it had progressed apace, and now affected both sides. There was very little tremor, just an overall immobility, a lack of motor initiative. And now, John showed me, there were the beginnings of a gaze palsy, too (an indication of yet a fourth form of lytico-bodig).

Felipe's civility, his character, was perfectly preserved despite his disease, along with a sense of rueful insight and humour. When I turned to wave goodbye, Felipe had a cockerel perched on each arm. 'Come again soon,' he said, cheerfully. 'I won't remember you, so I'll have the pleasure of meeting you all over again.'

*

We returned to Umatac, this time stopping at the old graveyard on the hillside above the village. One of John's neighbours, Benny, who tends the graveyard – he cuts the grass, acts as a sexton in the little church, and as grave digger when needed – showed us around. Benny's family, John told me, is one of the most afflicted in Umatac and one of the three families which especially caught Kurland's attention when he came here forty years ago. It was one of his forebears, in fact, at the end of the eighteenth century, who was cursed after stealing some mangoes from the local priest, and told that his family would contract fatal paralyses generation after generation, until the end of time. This, at least, is the story, the myth, in Umatac.

We walked slowly with Benny among the limestone grave markers, the older ones crooked and sunken with time, the newer ones in the shape of simple white crosses, often embellished by plastic statues of the Virgin Mary or photographs of the deceased, some with fresh flowers on them. As Benny led the way, he pointed out individual stones: 'Here's Herman, he passed away from it . . . and my cousin, that one here . . . another cousin is the one down here. And one of the couple here, the wife, passed away from that . . . yeah, they all passed away from the lytico-bodig. And up here – my sister's father-in-law passed away from the same disease . . . my cousin and her dad and mum, the same thing. . . . the mayor's sister, same problem . . . got a cousin here passed away too. Yes, here's another cousin, Juanita, and her dad, they both had it. My uncle Simon, right here – he was the oldest in the family who passed away from the lytico-bodig . . . and another cousin, he just passed away a couple of months ago. Another uncle, same problem – and the wife, same disease; I forget his first name. I didn't really know him, he just passed away before I got to know him.'

Benny went on, leading us from one grave to another, continuing his endless, tragic litany – here's my uncle, here's my cousin, and his wife; here's my sister, and here's my brother . . . and here (one seemed to hear, intimated in his voice, necessitated by the tragic logic of it all), here too I will lie, among all my family, my community of Umatac, dead of the lytico-bodig, in this graveyard by the sea. Seeing the same names again and again, I felt that the entire graveyard was devoted to lytico-bodig, and that everyone here belonged to a single family, or perhaps two or three inter-related families, which all shared the same curse.

As we walked slowly among the stones, I remembered another graveyard, also by the sea, which I had visited in up-island Martha's Vineyard. It was a very old one, going back to the end of the seventeenth century, and there I also saw the same names again and again. In Martha's

Vineyard, this was a graveyard of the congenitally deaf; here in Umatac, it was a graveyard of the lytico-bodig.

When I visited Martha's Vineyard, there were no longer any deaf people left – the last had died in 1952 – and with this, the strange deaf culture which had been such a part of the island's history and community for more than two hundred years had come to an end, as such isolates do. So it was with Fuur, the little Danish island of the colour-blind; so, most probably, it will be with Pingelap; and so, in all likelihood, it will be with Guam – odd genetic anomalies, swirls, transients, given a brief possibility, existence, by the nature of islands and isolation. But islands open up, people die or intermarry; genetic atten-uation sets in, and the condition disappears. The life of such a genetic disease in an isolate tends to be six or eight generations, two hundred years perhaps, and then it vanishes, as do its memories and traces, lost in the ongoing stream of time.

Rota

When I was five, our garden in London was full of ferns, a great jungle of them rising high above my head (though these were all uprooted at the start of the Second World War to make room for Jerusalem artichokes, which we were encouraged to grow for the war effort). My mother and a favourite aunt adored gardening, and were botanically inclined, and some of my earliest memories are of seeing them working side by side in the garden, often pausing to look at the young fronds, the baby fiddleheads, with great tenderness and delight. The memory of these ferns and of a quiet, idyllic botanizing became associated for me with the sense of childhood, of innocence, of a time before the war.

One of my mother's heroines, Marie Stopes (a lecturer in fossil botany before she turned to crusading for contraception), had written a book called *Ancient Plants*, which excited me strangely.[74] For it was here, when she spoke of 'the seven ages' of plant life, that I got my first glimpse of deep time, of the millions of years, the hundreds of millions, which separated the most ancient plants from our own. 'The human mind,' Stopes wrote, 'cannot comprehend the significance of vast numbers, of immense space, or of aeons of time'; but her book, illustrating the enormous range of plants which had once lived on the earth – the vast majority long extinct – gave me my first intimation of such aeons.[75] I would gaze at the book for hours, skipping over the flowering plants and going straight to the earliest ones – gingkos, cycads, ferns, lycopods, horsetails. Their very names held magic for me: *Bennettitales, Sphenophyllales,* I would say to myself, and the words would repeat themselves internally, like a spell, like a mantra.

During the war years, my aunt was headmistress of a school in Cheshire, a 'fresh-air school', as it was called, in the depths of Delamere Forest. It was she who first showed me living horsetails in the woods, growing a foot or two high in the wet ground by the sides of streams. She had me feel their stiff, jointed stems, and told me that they were among the most ancient of living plants – and that their ancestors had grown to gigantic size, forming dense thickets of huge, bamboolike trees, *Calamites,* twice as tall as the trees which now surrounded us. They had once covered the earth, hundreds of millions of years ago, when giant amphibians ploshed through the primordial swamps. She would show me how the horsetails were anchored by a network of roots, the pliant rhizomes which sent out runners to each stalk.[76]

Then she would find tiny lycopods to show me – club mosses or tassel ferns with their scaly leaves; these too, she told me, once took the form of immensely tall trees, more than a hundred feet high, with huge scaly trunks supporting tasselled foliage, and cones at their summits. At night I dreamed of these silent, towering giant horse-

Giant club-mosses of the Devonian

tails and club mosses, the peaceful, swampy landscapes of 350 million years ago, a Palaeozoic Eden – and I would wake with a sense of exhilaration, and loss.

I think these dreams, this passion to regain the past, had something to do with being separated from my family and evacuated from London (like thousands of other children) during the war years. But the Eden of lost childhood, childhood imagined, became transformed by some leger-demain of the unconscious to an Eden of the remote past, a magical 'once', rendered wholly benign by the omission, the editing out, of all change, all movement. For there was a peculiar static, pictorial quality in these dreams, with at most a slight wind rustling the trees or rippling the water.

Lepidodendra and *Calamites* of the Carboniferous

They neither evolved nor changed, nothing ever happened in them; they were encapsulated as in amber. Nor was I myself, I think, ever present in these scenes, but gazed on them as one gazes at a diorama. I longed to enter them, to touch the trees, to be part of their world – but they allowed no access, were as shut off as the past.

My aunt often took me to the Natural History Museum in London, where there was a fossil garden full of ancient lycopod trees, *Lepidodendra*, their trunks covered with rugged rhomboid scales like crocodiles, and the slender trunks of tree horsetails, *Calamites*. Inside the museum, she took me to see the dioramas of the Palaeozoic (they had titles like 'Life in a Devonian Swamp') – I loved these even more than the pictures in Marie Stopes' book, and they became my new dreamscapes. I wanted to see these giant plants *alive*, straightaway, and felt heartbroken when she told me that there were no more tree horsetails, no more club-moss trees, the old giant flora was all gone, vanished – though much of it, she added, had sunk into the swamps, where it had been compressed and trans-formed into coal over the aeons (once, at home, she split a coal ball and showed me the fossils inside).

Then we would move ahead 100 million years, to the dioramas of the Jurassic ('The Age of Cycads'), and she would show me these great robust trees, so different from the Palaeozoic ones. The cycads had huge cones and massive fronds at their tops – they were the dominant plant form once, she would say; pterodactyls flew among them, they were what the giant dinosaurs munched on. Although I had never seen a living cycad, these great trees with their thick, solid trunks seemed more believable, less alien, than the unimaginable *Calamites* and *Cordaites* which had preceded them – they looked like a cross between ferns and palms.[77]

On summer Sundays, we would take the old District Line to Kew – the line had been opened in 1877, and many of the original electric carriages were still in use. It cost 1d. to enter, and for this one had the whole sweep of the Garden, its broad walks, its dells, the eighteenth-century Pagoda, and my favourites, the great glass and iron conservatories.

A taste for the exotic was fostered by visits to the giant water lily *Victoria regia*, in its own special house – its vast leaves, my aunt told me, could easily bear the weight of a child. It had been discovered in the wilds of Guiana, she said, and given its name in honour of the young queen.[78]

I was even more taken by the grotesque *Welwitschia mirabilis*, with its two long, leathery, writhingly coiled leaves – it looked, to my eyes, like some strange vegetable octopus. *Welwitschia* is not easy to grow outside its natural habitat in the Namibian desert, and the large specimen at Kew was one of the few which had been successfully cultivated, a very special treasure. (Joseph Hooker, who named it and obtained the original material from the euphonious Welwitsch, thought it the most interesting, though ugliest, plant ever brought into Britain; and Darwin, fascinated by its mixture of advanced and primitive characteristics, called it 'the vegetable *Ornitho-rhynchus*', the platypus of the plant kingdom.)[79]

My aunt especially loved the smaller fern houses, the ferneries. We had ordinary ferns in our garden, but here, for the first time, I saw tree ferns, rearing themselves twenty or thirty feet up in the air, with lacy arching fronds at their summits, their trunks buttressed by thick cably roots – vigorous and alive, and yet hardly different from the ones of the Palaeozoic.

And it was at Kew that I finally saw living cycads, clustered as they had been for a century or more in a corner of the great Palm House.[80] They too were survivors from a long-distant past, and the stamp of their ancient-ness was manifest in every part of them – in their huge cones, their sharp, spiny leaves, their heavy columnar trunks, reinforced like mediaeval armour, by persistent leaf bases. If the tree ferns had grace, these cycads had grandeur and, to my boyish mind, a sort of moral dimension too. Widespread once, reduced now to a few genera – I could not help thinking of them as both tragic and heroic. Tragic in that they had lost the pre-modern world they had grown up in: all the plants they were intimately related to – the seed ferns, the *Bennettitales*, the *Cordaites* of the Palaeozoic – had long ago vanished from the earth, and now they found themselves rare, odd, singular, anomalous, in a world of little, noisy, fast-moving animals and fast-growing, brightly coloured flowers, out of synch with their own dignified and monumental timescale. But heroic too, in that they had survived the catastrophe which destroyed the dinosaurs, adapted to different climates and conditions (not least to the hegemony of birds and mammals, which the cycads now exploited to disperse their seeds).

The sense of their enduringness, their great phylogenetic age, was amplified for me by the age of some of the individual plants – one, an African *Encephalartos longifolius*, was said to be the oldest potted plant in Kew and had been brought here in 1775. If these wonders could be grown at Kew, I thought, why should I not grow them at home? When I was twelve (the war had just ended) I took the bus to a nursery in Edmonton, in north London, and bought two plants – a woolly tree fern, a *Cibotium*, and a small cycad, a *Zamia*.[81] I tried to grow them in our little glassed-in conservatory at the back of the house – but the house was too cold, and they withered and died.

When I was older, and first visited Amsterdam, I

discovered the beautiful little triangular Hortus Botanicus there – it was very old, and still had a mediaeval air, an echo of the herb gardens, the monastery gardens, from which botanical gardens had sprung. There was a conservatory which was particularly rich in cycads, including one ancient, gnarled specimen, contorted with age (or perhaps from its confinement in a pot and a small space), which was (also) said to be the oldest potted plant in the world. It was called the Spinoza cycad (though I have no idea whether Spinoza ever saw it), and it had been potted, if the information was reliable, near the middle of the seventeenth century; it vied, in this way, with the ancient cycad at Kew.[82]

But there is an infinite difference between a garden, however grand, and the wild, where one can get a feeling of the actual complexities and dynamics of life, the forces that press to evolution and extinction. And I yearned to see cycads in their own context, not planted, not labelled, not isolated for viewing, but growing side by side with banyans and screw pines and ferns all about them, the whole harmony and complexity of a full-scale cycad jungle – the living reality of my childhood dreamscape.

*

Rota is Guam's closest companion in the Marianas chain and is geologically similar, with a complex history of risings and fallings, reef makings and destructions, going back forty million years or so. The two islands are inhabited by similar vegetation and animals – but Rota, lacking Guam's size, its grand harbours, its commercial and agricultural potential, has been far less modernized. Rota has been largely left to itself, biologically and culturally, and it can perhaps give one some idea of how Guam looked in the sixteenth century, when it was still covered by dense forests of cycads, and this was why I wanted to come here.[83]

I would be meeting one of the island's few remaining medicine women, Beata Mendiola – John Steele had known her, and her son Tommy, for many years. 'They know more about cycads, about all the primitive plants and foods and natural medicines and poisons here,' he said, 'than anyone I know.' They met me at the landing strip – Tommy is an engaging, intelligent man in his late twenties or early thirties, fluent in Chamorro and English. Beata, lean, dark, with an aura of power, was born during the Japanese occupation, and speaks Chamorro and Japanese only, so Tommy had to interpret for us.

We drove a few miles down a dirt road to the edge of the jungle and then went on by foot, Tommy and his mother with machetes, leading the way. The jungle was so dense in places that light could hardly filter through, and I had the sense, at times, of a fairy wood, with every tree trunk, every branch, wreathed in epiphytic mosses and ferns.

I had seen only isolated cycads on Guam, perhaps two or three close together – but here there were hundreds, dominating the jungle. They grew everywhere, some in clumps, some as isolated trunks reaching, here and there, twelve or fifteen feet in height. Most, though, were relatively low – five or six feet tall, perhaps – and surrounded by a thick carpet of ferns. Thickened and strengthened with the scars of old leaves, leaf scales, these trunks looked mighty as locomotives or stegosaurs. High winds and typhoons beat through these islands regularly, and the trunks of some of them were bent at all angles, sometimes even prostrate on the ground. But this, if anything, seemed to increase their vitality, for where they were bent, especially at the base, new growths, bulbils, had erupted in scores, bearing their own crowns of young leaves, still pale green and soft. While most of the cycads around us were tall, unbranched ones whose life force seemed to be pouring upward to the sky, there were others, almost monstrous, which seemed to be running riot, exploding in all directions, full of anarchic vitality, sheer vegetable exuberance, hubris.

Beata pointed out the stiff reinforcing leaf bases which ringed each tree trunk – as each new crown of leaves had sprouted at the top, the older leaves had died off, but their bases remained. 'We can estimate the age of a cycad by counting these leaf scales,' said Beata. I started to do this, with one huge prostrate tree, but Tommy and Beata smiled as I did so. 'It is easier,' she said, 'if you look at the trunks – many of the older ones have a very thin ring in 1900, because that was the year of the great typhoon; and another thin ring in 1973, when we had very strong winds.'

'Yeah,' inserted Tommy, 'those winds got to two hundred miles per hour, they say.'

'The typhoon strips all the leaves off the plant,' Beata explained, 'so they can't grow as much as usual.' Some of the oldest trees, she thought, were more than a thousand years old.[84]

A cycad forest is not lofty, like a pine or oak forest. A cycad forest is low, with short stumpy trees – but the trees give an impression of immense solidity and strength. They are heavy-duty models, one feels – not tall, not flashy, not capable of rapid growth, like modern trees, but built to last, to withstand a typhoon or a drought. Heavy, armoured, slow growing, gigantic – they seem to bear, like dinosaurs, the imprint of the Mesozoic, the 'style' of two hundred million years ago.

Male and female cycads are impossible to tell apart until they mature and produce their spectacular cones. The male *Cycas* has an enormous upright cone, a foot or more in length and weighing perhaps thirty pounds, like a monstrous pinecone, tessellated, with great chunky cone scales sweeping round the axis of the cone in elegant spiral curves.[85] The female of the *Cycas* genus, in contrast, lacks a proper cone, but produces a great central cluster of soft woolly leaves instead – megasporophylls, specialized for reproduction – orange in colour, velvety, notched; and hanging below each leaf, eight or ten slate-coloured ovules – microscopic structures in most organisms, but here the size of juniper berries.

We stopped by one cone, half a yard high, ripe and full of pollen. Tommy shook it, and a cloud of pollen came out; it had a powerful, pungent smell and set me tearing and sneezing. (The cycad woods must be thick with pollen in the windy season, I thought, and some researchers have even wondered whether the lytico-bodig could be caused by inhaling it.) The smell of the male cones is generally rather unpleasant for human beings – as far back as 1795, there were ordinances in Agana requiring inhabitants to remove the cones if they grew male plants in their garden. But, of course, the smell is not for *us*. Ants are drawn by the powerful smell, said Tommy; sometimes a horde of tiny, biting ones will fly out as the tree is poked. 'Look!' he said. 'See this little spider? We call him paras ranas in Chamorro, "the one that weaves the web". This type of spider is mostly found on the cycad; it eats the ants. When the cycad is young and green, the spider is green too. When the cycad starts to become brown, the spider takes that colour too. I am glad when I see the spiders, because it means there will be no ants to bite me when I pick the fruits.'

Brilliantly coloured fungi sprouted in the wet earth – Beata knew them all, which were poisonous, and what remedy to use if poisoned; which were hallucinogenic; which were good to eat. Some of them, Tommy told me, were luminous at night – and this was also true of some of the ferns. Looking down among the ferns, I spotted a low, whisklike plant, *Psilotum nudum* – inconspicuous, with stiff leafless stems the diameter of a pencil lead, forking every few inches like a miniature tree, bifurcating its way through the undergrowth. I bent down to examine it, and saw that each tiny fractal branch was capped with a yellow three-lobed sporangium no bigger than a pin-head, containing all the spores. *Psilotum* grows all over Guam and Rota – on riverbanks, in the savannah, around buildings, and often on trees, as an epiphyte drooping like

Spanish moss from their branches – and seeing it in its natural habitat gave me a peculiar thrill. No one notices *Psilotum*, no one collects it, esteems it, respects it – small, plain, leafless, rootless, it has none of the spectacular features which attract collectors. But for me it is one of the most exciting plants in the world, for its ancestors, the psilophytes of the Silurian, were the first plants to develop a vascular system, to free themselves from the need to live in water. From these pioneers had come the club mosses, the ferns, the now-extinct seed ferns, the cycads, the conifers, and the vast range of flowering plants which subsequently spread all over the earth. But this originator, this dawn-plant, still lives on, humbly, inconspicuously co-existing with the innumerable species it has spawned – had Goethe seen it, he would have called this his *Ur-pflanze*.[86]

*

If the cycads conjured up for me the lush forests of the Jurassic, a very different, much older vision rose before me with the *Psilotum*: the bare rocks of the Silurian – a quarter of a billion years earlier, when the seas teemed with great cephalopods and armoured fish and eurypterids and trilobites, but the land, apart from a few mosses and lichens, was still uninhabited and empty.[87] Psilophytes, stiff stemmed as no alga had ever been, were among the first colonizers of the bare land. In the dioramas of 'The First Life on Land' I so loved as a child, one could see panting lungfish and amphibious tetrapods emerging from the primordial waters, climbing aboard the now-green margins of the land. Psilophytes, and other early land plants, provided the soil, the moisture, the cover, the pasture, without which no animal could have survived on land.

*

A little farther on, I was startled to see a large accumulation of empty, broken coconut shells on the ground, but when I looked around, there were no coconut palms to be seen, only cycads and pandanus. Filthy tourists, I thought – must have come in and thrown these husks here; but there were few tourists on Rota. It seemed odd that the Chamorros, who are so respectful of the jungle, would leave a pile of refuse here. 'What is this?' I asked Tommy. 'Who brought all these shells here?'

'Crabs,' he said. Seeing my confusion, he elaborated. 'These large coconut crabs come in. The coconut trees are over there.' He gestured toward the beach, a few hundred yards away, where we could just see a grove of palm trees. 'The crabs know they will be disturbed if they eat them by the beach, so they bring them over here to eat.'[88]

One shell had a huge hole, as if it had been bitten in half. 'This must have been a real big crab to do this,' Tommy observed, 'a monster! The crab hunters know when they find coconut shells like this that there are coconut crabs all around, and then we search, and then we eat *them* – I would like to catch the crab that did this!

'Coconut crabs love the cycads, too. So when I come out to gather the cycad fruit, I bring along a bag for crabs too.' With his machete, Tommy cut through the under-growth, making a path. 'This is good for the cycads – it gives them room to grow.'

*

'Feel this cone!' Tommy said, as we came to a large male plant – I was surprised to find it warm to the touch. 'It is like a furnace,' said Tommy. 'Making the pollen gives it heat – you can really feel it as the day cools, in the evening.' Botanists have known for about a century (and cycad gatherers, of course, for much longer) that the cones may generate heat – sometimes twenty degrees or more above the ambient temperature – as they ready for polli-nation. The mature cones produce heat for several hours each day by breaking down lipids and starches within the cone scales; it is thought that the heat increases the release of insect-attracting odours, and thus helps in the distribu-tion of pollen. Intrigued by the almost-animal warmth of the cone, I hugged it, impulsively, and almost vanished in a huge cloud of pollen.

*

In his *Useful Plants of the Island of Guam* Safford has much to say about *Cycas circinalis* – its role in Chamorro culture, its use as food; but 'its chief interest,' he adds (one remembers that he is a botanist here), 'lies in the structure of its inflorescence and the manner of its fructification.' At this point he cannot suppress a special enthusiasm and excitement. He describes how the pollen settles on the naked ovules and sends a tube down into them, within which the male germ cells, the spermatozooids, are produced. The mature spermatozooids are 'the largest known to occur in any animal or plant. They are even visible to the naked eye.' He goes on to describe how the spermatozooids, which are motile, powered by cilia, enter the egg cell and fuse with it totally, 'cytoplasm with cytoplasm, nucleus with nucleus'.

These observations were quite new at the time he was writing; for though cycads had been described by Europeans in the seventeenth century, there had been much confusion as to their origins and place in the vegetable kingdom. It was only the discovery of their motile spermatozooids, by Japanese botanists in 1896, that afforded the first absolutely clear evidence of their kinship (and thus of their whole group, the gymnosperms) with ferns and other 'lower' spore-bearing plants (which also have motile spermatozooids). The importance of these discoveries, made only a few years before he wrote, is strong and fresh for Safford, and enriches his account with a feeling of intellectual fervour. Longing to see this visible act of fecundation for myself, I pulled out my hand lens and peered into the male cone, then into the notched ovules, as if the whole drama might be enacted before my eyes.

Tommy and Beata seemed amused by my barmy enthusiasm, and burst out laughing – for them, basically, cycads are food. Their interest is not in the male plant, its pollen, or the giant spermatozooids which are produced within the ovules – these, so far as they are concerned, are just instrumental in getting the female plants fertilized, so that they may bear their great, glossy, plum-sized seeds. These they will gather, and slice, and wash, and wash again, and finally dry and grind to form the finest fadang flour. Like connoisseurs, choosing only the best, Tommy and his mother went from tree to tree – this one was unfertilized, that one unripe, but there was a carpophyll of heavy ripe seeds, a cluster of a dozen or more. Tommy sliced the machete, and caught the cluster as it fell. He poked another cluster, too high to chop, with a stick he was carrying, and asked me to catch the seeds as they fell. I found my fingers covered with sticky white sap. 'That's really poisonous,' said Tommy. 'Don't lick your fingers.'

*

It was not just the reproductive structures of cycads which so fascinated me as a boy, or the sheer gigantism that seemed characteristic of the group (the biggest spermatozooids, the biggest egg cells, the biggest growing apices, the biggest cones, the biggest everything in the vegetable world) – though (I could not deny it) these had a certain appeal. It was rather the sense that cycads were brilliantly adaptable and resourceful life-forms, full of unusual capacities and developments which had enabled them to survive for a quarter of a billion years, when so many of their contemporaries had fallen by the way. (Maybe they had been so poisonous to fend off the dinosaurs which ate them, I used to speculate as a child – maybe they had been responsible for the dinosaurs' extinction!)

It was true that cycads had the largest growing apices of any vascular plant, but, equally to the point, these delicate apices were beautifully protected by persistent leaf bases, enabling the plants to be fire resistant, everything resistant, to an unusual degree, and to reshoot new fronds, after a catastrophe, sooner than anything else. And if something did none the less befall the growing apices, the plants had an alternative, bulbils, which they could fall back on. Cycads could be pollinated by wind – or insects, they were not choosy: they had avoided the path of overspecialization which had done in so many species over the last half-billion years.[89] In the absence of fertilization, they could propagate asexually, by offsets and suckers (there was a suggestion too that some plants were able to spontaneously change sex). Many cycad species had developed unique 'corraloid' roots, where they symbiosed with blue-green algae, which could fix atmospheric nitrogen for them, rather than relying solely on organic nitrogen from the soil. This struck me as particularly brilliant – and highly adaptive should the seeds fall on impoverished soils; it had taken legumes, flowering

plants, another hundred million years to achieve a similar trick.[90]

Cycads had huge seeds, so strongly constructed and so packed with nourishment that they had a very good chance of surviving and germinating. And they could call on not just one but a variety of vectors for their dispersal. All sorts of smaller animals – from bats to birds to marsupials to rodents – attracted by the brightly coloured, nutritious outer coat, would carry them off, nibble at them, and then discard the seed proper, the essential inner core, unharmed. Some rodents would squirrel them away, bury them – in effect, plant them – increasing their chances of successful germination. Large mammals might eat the entire seed – monkeys eating individual seeds, elephants entire cones – and void the endosperm, in its tough nut, unharmed in their dung, often in quite far-removed places.

Beata was examining another cycad plant, speaking softly in Chamorro to her son. When the rains come, she was saying, the seeds can float. You can tell where they float to in the jungle, because new cycad plants sprout up all along the little rivers and streams. She thinks they float in the sea as well, and that this is how they get to other islands. As she spoke she split open a seed, and showed me the spongy flotation layer just beneath the seed coat – a feature peculiar to the Marianas cycad and the other littoral species of *Cycas*, which grow in coastal and near-coastal forests.

*

Cycads have spread to many different ecoclimes, from the humid tropical zones they flourished in during the Jurassic, to near deserts, savannahs, mountains, and seashores. It is the littoral species which have achieved the widest distribution, for their seeds can float and travel great distances on ocean currents. One of these species, *Cycas thouarsii*, has spread from the east coast of Africa to Madagascar, to the Comoros and the Seychelles. The other littoral species, *C. circinalis* and *C. rumphii*, seem to have originated in the coastal plains of India and South-east Asia. From here their seeds, borne on ocean currents, have fanned out across the Pacific, colonizing New Guinea, the Moluccas, Fiji, the Solomon Islands, Palau, Yap, some of the Carolines and Marshalls – and, of course, Guam and Rota. And as the buoyant seeds of the ancestral species have settled on different islands, they have begotten striking variants, some of which have diverged now, in a manner which would have delighted Darwin, to half a dozen new species or more.[91]

Although cycads vary greatly in size and character, from sixty-foot trees to delicate plants with underground rhizomes, many of the sixty-odd species of *Cycas* do not look that different (as opposed, say, to the species of *Zamia*, which vary so widely, and wildly, in appearance that one has difficulty believing they all belong to the same genus) – and that one of these species should be mistaken for another is very understandable. Indeed, I had been surprised, after my Guam visit, when I went into a nursery in San Francisco – thinking to buy a *Cycas circinalis* for a wedding present – and was shown a plant which was clearly different from the Guam one. When I queried the nursery owner, she indignantly insisted that it was a *circinalis*, and suggested that perhaps what I had seen in Guam was not. It seemed astonishing that there should be such confusion even among plant experts – but David Jones, in his *Cycads of the World*, speaks of the complexities of identifying the island cycads:

> The plants adapt over generations in various small ways to their own particular environmental circumstances and local climate. . . . The situation is further complicated by new arrivals being regularly carried on ocean currents. On reaching maturity these recent plants can hybridize with existing plants and the resulting complex range of variation may defy taxonomic separation. Thus *C. circinalis* must be regarded as an extremely variable species.

And indeed, since I returned from Guam, I have learned that the cycad peculiar to Guam and Rota, regarded for centuries as a variety of *C. circinalis*, has recently been reclassified as a distinct species within the *C. rumphii* 'complex', and renamed *C. micronesica*.[92]

C. micronesica, it seems, is distinctive not only morphologically, but chemically and physiologically too – with a notably higher content of carcinogenic and toxic substances (in particular, of cycasin and BMAA) than any other cycad which has been analysed. Thus cycad eating, relatively benign elsewhere, may be peculiarly dangerous on Guam and Rota – and the Darwinian process which has brought a new species into the world may also, conceivably, be contributing to a new human disease.

*

I find myself walking softly on the rich undergrowth beneath the trees, not wanting to crack a twig, to crush or disturb anything in the least – for there is such a sense of stillness and peace that the wrong sort of movement, even one's very presence, might be felt as an intrusion, and, so to speak, anger the woods. Tommy's words, earlier, came back to me now. 'All my life,' he said, 'I was taught to walk backwards in the jungle, and not to destroy anything ... I have the attitude that these plants are alive. They have powers. They can invoke some kind of a disease to you if you do not respect them. . . .' The beauty of the forest is extraordinary – but 'beauty' is too simple a word, for being here is not just an aesthetic experience, but one steeped with mystery, and awe.

I would have similar feelings as a child, when I lay beneath the ferns, and later, when I entered through the massive iron gates at Kew – a place which was not just botanical for me, but had an element of the mystical, the religious too. My father once told me that the very word 'paradise' meant garden, spelling out for me the four letters (*pe resh dalet samech*) of *pardes*, the Hebrew word for garden. But gardens, Eden or Kew, are not the right metaphors here, for the primeval has nothing to do with the human, but has to do with the ancient, the aboriginal, the beginning of all things. The primeval, the sublime, are much better words here – for they indicate realms remote from the moral or the human, realms which force us to gaze into immense vistas of space and time, where the beginnings and originations of all things lie hidden. Now, as I wandered in the cycad forest on Rota, it seemed as if my senses were actually enlarging, as if a new sense, a time sense, was opening within me, something which might allow me to appreciate millennia or aeons as directly as I had experienced seconds or minutes.[93]

*

I live on an island – City Island in New York – surrounded by the brilliant transient artefacts of man. And yet each June, without fail, horseshoe crabs come up from the sea, crawl on the beach, mate, deposit eggs, and then slowly swim away again. I love to swim in the bay alongside them; they permit this, indifferently. They have crawled up to the shores and mated every summer as their ancestors have done since the Silurian, four hundred million years ago. Like the cycads, the horseshoe crabs are rugged models, great survivors which have endured. When he saw the giant tortoises of the Galapagos, Melville wrote (in 'The Encantadas'):

> The great feeling inspired by these creatures was that of age – dateless, indefinite endurance. They seemed newly crawled from beneath the foundations of the world.

Such is the feeling inspired, for me, by the horseshoe crabs each June.

The sense of deep time brings a deep peace with it, a detachment from the timescale, the urgencies, of daily life. Seeing these volcanic islands and coral atolls, and wandering, above all, through this cycad forest on Rota, has given me an intimate feeling of the antiquity of the earth, and the slow, continuous processes by which different forms of life evolve and come into being. Standing here in the jungle, I feel part of a larger, calmer identity; I feel a profound sense of being at home, a sort of companionship with the earth.[94]

*

It is evening now, and as Tommy and Beata go off to gather some medicinal plants, I sit on the beach, looking out to sea. Cycads come down almost to the water's edge, and the strand is littered with their gigantic seeds, along with the tough egg cases of sharks and rays, which are shaped like bizarre fortune cookies. A light wind has sprung up, rustling the leaves of the cycads, blowing up little ripples on the water. Ghost crabs and fiddler crabs, hidden in the heat of the day, have emerged and are darting to and fro. The chief sound is the lapping of waves on the shore, lapping as they have done for billions of years, ever since land rose out of the water – an ancient, soothing, hypnotic sound.

I look at the cycad seeds curiously, thinking of Beata's words, how they float and can perhaps survive long immersion in seawater. Most, no doubt, have dropped from the trees above me, but some, perhaps, are nomads, brought here across the sea from Guam, or more distant islands – perhaps even Yap or Palau, or beyond.

A large wave comes in, lifts a couple of the seeds, and they float, bobbing, by the shore. Five minutes later, one of the seeds has been cast up again on the shore, but the other is still bobbing atop the waves, a few feet from land. I wonder where it will go, whether it will survive, will be cast back here on Rota, or taken hundreds, perhaps thousands, of miles to another island in the Pacific. Ten minutes more and I can no longer see it – it is launched, like a little ship, on its journey on the high seas.

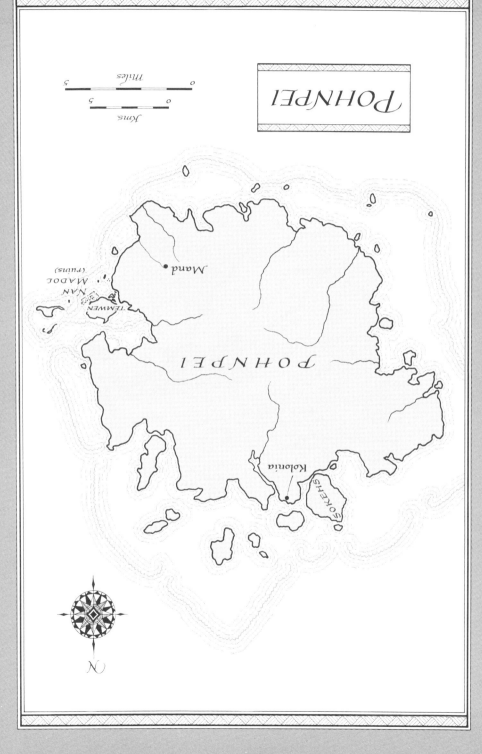

STATE OF POHNPEI

Kapingamarangi

Reefs

Kms
Miles
0   150
0   150

Nukuoro

Sapwuahfik (Ngatik)

Kosrae

Pingelap

Detail on Facing Page

Mokil (Mwoakilloa)

Pohnpei   Pakin   Ant

Oroluk

PACIFIC OCEAN

Eniwetok

N

Notes

*

1. Most of the statues of Easter Island do not, in fact, face
the sea; they face away from the sea, toward what used to
be the exalted houses of the island. Nor are the statues
eyeless – on the contrary, they originally had startling,
brilliant eyes made of white coral, with irises of red
volcanic tuff or obsidian; this was only discovered in
1978. But my children's encyclopaedia adhered to the
myth of the blind, eyeless giants staring hopelessly out
to sea – a myth which seems to have had its origin,
through many tellings and retellings, in some of the early
explorers' accounts, and in the paintings of William
Hodges, who travelled to Easter Island with Captain Cook
in the 1770s.

*

2. Humboldt first described the enormous dragon tree,
very briefly, in a postscript to a letter written in June 1799
from Teneriffe:

In the district of Orotava there is a dragon-tree measuring

forty-five feet in circumference. . . . Four centuries ago the girth was as great as it is now.

In his *Personal Narrative*, written some years later, he devoted three paragraphs to the tree, and speculated about its origin:

> It has never been found in a wild state on the continent of Africa. The East Indies is its real country. How has this tree been transplanted to Teneriffe, where it is by no means common?

Later still, in his 'Physiognomy of Plants' (collected, with other essays, in *Views of Nature*) he devoted nine entire pages to 'The Colossal Dragon-Tree of Orotava', his original observations now expanded to a whole essay of rich and spreading associations and speculations:

> This colossal dragon-tree, Dracaena draco, stands in the garden of M. Franqui, in the little town of Orotava ... one of the most charming spots in the world. In June 1799, when we ascended the peak of Teneriffe, we found that this enormous tree measured 48 feet in circumference.... When we remember that the dragon-tree is everywhere of very slow growth, we may conclude that the one at Orotava is of extreme antiquity.

He suggests an age of about six thousand years for the tree, which would make it 'coeval with the builders of the Pyramids ... and place its birth ... in an epoch when the Southern Cross was still visible in Northern Germany.' But despite its vast age, the tree still bore, he remarks, 'the blossom and fruit of perpetual youth'.

Humboldt's *Personal Narrative* was a great favourite of Darwin's. 'I will never be easy,' he wrote to his sister Caroline, 'till I see the peak of Teneriffe and the great Dragon tree.' He planned to visit it with his teacher, Henslow, but they were not permitted to land at Tenerife because of a quarantine. He did, however, take the *Personal Narrative* with him on the *Beagle* (along with Lyell's *Principles of Geology*), and when he was able to retrace some of Humboldt's travels in South America, his enthusiasm knew no bounds. 'I formerly admired Humboldt,' he wrote. 'Now I almost adore him.'

*

3. Remarkable specializations and evolutions may occur not only on islands, but in every sort of special and cut-off environment. Thus a unique stingless jellyfish was recently discovered in an enclosed salt-water lake in the interior of Eil Malk, one of the islands of Palau, as Nancy Barbour describes:

> The jellyfish in the lake are members of the genus *Mastigias*, a jellyfish commonly found in the Palau Lagoon whose powerful stinging tentacles are used for protection and for capturing planktonic prey. It is believed that the ancestors of these *Mastigias* jellyfish became trapped in the lake millions of years ago when volcanic forces uplifted Palau's submerged reefs, transforming deep pockets in the reefs into landlocked salt-water lakes. Because there was little food and few predators in the lake, their long, clublike tentacles gradually evolved into stubby appendages unable to sting, and the jellyfish came to rely on the symbiotic algae living within their tissues for nutrients. The algae capture energy from the sun and transform it into food for the jellyfish. In turn, the jellyfish swim near the surface during the day to ensure that the algae receive enough sunlight for photosynthesis to occur. . . . Every morning the school of jellyfish, estimated at more than 1.6 million, migrates across the lake to the opposite shore, each jellyfish rotating counter-clockwise so that the algae on all sides of its bell receive equal sunlight. In the afternoon the jellyfish turn and swim back across the lake. At night they descend to the lake's middle layer, where they absorb the nitrogen that fertilizes their algae.

*

4. 'I had been lying on a sunny bank,' Darwin wrote of his travels in Australia, 'reflecting on the strange character of the animals of this country as compared to the rest of the World.' He was thinking here of marsupials as opposed to placental animals; they were so different, he felt, that

> an unbeliever in everything beyond his own reason might exclaim, 'Surely two distinct Creators must have been at work.'

Then his attention was caught by a giant lion-ant in its conical pitfall, flicking up jets of sand, making little avalanches, so that small ants slid into its pit, exactly like lion-ants he had seen in Europe:

> Would any two workmen ever hit on so beautiful, so simple, and yet so artificial a contrivance? It cannot be thought so. The one hand has surely worked throughout the universe.

*

5. Frances Futterman also describes her vision in very positive terms:

> Words like 'achromatopsia' dwell only on what we lack. They give no sense of what we have, the sort of worlds we appreciate or make for ourselves. I find twilight a magical time – there are no harsh contrasts, my visual field expands, my acuity is suddenly improved. Many of my best experiences have come at twilight, or in moonlight – I have toured Yosemite under the full moon, and one achromatope I know worked as a night-time guide there;

some of my happiest memories are of lying on my back among the giant redwood trees, looking up at the stars.

As a kid I used to chase lightning bugs on warm summer nights; and I loved going to the amusement park, with all the flashing neon lights and the darkened fun house – I was never afraid of that. I love grand old movie theatres, with their ornate interiors, and outdoor theatres. During the holiday season, I like to look at all the twinkling lights decorating store windows and trees.

*

6. The caption on this postcard of Darwin suggested that he had 'discovered' his theory of coral atolls here in Majuro; though in fact he conceived it before he had ever seen an atoll. He never actually visited Majuro, nor any of the Marshalls or the Carolines (though he did go to Tahiti). He does, however, make brief reference in *Coral Reefs* to Pohnpei (as Pouynipête, or Senyavine) and even mentions Pingelap (by its then usual name, Macaskill).

*

7. Ebeye can be seen, perhaps, as a sort of end-point, an end-point characterized not only by desperate overcrowding and disease, but by loss of cultural identity and coherence, and its replacement by an alien and frenzied consumerism, a cash economy. The ambiguous processes of colonization showed their potential right from the start – thus Cook, visiting Tahiti in 1769, only two years after its 'discovery', could not help wondering, in his journals, whether the arrival of the white man might spell doom for all the Pacific cultures:

We debauch their morals, and introduce among them wants and diseases which they never had before, and which serve only to destroy the happy tranquillity they and their forefathers had enjoyed. I often think it would have been better for them if we had never appeared among them.

*

8. A pioneer in the use of streptomycin, Bill Peck joined the Micronesian Health Service in the 1950s and was an official observer of the atomic tests in the Marshalls. He was one of the first to record the great incidence of thyroid cancer, leukaemia, miscarriage, etc., in the wake of the tests, but was not allowed to publish his observations at the time. In his book *A Tidy Universe of Islands*, he gives a vivid description of the fallout on Rongelap after the detonation of the atomic bomb Bravo in Bikini:

The fallout started four to six hours after the detonation and appeared first as an indefinite haze, rapidly changing to a white, sifting powder: like snow, some of them said who had seen movies at Kwajalein. Jimaco and Tina romped through the village with a troop of younger children, exulting in the miracle and shouting, 'Look, we are like a Christmas picture, we play in snow,' and they pointed with glee at the sticky powder that smeared their skin, whitened their hair, and rimed the ground with hoarfrost.

As evening came on the visible fallout diminished until finally all that remained was a little unnatural lustre in the moonlight. And the itching. Almost everyone was scratching. . . . In the morning they were still itching, and several of them had weeping eyes. The flakes had become grimy and adherent from sweat and attempts to wash them off in cold water failed. Everyone felt a little sick, and three of them vomited.

*

9. Obesity, sometimes accompanied by diabetes, affects an overwhelming majority of Pacific peoples. It was suggested by James Neel in the early 1960s that this might be due to a so-called 'thrifty' gene, which might have evolved to allow the storage of fat through periods of famine. Such a gene would be highly adaptive, he posited, in peoples living in a subsistence economy, where there might be erratic periods of feast and famine, but could prove lethally maladaptive if there was a shift to a steady high-fat diet, as has happened throughout Oceania since the Second World War. In Nauru, after less than a generation of Westernization, two-thirds of the islanders are obese, and a third have diabetes; similar figures have been observed on many other islands. That it is a particular conjunction of genetic disposition and lifestyle which is so dangerous is shown by the contrasting fates of the Pima Indians. Those living in Arizona, on a steady high-fat diet, have the highest rates of obesity and diabetes in the world, while the genetically similar Pima Indians of Mexico, living on subsistence farming and ranching, remain lean and healthy.

NOTES TO *PINGELAP*

*

10. A similar feeling of kinship may occur for a deaf traveller, who has crossed the sea or the world, if he lights upon other deaf people on his arrival. In 1814, the deaf French educator Laurent Clerc came to visit a deaf school in London, and this was described by a contemporary:

> As soon as Clerc beheld this sight [of the children at dinner] his face became animated: he was as agitated as a traveller of sensibility would be on meeting all of a sudden in distant regions, a colony of his countrymen. . . . Clerc approached them. He made signs and they answered him by signs. This unexpected communication caused a most delicious sensation in them and for us was a scene of expression and sensibility that gave us the most heartfelt satisfaction.

And it was similar when I went with Lowell Handler, a friend with Tourette's syndrome, to a remote Mennonite community in northern Alberta where a genetic form of Tourette's had become remarkably common. At first a bit tense, and on his best behaviour, Lowell was able to suppress his tics; but after a few minutes he let out a loud Tourettic shriek. Everyone turned to look at him, as always happens. But then everybody smiled – they understood – and some even answered Lowell with their own tics and noises. Surrounded by other Touretters, his

Tourettic brethren, Lowell felt, in many ways, that he had 'come home' at last – he dubbed the village 'Tourettes-ville', and mused about marrying a beautiful Mennonite woman with Tourette's, and living there happily ever after.

*

11. R. L. Stevenson writes about pigs in his memoir of Polynesia, *In the South Seas*:

> The pig is the main element of animal food among the islands. . . . Many islanders live with their pigs as we do with our dogs; both crowd around the hearth with equal freedom; and the island pig is a fellow of activity, enter-prise, and sense. He husks his own cocoa-nuts, and (I am told) rolls them into the sun to burst. . . . It was told us in childhood that pigs cannot swim; I have known one to leap overboard, swim five hundred yards to shore, and return to the house of his original owner.

*

12. It was striking how green everything was in Pingelap, not only the foliage of trees, but their fruits as well – breadfruit and pandanus are both green, as were many varieties of bananas on the island. The brightly coloured red and yellow fruits – papaya, mango, guava – are not native to these islands, but were only introduced by the Europeans in the 1820s.

J. D. Mollon, a preeminent researcher on the mechan-isms of colour vision, notes that Old World monkeys 'are particularly attracted to orange or yellow fruit (as opposed to birds, which go predominantly for red or purple fruit)'.

Most mammals (indeed, most vertebrates) have evolved a system of dichromatic vision, based on the correlation of short- and medium-wavelength information, which helps them to recognize their environments, their foods, their friends and enemies, and to live in a world of colour, albeit of a very limited and muted type. Only certain primates have evolved full trichromatic vision, and this is what enables them to detect yellow and orange fruits against a dappled green background; Mollon suggests that the coloration of these fruits may indeed have coevolved with such a trichromatic system in monkeys. Trichromatic vision enables them too to recognize the most delicate facial shades of emotional and biological states, and to use these (as monkeys do, no less than humans) to signal aggression or sexual display.

Achromatopes, or rod-monochromats (as they are also called), lack even the primordial dichromatic system, considered to have developed far back in the Palaeozoic. If 'human dichromats,' in Mollon's words, 'have especial difficulty in detecting coloured fruit against dappled foliage that varies randomly in luminosity', one would expect that monochromats would be even more profoundly disabled, scarcely able to survive in a world geared, at the least, for dichromats. But it is here that adaptation and compensation can play a crucial part. This quite different mode of perception is well brought out by Frances Futterman, who writes:

When a new object would come into my life, I would have a very thorough sensory experience of it. I would savour the feel of it, the smell of it, and the appearance of it (all the visible aspects except colour, of course). I would even stroke it or tap it or do whatever created an auditory experience. All objects have unique qualities which can be savoured. All can be looked at in different lights and in different kinds of shadows. Dull finishes, shiny finishes, textures, prints, transparent qualities – I scrutinized them all, up close, in my accustomed way (which occurred because of my visual impairment but which, I think, provided me with more multi-sensory impressions of things). How might this have been different if I were seeing in colour? Might the colours of things have dominated my experience, preventing me from knowing so intimately the other qualities of things?

*

13. Darwin's friend and colleague John Judd recorded that Lyell, the strongest proponent of the submerged volcano theory, 'was so overcome with delight' when the young Darwin told him of his own subsidence theory, 'that he danced about and threw himself into the wildest contortions'. But he went on to warn Darwin: 'Do not flatter yourself that you will be believed till you are growing bald like me with hard work and vexation at the incredulity of the world.'

*

14. The coconut palm, which Stevenson called 'that giraffe of vegetables . . . so graceful, so ungainly, to the European eye so foreign', was the most precious possession of the Polynesians and Micronesians, who brought it with them

to every new island they colonized. Melville describes this in *Omoo*:

> The blessings it confers are incalculable. Year after year, the islander reposes beneath its shade, both eating and drinking of its fruit. He thatches his hut with its boughs and weaves them into baskets to carry his food. He cools himself with a fan platted from the young leaflets and shields his head from the sun by a bonnet of the leaves. Sometimes he clothes himself with the cloth-like substance which wraps round the base of the stalks. The larger nuts, thinned and polished, furnish him with a beautiful goblet; the smaller ones, with bowls for his pipes. The dry husks kindle his fires. Their fibers are twisted into fishing lines and cords for his canoes. He heals his wounds with a balsam compounded from the juice of the nut and with the oil extracted from its meat embalms the bodies of the dead.
>
> The noble trunk itself is far from being valueless. Sawed into posts, it upholds the islander's dwelling. Converted into charcoal, it cooks his food. . . . He impels his canoe through the water with a paddle of the same wood and goes to battle with clubs and spears of the same hard material. . . .
>
> Thus, the man who but drops one of these nuts into the ground may be said to confer a greater and more certain benefit upon himself and posterity than many a life's toil in less genial climes.

*

15. The sort of divergence which has made Pingelapese a distinct dialect of Pohnpeian has occurred many times

throughout the scattered islands of Micronesia. It is not always clear at what point the line between dialect and language has been crossed, as E. J. Kahn brings out, in *A Reporter in Micronesia*:

In the Marshalls, Marshallese is spoken, and in the Marianas, Chamorro. From there on, things start to get complicated. Among the languages ... is a rare one used by the eighty-three inhabitants of Sonsorol and the sixty-six of Tobi, two minute island groups in the Palau district but far off the beaten Palauan track. It has been argued that the Sonsorolese and Tobians don't really have a language at all but merely speak a dialect of Palauan, which is that district's major tongue. Yapese is another major one, and a complex one, with thirteen vowel sounds and thirty-two consonants. The Ulithi and Woleai atolls in the Yap district have their own languages, provided one accepts Woleaian as such and not as a dialect of Ulithian. The speech of the three hundred and twenty-one residents of still another Yap district atoll, Satawal, may also be a separate language, though some assert that it is simply a dialect of Trukese, the main language of Truk.

Not counting Satawalese, there are at least ten distinctive dialects of Trukese, among them Puluwatese, Pulapese, Pulusukese, and Mortlockese. (A number of scholars insist that the tongue of the Mortlock Islands, named for an eighteenth-century explorer, is a bona fide separate language.) In the Ponape district, in addition to Ponapean, there is Kusraiean; and because the Ponapean sector of Micronesia contains the two Polynesian atolls, Nukuoro and Kapingamarangi, there is a language that is used in those places – with considerable dialectical variations between the version in the one and that in the other. And, finally, there are linguists who maintain that the languages spoken in still two more Ponapean island groups, Mokil and Pingelap, are not, as other linguists maintain, mere variations of standard Ponapean, but authentic individualistic tongues called Mokilese and Pingelapese.

'Some Micronesians,' he goes on, 'have become remarkably versatile linguists.'

One cannot but be reminded of how animals and plants diverge from the original stock, first into varieties, and then into species – a speciation intensely heightened by the unique conditions on islands, and so most dramatic in the contiguous islands of an archipelago. Cultural and linguistic evolution, of course, normally proceeds much faster than Darwinian, for we directly pass whatever we acquire to the next generation.

*

16. There are two kerosene generators on Pingelap: one for lighting the administration building and dispensary and three or four other buildings, and one for running the island's videotape recorders. But the first has been out of action for years, and nobody has made much effort to repair or replace it – candles or kerosene lamps are more reliable. The other dynamo, however, is carefully tended, because the viewing of action films from the States exerts a compulsive force.

*

17. William Dampier was the first European to describe breadfruit, which he saw in Guam in 1688:

> The fruit grows on the boughs like apples; it is as big as a penny loaf, when wheat is at five shillings the bushel; it is of a round shape, and hath a thick, tough rind. When the fruit is ripe, it is yellow and soft, and the taste is sweet and pleasant. The natives of Guam use it for bread. They gather it when full grown, while it is green and hard; then they bake it in an oven, which scorcheth the rind and maketh it black; but . . . the inside is soft, tender and white, like the crumb of a penny-loaf. There is *neither seed nor stone* in the inside, but all of a pure substance, like bread. It must be eaten new, for if it be kept above twenty-four hours, it grows harsh and choky, but it is very pleasant before it is too stale. This fruit lasts in season *eight months* in the year, during which the natives eat no other sort of bread-kind.

*

18. Many holothurians have very sharp, microscopic spicules in their body walls; these spicules take all sorts of shapes – one sees buttons, granules, ellipsoids, bars, racquets, wheel forms with spokes, and anchors. If the spicules (especially the anchor-shaped ones, which are as perfect and sharp as any boat anchor) are not dissolved or destroyed (many hours, or even days, of boiling may be needed), they may lodge in the gut lining of the unfortunate eater, causing serious but invisible bleeding. This has been used to murderous effect for many centuries in China, where trepang is regarded as a great delicacy.

*

19. Irene Maumenee Hussels and her colleagues at Johns Hopkins have taken samples of blood from the entire population of Pingelap and from many Pingelapese in Pohnpei and Mwoakil. Using DNA analysis, they hope it will be possible to locate the genetic abnormality which causes the maskun. If this is achieved, it will then be possible to identify carriers of the disease – but this, Maumenee Hussels points out, will raise complex ethical and cultural questions. It may be, for example, that such identification would militate against chances of marriage or employment for the thirty per cent of the population that carries the gene.

*

20. In 1970 Maumenee Hussels and Morton came to Pingelap with a team of geneticists from the University of Hawaii. They came on the MS *Microglory*, bringing sophisticated equipment, including an electroretinogram for measuring the retina's response to flashes of light. The retinas of those with the maskun, they found, showed normal responses from the rods, but no response whatever from the cones – but it was not until 1994 that Donald Miller and David Williams at the University of Rochester described the first direct observation of retinal cones in living subjects. Since then, they have borrowed techniques from astronomy, adaptive optics, to allow routine imaging of the eye. This equipment has not yet been used to examine any congenital achromatopes, but it would be

interesting to do so, to see whether the absence or defect of cones can be visualized directly.

*

21. 'Cannibalism,' wrote Stevenson, 'is traced from end to end of the Pacific, from the Marquesas to New Guinea, from New Zealand to Hawaii. . . . All Melanesia appears tainted . . . [but] in Micronesia, in the Marshalls, with which my acquaintance is no more than that of a tourist . . . I could find no trace at all.'

But Stevenson never visited the Carolines, and O'Connell does claim to have witnessed cannibalism on one of Pingelap's sister atolls, Pakin (which he calls Wellington Island):

> I did not believe, till my visit, that the natives of Wellington Island were cannibals; then I had ocular demonstration. It seemed with them an ungovernable passion, the victims being not only captives, but presents to the chiefs from parents, who appeared to esteem the acceptance of their children, for a purpose so horrid, an honor. Wellington Island . . . is, in fact, three islands, bounded by a reef. One of them is inhabited, and the other two are uninhabited spots, claimed by different chiefs, as if to afford a pretext for war, and the gratification of their horrible passion for human flesh.

*

22. The legendary history of Pingelap is told in the *Liam-weiwei*, an epic or saga which had been transmitted to

each generation for centuries as a recitation or chant. In the 1960s, only the nahnmwarki knew all 161 verses; and if Jane Hurd had not transcribed these, this epic history would now be lost.

But an anthropologist, however sympathetic, tends to treat an indigenous chant or rite as an object, and may not be able to fully enter its inwardness, its spirit, the perspective of those who actually sing it. An anthropologist sees cultures, one wants to say, as a physician sees patients. The penetration, the sharing, of different consciousnesses and cultures needs skills beyond those of the historian or the scientist; it needs artistic and poetic powers of a special kind. Auden, for instance, identified with Iceland (his first name, Wystan, was Icelandic; and an early book was his *Letters from Iceland*) – but it is his linguistic and poetic powers which make his version of the Elder Edda, the great saga of Iceland, such an uncanny recreation of the original.

And it is this which gives unique value to the work of Bill Peck, a physician and poet who has spent the last thirty-five years living and working in Micronesia. As a young doctor in southern Africa, he had developed a deep interest in folklore and aboriginal art and a deep sympathy for the local culture; when he came to Micronesia as an official observer of the atomic tests, he was appalled by the treatment of the islanders. Later, as commissioner of health for the Trust Territory of the Pacific Islands (as Micronesia was called), he attracted energetic and romantic physicians (including John Steele and later Greg Dever) to help him develop new health services (now the

Micronesian Health Service) and train native nurses to be physician's aides.

Living in Chuuk in the early 1970s, he became increasingly conscious of the ancient traditions and myths of the Chuukese, and had a 'conversion experience' when he met Chief Kintoki Joseph of Udot. He spent several weeks with the chief, listening, recording. This, he says, was

> like discovering the Dead Sea Scrolls or the Book of Mormon. . . . Chief Kintoki would sit quietly, almost in a trance, nodding rhythmically as he recalled a prayer or chant. Then, gesturing, he would recite it dramatically in Ittang, his voice rising and falling as the glory or awe or fright of his vision impelled him. . . . Chief Kintoki said to me, 'Each time I recite these poems I believe, for the moment, that I am the ancient prophet who first revealed them.'

This encounter opened a new dedication for Bill – to record and preserve, to recreate for posterity, the songs and myths of Chuuk and of all the Micronesian cultures (though only a fraction of his work has been published, in his *Chuukese Testament* and *I Sing the Beginning*, as well as a handful of articles and poems). His is a voice, a scientific and poetic transparency, as remarkable as any in Micronesia. In Rota, where he has retired to live and write (and where I met him), he is an honorary citizen, the only non-Chamorro ever accorded this honour. 'Here I am,' he said as I finally left him, 'an old doctor, an old poet, in my eighty-third year, translating, preserving the old legends for the future – trying to give back to these people some of the gifts they have given me.'

*

23. There may be as many as thirty thousand of these tiny bioluminescent creatures in a cubic foot of seawater, and many observers have attested to the extraordinary brilliance of seas filled with *Noctiluca*. Charles Frederick Holder, in his 1887 *Living Lights: A Popular Account of Phosphorescent Animals and Vegetables*, relates how M. de Tessan described the phosphorescent waves as 'appearing like the vivid flashes of lightning', giving enough illumination to read by:

> It lighted up the chamber that I and my companions occupied [de Tessan wrote] ... though it was situated more than fifty yards distant from the breakers. I even attempted to write by the light, but the flashes were of too short duration.

Holder continues his account of these 'living asteroids':

> When a vessel is ploughing through masses of these animals, the effect is extremely brilliant. An American captain states that when his ship traversed a zone of these animals in the Indian Ocean, nearly thirty miles in extent, the light emitted by these myriads of fire-bodies ... eclipsed the brightest stars; the milky way was but dimly seen; and as far as the eye could reach the water presented the appearance of a vast, gleaming sea of molten metal, of purest white. The sails, masts, and rigging cast weird shadows all about; flames sprang from the bow as the ship

M. DE TESSAN READING BY LIGHT OF
PHOSPHORESCENT SEA.

surged along, and great waves of living light spread out ahead – a fascinating and appalling sight. . . .

The light of Noctilucae in full vigour is a clear blue; but, if the water is agitated, it becomes nearly, if not quite white, producing rich silvery gleams sprinkled with greenish and bluish spangles.

Humboldt also described this phenomenon, in his *Views of Nature*:

In the ocean, gelatinous sea-worms, living and dead, shine like luminous stars, converting by their phosphorescent light the green surface of the ocean into one vast sheet of fire. Indelible is the impression left on my mind by those calm tropical nights in the Pacific, where the constellation of Argo in its zenith, and the setting Southern Cross, pour their mild planetary light through the ethereal azure of the sky, while dolphins mark the foaming waves with their luminous furrows.

NOTES TO *POHNPEI*

*

24. Although O'Connell's story sounds more like a fantasy, it tallies with Melville's experiences a decade later and William Mariner's several decades before. Thus Finau Ulukalala II, the most powerful chief in Tonga, took a great liking to Mariner, a young English sailor who had survived the massacre of half of his crewmates in 1806.

The chief appointed one of his wives as Mariner's 'mother' and teacher, had him indoctrinated in the ways of the tribe, and then adopted him into his own household, giving him the name of his deceased son. Similarly, when Melville jumped ship in the Marquesas in 1842 and wound up in the valley of the Typee, the most powerful chief in the valley, Mehevi, adopted him, and gave him his daughter Pe'ue (Fayaway) as teacher and lover.

Melville's story, while it charmed readers, was generally seen as romantic fiction, although Melville himself always insisted on its veracity – a century later anthropologists were able to confirm his story, which had been indelibly recorded in the oral history of the remaining Typee. It was easier for O'Connell to obtain credence for his story, for he arrived back in the United States tattooed from top to toe; indeed, he went on to tell his story all over the country, billed as 'the Tattooed Irishman'.

*

25. The way in which human populations have met 'mysterious ends on over a dozen Polynesian islands' has been investigated by M. I. Weisler, particularly in relation to Pitcairn and Henderson, which are among the world's most remote and isolated islands. Both of these were colonized from the parent island, Mangareva, around AD 1000. Henderson, a coral atoll with little soil and no permanent fresh water, could not support more than fifty people, but Pitcairn, a volcanic island, was able to support several hundred. At first, when these two populations remained in touch with each other and with the parent

colony on Mangareva, and the populations did not exceed their resources, they were able to maintain a social and ecological balance. But expanding populations, hypothesizes Weisler, deforested Mangareva and Pitcairn and drove the seabirds and tortoises on Henderson to near-extinction. Mangareva's population survived, but 'descended into an orgy of war and cannibalism', in Jared Diamond's words, and fell out of contact with Henderson and Pitcairn around 1450. Without the physical and cultural contact of Mangareva, these populations were now doomed, shrank into themselves, and finally vanished around 1600. Diamond speculates on what may have occurred in these last, pathetic years:

> No potential marriage partners could have remained who did not violate incest taboos . . . climatic variations in an already marginal environment may have driven the islanders to starvation. . . . The people of Henderson may have [turned to] murder and cannibalism (like those on Mangareva, and Easter Island). . . . The islanders may have become insane from social deprivation.

If they managed to avoid all these gruesome fates, Diamond stresses, the islanders 'would have run up against the problem that fifty people are too few to constitute a viable population'. Even a society of several hundred 'is insufficient to propel human culture indefinitely', if it is isolated; even if it survives physically, it will become stagnant and uncreative, regressed and culturally 'inbred'.

When I collected stamps as a boy, I was especially pleased by the stamps of Pitcairn, and the idea that this remote island was populated by only seventy people, all descendants of the *Bounty* mutineers. But of course, the Pitcairners now have access to the larger world, with modern communications and frequent ship and air traffic.

*

26. Darwin marvelled at the survival of these fragile atolls:

> These low hollow islands bear no proportion to the vast ocean out of which they abruptly rise; and it seems wonderful, that such weak invaders are not overwhelmed, by the all-powerful and never-tiring waves of that great sea, miscalled the Pacific.

*

27. Cook learned of many instances of accidental migrations, often due to the strong westward trade winds. Landing at Atiu, he found three survivors who had been cast ashore from Tahiti, seven hundred miles away. They had set out in a party of twenty, expecting to make a brief journey from Tahiti to Raiatéa, a few miles away, but had been blown off course. Similar unintentional voyages, he thought, might explain 'how the South Seas, may have been peopled; especially those [islands] that lie remote from any inhabited continent, or from each other.'

*

28. I thought of Montaigne's words in relation to Knut that day:

A man must have experienced all the illnesses he hopes to cure and all the accidents and circumstances he is to diagnose. . . . Such a man I would trust. For the rest guide us like the person who paints seas, rocks and harbours while sitting at his table and sails his model of a ship in perfect safety. Throw him into the real thing, and he does not know where to begin.

*

29. Like Knut, Frances Futterman has acquired an enormous catalogue of information about colour, its physical and neurological basis, its meaning and value for other people. She is curious about (and finds that other achromatopes are intrigued by) its meaning and value, and I was especially struck by this when I visited her office in Berkeley, which was filled with bookshelves containing the hundreds of volumes she has collected. Many of these she acquired during her years of special education and rehabilitation teaching with the blind and partially sighted – others deal with scotopic or night vision. Thus on one wall, I saw titles like *The World of Night: The Fascinating Drama of Nature as Enacted between Dusk and Dawn*; *Nature by Night*; *The Coral Reef by Night*; *After the Sun Goes Down: The Story of Animals at Night*; *The Shadow Book* (a photographic-aesthetic study); *Images from the Dark*; *Night Eyes*; *Black is Beautiful* (black-and-white landscape photos) – books about the world she loves and knows.

On the other wall there were several shelves of books about colour, that strange phenomenon which she can never perceive and never really know, but about which she is endlessly curious. Some of these were scientific studies on the physics of colour or the physiology of vision; others dealt with linguistic aspects of colour – *The 750 Commonest Colour Metaphors in Daily Life*; *Seeing Red and Tickled Pink: Colour Terms in Everyday Language*. There were books on the aesthetics and philosophy of colour, ranging from anthropological treatises to Wittgenstein on colour. Others, she told me, had been collected simply for their colourful titles (*Colour Me Beautiful: Discover Your Natural Beauty through the Colours that Make You Look Great and Feel Fabulous*). There was a variety of books for younger ages, with titles like *Hello Yellow*, *Ant and Bee and Rainbow: A Story about Colours*, and her favourite, *Hailstones and Halibut Bones: Adventures in Colour*. She often recommends these for achromatopic children, so that they can 'learn' the colours of common objects, and the emotional 'valence' of different colours – necessary knowledge in a chromatopic world.

Frances is also hugely knowledgeable about specialized sunglasses for visually impaired people, and had advised us on which type to bring to Pingelap. 'She has collated a huge amount of practical information on all kinds of aids for achromatopic people,' Knut remarked, 'and although she repeatedly refers to herself as a non-scientific person, I regard her as a genuine investigator in the real meaning of the term.'

*

30. This is very much what happened with Virgil, a man virtually blind from birth whom Bob and I had worked with (his case history, 'To See and Not See', is given in *An Anthropologist on Mars*). When it was suggested that Virgil's sight might be restored by surgery, he could not help being intrigued and excited by the prospect of seeing. But after the operation, which was seen, medically, as 'successful', the reality, for Virgil, was bewildering. He had built up his world entirely from non-visual information, and the sudden introduction of visual stimuli threw him into a state of shock and confusion. He was overwhelmed by new sensations, visual sensations, but he could make no sense of them, he could not give them any order or meaning. The 'gift' of sight disturbed him profoundly, disturbed a mode of being, habits and strategies he had had for fifty years; and, increasingly, he would shut his eyes, or sit in the darkness, to shut out this frightening perceptual assault, and regain the equilibrium which had been taken from him with the surgery.

On the other hand, I recently received a fascinating letter from a deaf man who received a cochlear implant in middle age. Though he experienced many difficulties and confusions, analogous to those of Virgil (and though the use of cochlear implants can often be fraught with problems), he can now enjoy melodies and harmonies, which before he could neither perceive nor imagine.

*

31. Traditionally, very few of the islanders who enter medical schools have got their degrees, and Greg Dever

has worked to develop a curriculum relevant to the resources and needs of the Pacific – he was very proud of his first class, of which two-thirds of the entering students had been graduates, including the first women physicians from Pohnpei.

*

32. Kahn notes that 'the major credit for smallpox is usually ceded to Spain, for leprosy to Germany, for dysentery to England, for venereal disease to the US, and for tuberculosis to Japan'. Leprosy was, indeed, widespread throughout the Pacific: there was, until fairly recently, a leper colony on Pingelap; and for many years, a large leper colony on Guam; and, of course, there was the infamous leper colony of the Hawaiian Islands, on Molokai, which Jack London wrote about in 'The Sheriff of Kona' and 'Koolau the Leper'.

*

33. Melville includes a footnote on this term in *Omoo*:

> *Beach-comber:* This is a term much in vogue among sailors in the Pacific. It is applied to certain roving characters, who, without attaching themselves permanently to any vessel, ship now and then for a short cruise in a whaler; but upon the condition only of being dishonorably discharged the very next time the anchor takes hold of the bottom; no matter where. They are, mostly, a reckless, rollicking set, wedded to the Pacific, and never dreaming of ever doubling Cape Horn again on a homeward-bound passage. Hence, their reputation is a bad one.

*

34. Our Western diseases have had a disastrous effect on the native populations of the Pacific – scarcely less disastrous than those of military conquest, commercial exploitation, and religion. Jack London, visiting the valley of Typee sixty-five years after Melville, found the splendid physical perfection of which Melville spoke almost entirely destroyed:

> And now ... the valley of Typee is the abode of some dozen wretched creatures, afflicted by leprosy, elephantiasis, and tuberculosis.

Wondering what had befallen the Typee, London speaks of both immunity and evolution:

> Not alone were the Typeans physically magnificent; they were pure. Their air did not contain the bacilli and germs and microbes of disease that fill our own air. And when the white men imported in their ships these various micro-organisms of disease, the Typeans crumpled up and went down before them. . . .
>
> Natural selection, however, gives the explanation. We of the white race are the survivors and the descendants of the thousands of generations of survivors in the war with the micro-organisms. Whenever one of us was born with a constitution peculiarly receptive to these minute enemies, such a one promptly died. Only those of us survived who could withstand them. We who are alive are the immune, the fit – the ones best constituted to live in a world of hostile micro-organisms. The poor Marquesans had undergone no such selection. They were not immune. And

they, who had made a custom of eating their enemies, were now eaten by enemies so microscopic as to be invisible, and against whom no war of dart and javelin was possible.

*

35. Both Joakim and Valentine displayed in a high degree what the naturalist E. O. Wilson calls 'biophilia'. He defines this as an 'inborn affinity human beings have for other forms of life' – an affinity which can extend itself to an ecological feeling, a feeling for habitat. Howard Gardner, well known for his theory of multiple intelligences (mathematico-logical, visuo-spatial, kinaesthetic, social, etc.) is now inclined to recognize such a 'biological' intelligence as a distinctive one. Though such an intelligence may be enormously developed in a Darwin or a Wallace, it is present to varying degrees in us all. Others besides naturalists may be richly endowed with it and may express it in their vocations or avocations: gardeners, foresters, farmers, and horticulturalists; fishermen, horsemen, cattlemen, animal trainers, birdwatchers. Many artists express this in their work – D. H. Lawrence, to my mind, is miraculous here and seems to know directly, by a sort of connaturality, what it is like to be a snake or mountain lion; to be able to enter the souls of other animals. Biophilia may run in families (one thinks of the Hookers, where both father and son were consummate biologists); and it may be unusually common in people with Tourette's syndrome or autism. One has to wonder whether it may not have – as linguistic competence and

musical intelligence have – a clear neurological basis, which may be more richly developed by experience and education, but is none the less innate.

*

36. Stevenson remarked on the 'attractive power' of the Pacific islands in *In the South Seas*:

Few men who come to the islands leave them; they grow grey where they alighted; the palm shades and the trade-winds fan them till they die, perhaps cherishing to the last the fancy of a visit home. . . . No part of the world exerts the same attractive power.

*

37. Two-thirds of Krakatau Island, originally six miles long and clothed in tropical rain forest, disappeared in the huge eruption of 1883, but a remnant of the southern volcano was left standing, along with two close neigh-bours, Sertung and Panjang. All of these were covered by a thirty-foot blanket of hot ash, so that 'not a plant, not a blade of grass, not a fly, survived', in Ian Thornton's account. Three years later, ferns were the first plants to recolonize the island. These were followed by casuarinas, birds which had migrated from Australia, and a monitor lizard.

*

38. Biologically, as well as geologically, continental islands (such as, for instance, New Zealand, Madagascar,

or New Guinea) are entirely different from oceanic ones. For continental islands *are* broken-off pieces of the main and (at least initially) may have all the species of the parent continent. Once broken off, of course, they become as isolated as any other island, and their isolation (and altered conditions) may promote the most extravagant speciation, as with the unique primates of Madagascar or the flightless birds of New Zealand.

*

39. More than forty varieties of banana are grown on Pohnpei, and some of these seem to be unique to the island. The banana has a remarkable tendency to somatic mutation, to 'sports' – some of these are disadvantageous, but others may lead to plants which are more disease resistant, or fruit which is more delectable in one way or another; and this has stimulated cultivation of some five hundred varieties worldwide.

The major banana sports are regarded as species (and given binomial, Linnaean names), the minor sports as varieties only (which bear only local names). But the difference, as Darwin remarks, is only one of degree: 'Species and variations', he writes in the *Origin*, 'blend into each other by an insensible series; and a series impresses the mind with the idea of an actual passage.' In time, many varieties will diverge sufficiently to become distinct species.

The importation of bananas onto islands, as it happens, has also shown us something of the rate of evolution in sympatric species. Thus, as H. W. Menard notes, 'Five new species of banana moths have evolved in Hawaii since the

Polynesians introduced the banana to Hawaii only about one thousand years ago.' For islands are forcing grounds for evolutionary change, whether of plants or animals, insects or microbes; under the special conditions of island life, the slow processes of mutation and specialization may be amplified and accelerated to a spectacular degree.

J. B. S. Haldane once proposed a way of quantifying the rate of change of any variable – a bird's beak, an ammonite's whorl – as it evolved, suggesting that a change of one per cent per million years be called a 'darwin'. Evolution generally proceeded, he thought, in 'millidarwins', and he imagined (as Darwin himself did) that with this infinitesimal rate evolution could never actually be seen. But we are now finding (as Jonathan Weiner recounts in *The Beak of the Finch*) that evolution can occur at a very much faster rate in rapidly changing circumstances when selection pressures are high. This has been studied by Peter and Rosemary Grant, with the very finch populations Darwin himself observed on the small Galapagos island of Daphne Major. Following a catastrophic drought, the finch population showed clear evolutionary changes (in beak and body size) in a matter of months, an 'evolutionary rate', Weiner calculates, of 25,000 darwins.

One does not need to deal only with rare and catastrophic circumstances to see evolution in action. A beautiful example has recently been observed by Martin Cody and Jacob Overton with the seeds of some daisies, which are blown by the wind to small islets off the Pacific coast of Canada. A fluffball or pappus holds the seed aloft, and its size determines, other things being equal, how far the seed is liable to be carried. Once the plants have settled on an island, their pappi become shorter, so they are less liable to be dispersed. These changes, like those of finches, have been observed within the span of a year or two.

But the most astounding example of very rapid, massive evolution relates to the more than three hundred species of cichlid fish unique to Lake Victoria. DNA studies (by Axel Meyer) have indicated that these species diverged very recently in evolutionary terms, and there is now strong geologic evidence that the lake itself is only twelve thousand years old. While Darwin's Galapagos finches evolved perhaps twenty different species over four million years, the cichlids of Lake Victoria have shown a rate of speciation more than five thousand times greater.

*

40. Jack London, in Uaitape, found Bora-Borans dancing 'with strange phosphorescent flowers in their hair that pulsed and dimmed and glowed in the moonlight'.

*

41. Paul Theroux has called sakau (known on many islands as kava) 'the most benign drug in the world'. Its benignness was also stressed by Cook when he encountered it on his first visit to Tahiti (a related variety of pepper in New Zealand is now named *captaincookia* in his honour). Though it was described by naturalists on Cook's first voyage, credit for its 'discovery' is usually given to the Forsters, the botanical father and son who accompanied Cook on his second voyage, and the plant

has since been known by the name they gave it, *Piper methysticum* Forst.

An eloquent description of its effects was given by L. Lewin in his *Phantastica*; I had read this years before, as a student, and had been curious to try it myself. All is benign, stresses Lewin, if one does not overdo it:

> When the mixture is not too strong, the subject attains a state of happy unconcern, well-being and contentment, free of physical or psychological excitement. . . . The drinker never becomes angry, unpleasant, quarrelsome or noisy, as happens with alcohol. . . . The drinker remains master of his conscience and his reason. When consumption is excessive, however, the limbs become tired, the muscles seem no longer to respond to the orders and control of the mind, walking becomes slow and unsteady and the drinker looks partly inebriated. He feels the need to lie down. The eyes see the objects present, but cannot or do not want to identify them accurately. The ears also perceive sounds without being able or wanting to realize what they hear. Little by little, objects become vaguer and vaguer . . . [until] the drinker is overcome by somnolence and finally drifts off to sleep.

We had all been struck, when we arrived in Pohnpei, by the extraordinary slowness of drivers and pedestrians in Kolonia, but put this down to unhurriedness, a sense of leisure, 'island time'. But some of this slowness was clearly physiological, a sakau-induced psychomotor retardation. Sakau use and abuse is widespread here, although the effects of this are generally not dangerous. Dr G. A. Holland mentions having seen only one sakau-related accident in his many years of practice in Micronesia; this was an elderly man who stumbled while returning home from a sakau party, fell, and broke his neck.

It was remarked even in the last century that sakau was incompatible with alcohol, but in recent years, its use has been much less restrained by tradition, and some younger Pohnpeians have taken to drinking it with beer, which can produce drastic changes in blood pressure and even sudden death. Chronic sakau drinkers, moreover, may develop a hard, scaly skin; we saw many older Pohnpeians with ichthyosis, or 'fish' skin.

*

42. John Updike, in *In the Beauty of the Lilies*, re-reverses the foreground/background reversal of Joyce's image, and writes of a 'humid blue-black sky and its clusters of unreachable stars'.

*

43. I had not heard of these effects normally occurring after sakau. But I had had a low-level visual migraine for the last three days; I had been seeing squiggles and patterns since landing in Pingelap, and the sakau seemed to have exacerbated this. Knut told me that he sometimes had attacks of migraine too, and I wondered whether a direct stimulation of the colour areas in the brain, as may occur in a visual migraine, could evoke colour even in someone with no normal experience of it. Someone had once asked him if he saw migraine phosphenes in colour – but he had replied, 'I would not know how to answer.'

*

44. There was, I had been told, a cluster of houses near the Edwards' on Pingelap, all of which belonged to achromatopic families – but it was unclear whether these families had clustered together because they were related (as virtually everyone on Pingelap is) or because they all shared the maskun.

NOTES TO *GUAM*

*

45. A vast epidemic of viral sleepy-sickness, encephalitis lethargica, starting in Europe in the winter of 1916–17, swept through the world in the following years, coming to an end in the mid-1920s. Many patients seemed to recover from the acute illness entirely, only to fall victim, years or decades later, to strange (and sometimes progressive) post-encephalitic syndromes. There were thousands of such patients before the 1940s, and every neurologist at the time had a vivid idea of these syndromes. But by the 1960s, there were only a few hundred of these patients left – most very disabled and forgotten in chronic hospitals; and neurologists training at this time were scarcely aware of them. In 1967, when L-DOPA became available for treating parkinsonism, there were only, to my knowledge, two 'colonies' or communities of post-encephalitic

patients left in the world (at Beth Abraham Hospital in the Bronx and the Highlands Hospital in London).

*

46. Zimmerman's brief report, in fact, was written up for the US Navy, but not available generally; its existence was virtually unknown for almost a decade. It was not until the late 1950s that his paper was recognized as the first to report on the Guam disease.

*

47. Hirano's visit to Guam is still vivid for him thirty-five years later – the long and complex journey there, his delight in the island, the patients he saw, the autopsies he performed, the microscopic sections he prepared. He presented his findings at the 1961 annual meeting of the American Association of Neuropathologists – the same meeting at which, three years later, Steele, Olszewski, and Richardson presented their findings on progressive supranuclear palsy, another equally strange 'new' disease. Hirano was struck at the time by the fact that 'the histological and cytological features were essentially similar in the two', and concluded, in his remarks as a discussant of their paper, that

> The striking similarity of tissue response in these two disorders, occurring at two different geographical locations, certainly deserves attention, not only in the clinical and pathological sense, but also from the standpoint of their familial and epidemiological features.

*

48. It was Freycinet's impression that though the cycads had always been common on Guam, they had not been eaten 'until the Spanish taught the natives how to separate its substance from the poisonous juice it contained'. But this is a matter which has to be questioned, for in many other cultures the use of cycads and the knowledge of how to prepare and detoxify them go back to prehistoric times, as David Jones remarks in *Cycads of the World*:

> Studies suggest that Australian aborigines had developed the technology for the preparation of edible foods from cycads at least 13,000 years ago. . . . Perhaps toxic cycads were one of the first dangerous plants to be tamed by humans. . . . Nevertheless, in view of the presence of virulent toxins, the use of cycad parts by humans as food is quite extraordinary. . . . Although the techniques of preparation are relatively simple . . . there is room for error. It is tempting to speculate on the hit or miss learning procedure which must have preceded the successful development of such a methodology.

*

49. Cycads, properly speaking, do not have fruits, for fruits come from flowers, and cycads have no flowers. But it is natural to speak of 'fruits', for the seeds are enclosed in a brightly coloured, luscious outer tunic (or sarcotesta), which resembles a greengage or plum.

*

50. Raymond Fosberg spent his entire professional life studying tropical plants and islands. 'From a childhood fascination with islands,' he remarked in a 1985 commencement address at the University of Guam,

> [which] I gained from maps, in grade-school geography books, and a wonderful book, read at an early age, titled *Australia and the Islands of the Sea*, I gravitated toward islands at my first opportunity. This was a Sierra Club visit to Santa Cruz Island, off the California coast. The vision of [its] beauty . . . has never left me.

During the Second World War, he worked in the tropical jungles of Colombia in search of cinchona bark to provide quinine for combat troops in malarial areas and helped to export nine thousand tons of the bark. After the war, he devoted himself to the islands of Micronesia, cataloguing minutely their plant life and studying the effects of human development and the introduction of alien species upon the vulnerable habitats of islands with their native flora and fauna.

*

51. Botanists now recognize more than two hundred cycad species, and eleven genera – the newest genus, *Chigua*, was discovered in Colombia in 1990 by Dennis Stevenson of the New York Botanical Garden.

*

52. *Cycas revoluta* is sometimes called the sago palm (or king sago), and *C. circinalis* the false sago palm (or queen

sago). The word 'sago' is itself a generic one, referring to an edible starchy material obtained from any plant source. Sago proper, so to speak (such as English children in my generation were brought up on), is obtained from the trunks of various palms (especially *Metroxylon*), but it also occurs in the stems of cycads, even though they are botanically quite different. The male trunks of *C. revoluta* contain about fifty per cent starch, the female ones about half this. There is also a good deal of starch in their seeds – and the seeds, of course, are replenishable, whereas harvesting of the trunk kills the entire plant.

Similar considerations apply to 'arrowroot', which, properly speaking, is obtained from the rootstock of the arrowroot, *Maranta*, but is also extracted from other plants, including the cycad *Zamia*. The Seminole Indians in Florida had long made use of the *Zamia* (or koonti) which grew wild there, and in the 1880s a substantial industry was set up, producing twenty tons or more of 'Florida arrowroot' annually, for use in infant foods, biscuits, chocolates, and spaghetti. The industry closed down in the 1920s, after overharvesting the cycad almost to extinction.

*

53. The consumption of this sake prepared from *C. revoluta*, David Jones remarks,

> is almost as deadly as a game of Russian roulette, since it is slightly poisonous and occasionally a potent batch kills all who partake.

It would go well, one feels, with a meal of puffer fish or fugu.

*

54. Georg Rumpf (known to posterity as Rumphius), already a passionate naturalist and botanist in his twenties, enlisted with the Dutch East India Company and set sail for Batavia and the Moluccas in 1652. In the following decade he travelled widely in Southeast Asia, spending much time on the Malabar coast of India, where in 1658 he documented a new plant – this was the first cycad ever described, and the one which Linnaeus, a century later, was to call *Cycas circinalis*, and to take as the cardinal 'type' of all cycads. A few years later, Rumphius was appointed assistant to the Dutch governor of Ambon, in the Moluccas, where he embarked on his magnum opus, the *Herbarium Amboinense*, describing 1200 species of plants peculiar to Southeast Asia.

Though stricken by blindness in 1670, he continued his work, helped now by sighted assistants. H. C. D. de Wit, in a 1952 address on Rumphius at the Hortus Botanicus in Amsterdam (on the two hundred and fiftieth anniversary of Rumphius' death) described in detail his labours on the *Herbarium*, which were to take forty years and were punctuated by a relentless series of travails, including the death of his wife and daughter:

It was the 17th of February, 1674. In the gathering dusk Mrs Rumpf and her youngest daughter went for a visit to a Chinese friend to look at the Chinese New Year celebrations, a colourful procession through the streets, to be held later in the evening. They saw Rumphius [who was by now completely blind] passing by to take some air. Some minutes later a disastrous earthquake destroyed the larger part of the town.

Both women were killed by collapsing walls.

Rumphius returned to work on his manuscript, but in 1687 a calamitous fire burnt the town of Amboina to the ground, destroying his library and all his manuscripts. Still undaunted, and aided by his remarkable abilities and determination, he began rewriting the *Herbarium* and the original copy of the first six books finally started on its way to Amsterdam in 1692, only to be lost when the ship carrying it was sunk. (Fortunately, the governor-general of Batavia, Camphuys, had taken the precaution of having Rumphius' manuscript copied before shipping it on to Holland.) Rumphius continued working on the last six volumes, but suffered another setback when sixty-one coloured plates were stolen from his office in Batavia in 1695. Rumphius himself died in 1702, some months after completing the *Herbarium* – but his great work was not published until the middle of the century. The final work, despite all these mishaps, contains nearly 1700 pages of text and 700 plates, including half a dozen magnificent plates of cycads.

*

55. Sidney Parkinson, the artist who voyaged on the *Endeavour* with Cook, described the plants they encountered:

Of vegetables we found . . . Cicas circinalis, the kernels of which, roasted, tasted like parched peas; but it made some of our people sick, who ate it: of this fruit, they make a kind of sago in the East Indies.

Cycas circinalis does not occur in Australia, and the cycad which Cook's crew encountered there, David Jones suggests, was probably the native *C. media*.

*

56. Lathyrism is a form of paralysis long endemic in parts of India, where it is associated with eating the chickling pea, *Lathyrus sativa*; a little lathyrus does no harm, but sometimes it is the only food available – and then the hideous choice is to be paralysed or starve.

It was similar, in some ways, with the 'jake paralysis' which paralysed tens of thousands of Americans during Prohibition. Driven to seek some source of alcohol, these unfortunates turned to a readily available extract of Jamaica ginger (or 'jake'), not knowing it contained large quantities of a poison (later found to be a toxic organo-phosphorus compound) which could lead to paralysis. (My own research, as a student, was an attempt to elucidate its mechanism of action, using chickens as experimental animals.)

The Minamata Bay paralysis first became apparent in the mid-1950s, in Japanese fishing villages surrounding the bay. Those affected would first become unsteady, tremulous, and suffer various sensory disturbances, going on (in the worst cases) to become deaf, blind, and demented. There was a high incidence of birth defects, and domestic animals and seabirds seemed affected too. The local fish fell under suspicion, and it was found that when they were fed to cats, they indeed produced the same progressive and fatal neurological disease. Fishing was banned in Minamata Bay in 1957, and with this the disease disappeared. The precise cause was still a mystery, and it was only the following year that it was observed by Douglas McAlpine that the clinical features of the disease were virtually identical to those of methyl mercury poisoning (of which there had been isolated cases in England in the late 1930s). It took several more years to trace the toxin back to its source (Kurland, among others, played a part here): a factory on the bay was discharging mercuric chloride (which is moderately toxic) into the water, and this was converted by micro-organisms in the lake to methyl mercury (which is intensely toxic). This in turn was consumed by other micro-organisms, starting a long ascent through the food chain, before ending up in fish, and people.

*

57. That lytico or bodig can remain almost stationary for years in this way is utterly unlike the relentless progression of classical Parkinson's disease or ALS, but such an apparent halting of the disease process was sometimes seen in post-encephalitic parkinsonism or amyotrophy. Thus one patient I have seen, Selma B., immediately following the encephalitic epidemic in 1917, developed a mild parkinsonism on one side of her body, which has

remained essentially unchanged for more than seventy-five years. Another man, Ralph G., developed a gross, polio-like wasting of one arm as part of a post-encephalitic syndrome – but this has neither advanced nor spread in fifty years. (This is one reason why Gajdusek regards post-encephalitic syndromes not as active disease processes but as hypersensitivity reactions.) And yet such arrests are the exception, and lytico-bodig, in the vast majority of cases, is relentlessly progressive.

*

58. I was sorry to see that Darwin, who seems to love and admire every form of life, speaks (in *The Voyage of the Beagle*) of 'the slimy disgusting Holothuriae . . . which the Chinese gourmands are so fond of'. Indeed, they are not loved. Safford refers to seeing them 'creep about like huge brown slugs'. Jack London, in *The Cruise of the Snark*, speaks of them as 'monstrous sea-slugs' which 'ooze' and 'writhe' beneath his feet – the only negative note for him as he skims ('in a chromatic ecstasy') above the Pacific reef.

*

59. In his history of Pacific exploration, J. C. Beaglehole speaks of three phases – the Spanish explorations of the sixteenth century, 'animated by a mingled zeal for religion and gold'; the Dutch voyages of the seventeenth, undertaken for commercial reasons; and the final English and French ones, devoted expressly to the acquisition of knowledge – but he sees a spirit of curiosity and wonder,

no less than conquest, as animating all the explorations. Certainly this was true of Antonio Pigafetta, a gentleman-volunteer who joined Magellan, 'desirous of seeing the wonderful things of the ocean', and wrote the best history of the voyage. And it was true of the Dutch voyages, which took naturalists to never before explored parts of the world – thus Rumphius and Rheede, going to the Dutch East Indies in the seventeenth century, made major contributions to biological knowledge (and, specifically, provided the first descriptions and illustrations of cycads and other plants hitherto unknown in Europe). And it was especially true of Dampier and Cook, who were, in a sense, precursors of the great nineteenth-century naturalist-explorers.

But Magellan's reputation has not fared as well. His discovery of Guam, especially, took place under very adverse circumstances. His men were starving and sick with scurvy, reduced to eating rats and the hides which kept the rigging from chafing; they had been at sea for ninety-eight days before they finally sighted land on 6 March 1521. When they anchored in Umatac Bay and went ashore, the inhabitants stole their skiff and various odds and ends. Magellan, normally temperate, overreacted in a monstrous way, taking a large party of men ashore, burning forty or fifty houses, and killing seven Chamorros. He christened Guam (and Rota) the Ladrones, the Isles of Thieves, and treated their inhabitants with cruelty and contempt. Magellan's own death came soon afterward, at the hands of a crowd of infuriated natives he had provoked in the Philippines. And yet Magellan should not be judged entirely by his actions in the final months of his life. For his conduct up to this point had been both moderate and masterly, in his handling of sick, angry, impatient, and sometimes mutinous crews; in his brilliant discovery of the Strait of Magellan – and in his usually respectful feeling for the indigenous peoples he encountered. And yet, as with all the early Spanish and Portuguese explorers, a sort of zealous violence was built in – Beaglehole calls this 'a sort of Christian arrogance', and feels it overcame Magellan at the end.

This arrogance seems to have been wholly absent from the admirable Pigafetta, who (though himself wounded at the time of Magellan's death) described the entire voyage – its natural wonders, the peoples they visited, the desperation of the crew, and Magellan's own character, with its heroism, its candor, its mystical depths, its fatal flaws – with the sympathy of a naturalist, a psychologist, and a historian.

*

60. A frightful picture of leprosy on Guam is to be found in Arago's description of the Freycinet voyage:

> A few hundred yards from Anigua are several houses, in which are kept lepers of both sexes, whose disease is so virulent that it commonly deprives them of the tongue or some of their limbs, and is said to become a contagious distemper. I have delineated two of these unfortunate creatures, exhibiting to the eye the most hideous aspect of human misery. One shudders with horror on approaching these houses of desolation and despair. I am persuaded,

that by enlarging these paltry buildings, collecting in them all the persons in the island severely attacked by the leprosy, and prohibiting all communication with them from without, they might expel from the country this frightful disease; which, if it do not quickly cause the death of the patient, at least shortens his days, and perhaps leads him to curse them. (It is here called the disease of St Lazarus.) What a scene, to behold an infant, a few days old, calmly reposing in the arms of a woman devoured by the leprosy, who imprudently lavishes on it her caresses! Yet this occurs in almost every house; government opposes no obstacle to it; and the infant, while sucking in its mother's milk, inhales with it death and disease.

*

61. The rarity of Safford's understanding and sympathy is brought out by comparison with the almost contemporary account of Antoine-Alfred Marche. The Chamorros, Marche reported,

do not engage in any serious work. . . . The indigenes today are intelligent but very lazy, proud, and dishonest, incapable of gratitude, and, like their ancestors, without any moral sense. . . . All that is frivolous . . . attracts them . . . without limit or decency. . . . One finds a few individuals who have learned how to benefit from our civilization, but they are the few.

*

62. The little village of Umatac is strangely peaceful, a backwater now – though there is a memorial to Magellan

277

just outside town, remembering that momentous day in the spring of 1521 when he landed at Guam. For Julia Steele, a journalist and historian (and John's daughter), the village is symbolic of that moment of first contact:

> The more I thought about Umatac, the more I liked thinking about Umatac, this little town of such significance, a minor understudy thrust into a major role on history's stage: the first spot where island and Western cultures had clashed, in the first of thousands of conflicts that would be played out time and again throughout the Pacific and bring with them a cataclysm of change in island societies. Just as the Indies had been for Magellan, from that point on Umatac became for me a concept, a vehicle for thinking about the world and its structure.

*

63. Though Lake Fena is the largest above-ground reservoir on Guam, most of the fresh water is provided by an exceptionally large water lens which floats above the salt-water aquifer underlying the northern end of the island. Fena is a man-made lake whose waters add to this supply. It is rumoured that the lake was built as a 'quenching facility' to stop a chain reaction should an accident occur in the surrounding nuclear storage area.

*

64. In hindsight, John feels, it is far from clear whether these few non-Chamorro immigrants had true lytico-bodig or classical ALS or parkinsonism. But some of their offspring, half-Chamorro, have gone on to develop lytico-

bodig. And though Kurland could not pursue the genetic hypothesis with the technology of the 1950s, he and his colleague W. Weiderholt are now looking at the children of the Californian Chamorros, to see if lytico-bodig appears in any of them.

*

65. Kuru, a fatal neurological disease which had been endemic in the area for a century or more, could be transmitted, Gajdusek found, by the ritual practice of eating the brains of the dead. The disease agent was a newly discovered form of virus, a so-called slow virus which could remain latent in the tissues for years before giving rise to actual symptoms. Other slow viruses are responsible for various animal diseases (scrapie, in sheep, and bovine spongiform encephalitis, or mad cow disease); and human diseases (such as Creutzfeldt-Jakob disease). Some of these slow 'viruses' are now identified as prions, particles even smaller than viruses, and having no DNA of their own.

*

66. A very full discussion of the ecological disaster in Guam has recently been provided by David Quammen in his book *The Song of the Dodo: Island Biogeography in an Age of Extinction*. He describes how the native bird populations, which had been numerous and varied in 1960, were brought to the verge of extinction little more than twenty years later. No one at the time had any idea what was causing this:

Where had the birds gone? What was killing them? Had they been devastated by an exotic disease, as in Hawaii? Had they been poisoned by cumulative doses of DDT? Had they been eaten by feral cats and tree-climbing pigs and Japanese soldiers who refused to surrender?

It was only in 1986 that Guam's 'ecological murder mystery' was solved and the bird-eating tree snake, *Boiga irregularis*, was proved to be the culprit. There had been a spreading explosion of these snakes, starting in the southern savannahs in the 1950s, reaching the northern forests by 1980, correlating precisely with the wave of bird extinctions. It was estimated in the mid-eighties that there were now thirteen thousand snakes to the square mile, three million on the whole island. Having consumed all the birds by this time, the snakes turned to other prey – skinks, geckos, other lizards, and even small mammals – and these too have shown catastropic declines. Going with this there has been a vast increase in the numbers of orb-weaving spiders (I saw their intricate webs everywhere), probably due to the decline of the lizards. Thus the inauguration of what ecologists call a trophic cascade, the accelerating imbalance of a previously balanced ecosystem.

*

67. Lynn Raulerson had told me of something even rarer, an immense tassel fern, *Lycopodium phlegmaria*, which used to be common in the forest, but had now almost vanished, because most specimens had been poached for

cultivation as house plants. Both this and the great ribbon fern are also to be found in Australia, and Chamberlain, while cycad hunting there, was fascinated by these and wrote of them in his 1919 book *The Living Cycads*:

> The immense *Lycopodium phlegmaria*, the 'tassel fern', with tassel-like cluster of cones, and *Ophioglossum pendulum*, the 'ribbon fern', were the most interesting features of the epiphytic vegetation of the treetops. If a tree with such specimens was a foot or less in diameter the bushmen were likely to cut it down; if larger they would climb; but when they found that fine, uninjured specimens were worth three pence or even six pence, a climb of eighty feet was not at all objectionable.

*

68. It is sometimes said (the term goes back to Charcot) that patients with Parkinson's disease have a 'reptilian' stare. This is not just a picturesque (or pejorative) metaphor; normal access to the motor functions, which gives mammals their delicate motor flexibility, is impaired in parkinsonism; this leads to alternations of extreme immobility with sudden, almost explosive motion, which are reminiscent of some reptiles.

Parkinson himself was a palaeontologist, as well as a physician, and his 1804 book, *Organic Remains of a Former World*, is one of the great pioneer texts of palaeontology. One wonders whether he may have partly regarded parkinsonism as an atavism, a reversion, the uncovering, through disease, of an ancestral, 'an antediluvian' mode of function dating from the ancient past.

Whether or not this is so of parkinsonism is arguable, but one can certainly see reversion to, or disclosure of, a variety of primitive behaviours in post-encephalitic syndromes on occasion, and in a rare condition, branchial myoclonus, arising from lesions in the brain stem. Here there occur rhythmic movements of the palate, middle-ear muscles, and certain muscles in the neck – an odd and unintelligible pattern, until one realizes that these are the only vestiges of the gill arches, the branchial musculature, in man. Branchial myoclonus is, in effect, a gill movement in man, a revelation of the fact that we still carry our fishy ancestors, our evolutionary precursors, within us.

*

69. About five years ago, John became intrigued by the number of lytico-bodig patients with gaze palsies. His colleague Terry Cox, a neuro-ophthalmologist, confirmed this with further eye examinations and found that half of these patients also showed strange tortuous tracks in the retina (these cannot easily be seen with an ordinary ophthalmoscope, but only with indirect ophthalmoscopy – and thus would escape notice on a routine eye exam). The tracks seem to affect just the upper layer of retinal pigment, and to cause no symptoms.

'This retinal pigmentary epitheliopathy,' John said, 'is confined to the Chamorros – it has never been observed in a Caucasian immigrant, or in Filipinos, who have lived here since the 1940s. It's rare in anyone under fifty – the youngest person we've seen with it was born in 1957. It's present in twenty per cent of Chamorros over the age of fifty; but in fifty per cent of those with lytico-bodig. We have been following patients who showed RPE in the early 1980s, and more than two-thirds of them have gone on to develop lytico-bodig within ten years.

'The condition doesn't seem to be progressive; it's more like the scar of some trauma to the eye many decades ago. We wonder if it could be a marker for the lytico-bodig, something which came on at the same time as the disease – even though we are only picking it up now. We are checking now to see if there are any similar findings in patients with PSP or post-encephalitic parkinsonism.

'The tracks have some resemblance to those made by the larvae of a botfly, but we don't have any botflies on Guam. Maybe the tracks are made by the larvae of some other fly – perhaps one which transmitted a virus that caused the lytico-bodig. Or maybe it's an effect of a toxin. We don't yet know if it is unique to the lytico-bodig or not, or whether it is significant at all. But all these coincidences are tantalizing, and this is another thing that makes me think that the lytico-bodig could be caused by an organism, a virus – perhaps one transmitted by an otherwise unobjectionable parasite.'

*

70. The term 'cynomolgus' means, literally, 'dog-milking'. The Cynomolgi were an ancient human tribe in Libya. Why this name should be given to some macaques (which are also known as 'crab-eating macaques') is unclear, though John Clay suggests that a better translation might be 'dog-suckling', as macaques may indeed suckle other animals.

*

71. There was one report in a Japanese journal in the 1920s regarding an unusually high incidence of bulbar palsy in Saipan, though it is unclear whether this could have been a manifestation of lytico. Of the fifteen cases of lytico-bodig in Saipan described by Gajdusek *et al.*, all but two had been born before the First World War and the youngest had been born in 1929. In several cases, according to John, the parents of these patients had been born in Guam or Rota.

*

72. Research on cycad neurotoxicity, somewhat dormant since the 1960s, has again become very active in several places. Tom Mabry and Delia Brownson at the University of Texas at Austin are working on the relation between cycads and lytico-bodig, looking at the effect of the putative Guam neurotoxins on rat brain-cell preparations. And Alan Seawright at the (Australian) National Research Centre for Environmental Toxicity has been investigating the effects of MAM and BMAA in experimental animals.

*

73. Though there are rare forms of Alzheimer's disease, Parkinson's disease, and ALS with a simple Mendelian pattern, these are the exception and not the rule. Ordinary Alzheimer's, Parkinson's, and ALS, it seems, are complex disorders in which the actual expression of disease is

contingent on a variety of genetic and environmental factors.

NOTES TO *ROTA*

*

74. Marie Stopes was born in London in 1880, showed insatiable curiosity and scientific gifts as an adolescent, and despite strong disapprobation (similar to that which delayed the entry of women into medicine at the time) was able to enter University College, where she obtained a Gold Medal and a first-class degree in botany. Her passion for palaeobotany was already developing by this time, and after graduating she went to the Botanical Institute in Munich, where she was the only woman among five hundred students. Her research on cycad ovules earned her a Ph.D. in botany, the first ever given a woman.

In 1905 she received her doctorate in science from London University, making her the youngest D.Sc. in the country. The following year, while working on a massive two-volume *Cretaceous Flora* for the British Museum, she also published *The Study of Plant Life for Young People*, a delightful book which showed her literary power and her insight into youthful imaginations, no less than her botanical expertise. She continued to publish many scientific papers, and in 1910 another popular book, *Ancient Plants*. Other writings, romantic novels and poems, were also stirring in her at this time, and in *A Journal from Japan* she gave poignant fictional form to her own painfully frustrated love for an eminent Japanese botanist.

By this time other interests were competing with botany. Stopes wrote a letter to *The Times* supporting women's suffrage, and became increasingly conscious of how much sexually, as well as politically and professionally, women needed to be liberated. From 1914 on, though there was an overlap with palaeobotany for a few years, Stopes's work dealt essentially with human love and sexuality. She was the first to write about sexual intercourse in a matter-of-fact way, doing so with the same lucidity and accuracy she had in her description of the fertilization of cycad ovules – but also with a tenderness which was like a foretaste of D. H. Lawrence. Her books *Married Love* (1918), *A Letter to Working Mothers* (1919), and *Radiant Motherhood* (1920) were immensely popular at the time; no one else spoke with quite her accent or authority.

Later Stopes met Margaret Sanger, the great American pioneer of birth control, and she became its chief advocate in England. *Contraception, Its Theory, History and Practice* was published in 1923, and this led to the setting up of Marie Stopes clinics in London and elsewhere. Her voice, her message, had little appeal after the Second World War, and her name, once instantly recognized by all, faded into virtual oblivion. And yet, even in old age, her palaeobotanical interests never deserted her; coal balls, she often said, were really her first love.

*

75. The Copernican revolution in the sixteenth and seventeenth centuries, with its revelation of the immensity of space, dealt a profound blow to man's sense of being at the centre of the universe; this was voiced by no one more poignantly than Pascal: 'The whole visible world is but an imperceptible speck,' he lamented; man was now 'lost in this remote corner of Nature', closed into 'the tiny cell where he lodges'. And Kepler spoke of a 'hidden and secret horror', a sense of being 'lost' in the infinity of space.

The eighteenth century, with its close attention to rocks and fossils and geologic processes, was to radically alter man's sense of time as well (as Rossi, Gould, and McPhee, in particular, have emphasized). Evolutionary time, geologic time, deep time, was not a concept which came naturally or easily to the human mind, and once conceived, aroused fear and resistance.

There was great comfort in the feeling that the earth was made for man and its history coeval with his, that the past was to be measured on a human scale, no more than a few score of generations back to the first man, Adam. But now the Biblical chronology of the earth was vastly extended, into a period of aeons. Thus while Archbishop Ussher had calculated that the world was created in 4004 BC, when Buffon introduced his secular view of nature – with man appearing only in the latest of seven epochs – he suggested an unprecedented age of 75,000 years for the earth. Privately, he increased this time scale by forty – the original figure in his manuscripts was three million years – and he did this (as Rossi notes) because he felt that the larger figure would be incomprehensible to his contemporaries, would give them too fearful a sense of the 'dark abyss' of time. Less than fifty years later, Playfair was to write of how, gazing at an ancient geologic unconformity, 'the mind seemed to grow giddy by looking so far into the abyss of time'.

When Kant, in 1755, published his *Theory of the Heavens,* his vision of evolving and emerging nebulae, he envisaged that 'millions of years and centuries' had been required to arrive at the present state, and saw creation as being eternal and immanent. With this, in Buffon's words, 'the hand of God' was eliminated from cosmology, and the age of the universe enormously extended. 'Men in Hooke's time had a past of six thousand years,' as Rossi writes, but 'those of Kant's times were conscious of a past of millions of years.'

Yet Kant's millions were still very theoretical, not yet firmly grounded in geology, in any concrete knowledge of the earth. The sense of a vast geologic time filled with terrestrial events, was not to come until the next century, when Lyell, in his *Principles of Geology*, was able to bring into one vision both the immensity and the slowness of geologic change, forcing into consciousness a sense of older and older strata stretching back hundreds of millions of years.

Lyell's first volume was published in 1830, and Darwin took it with him on the *Beagle*. Lyell's vision of deep time was a prerequisite for Darwin's vision too, for the almost glacially slow processes of evolution from the animals of the Cambrian to the present day required, Darwin estimated, at least three hundred million years.

Stephen Jay Gould, writing about our concepts of time in *Time's Arrow, Time's Cycle*, starts by quoting Freud's famous statement about mankind having had to endure from science 'two great outrages upon its naïve self-love' – the Copernican and Darwinian revolutions. To these, Freud added ('in one of history's least modest pronouncements,' as Gould puts it) his own revolution, the Freudian one. But he omits from his list, Gould observes, one of the greatest steps, the discovery of deep time, the needed link between the Copernican and the Darwinian revolutions. Gould speaks of our difficulty even now in 'biting the fourth Freudian bullet', having any real, organic sense (beneath the conceptual or metaphoric one) of the reality of deep time. And yet this revolution, he feels, may have been the deepest of them all.

It is deep time that makes possible the blind movement of evolution, the massing and honing of minute effects over aeons. It is deep time that opens a new view of nature, which if it lacks the Divine fiat, the miraculous and providential, is no less sublime in its own way. 'There is grandeur in this view of life', wrote Darwin, in the famous final sentence of the *Origin*,

> that, whilst this planet has gone cycling on according to the fixed law of gravity, from so simple a beginning endless forms most beautiful and most wonderful have been, and are being, evolved.

*

76. Karl Niklas speculates on this:

One can only wonder at the lengths of the huge rhizomes that anchored *Calamites* to the ground. Interconnected by these subterranean roots, hundreds of *Calamites* trees actually made up single organisms, possibly the largest living things in Earth's history.

When I was in Australia I saw a forest of antarctic beech said to date back to the last Ice Age, and at twenty-four thousand years old to be the oldest organism on earth. It was called a single organism because all the trees were connected, and had spread by runners and offshoots into a continuous, if many trunked and many rooted, plant fabric. Recently a monstrous underground mat of fungus, *Armillaria bulbosa*, has been found in Michigan, covering thirty acres and weighing in excess of one hundred tons. The subterranean filaments of the Michigan mat are all genetically homogeneous, and it has therefore been called the largest organism on earth.

The whole concept of what constitutes an organism or an individual becomes blurred in such instances, in a way which hardly arises in the animal kingdom (except in special cases, such as that of the colonial coral polyps), and this question has been explored by Stephen Jay Gould in *Dinosaur in a Haystack*.

*

77. Though they are sometimes similar in appearance, ferns, palms, and cycads are unrelated and come from quite different plant groups. Indeed many of their 'common' features have evolved quite independently. Darwin was fascinated by such examples of convergent

evolution, in which natural selection, acting at different times, on different forms, in different circumstances, might reach analogous ways of solving the same problem.

Even so basic a feature as wood, Niklas has stressed, has arisen independently in numerous different plant families, whenever there has been a need for a light, stiff material to support an erect tree form. Thus tree horsetails, tree club mosses, cycads, pines, and oaks have all arrived at different mechanisms for wood formation, while tree ferns and palms, which have no true wood, have developed other ways of reinforcing themselves, using flexible but stringy stem tissue or outer roots to buttress their stems. Cycads produce a softer wood, which is not as strong, but they also reinforce their trunks with persistent leaf bases, which give them their armoured appearance. Other groups, like the long-extinct *Sphenophyllales*, developed dense wood without ever assuming an arboreal form.

One also sees convergent evolution in the animal kingdom, with the separate evolution of eyes, for example, in many different phyla – in jellyfish, in worms, in crustacea and insects, in scallops, and in cuttlefish and other cephalopods, as well as in vertebrates. All of these eyes are quite different in structure, as they are different in origin, and yet, they are all dependent on the operation of the same basic genes. The study of these PAX eye-coding genes, and other genes like the homebox genes, which determine the morphogenesis of bodies and organs, is revealing, more radically and deeply than anyone could have suspected, the fundamental unity of all life. Richard Dawkins has recently provided an excellent discussion of the development of eyes, in particular, in his book *Climbing Mount Improbable*.

*

78. Sir Robert Schomburg described his great excitement on finding *Victoria regia*:

> It was on the first of January 1837, while contending with the difficulties which, in various forms, Nature interposed to bar our progress up the Berbice River, that we reached a spot where the river expanded, and formed a currentless basin. Something on the other side of this basin attracted my attention; I could not form an idea of what it might be; but, urging the crew to increase the speed of their paddling, we presently neared the object which had roused my curiosity – and lo! a vegetable wonder! All disasters were forgotten; I was a botanist, and I felt myself rewarded. There were gigantic leaves, five to six feet across, flat, with a deep rim, light green above and vivid crimson below, floating upon the water; while in keeping with this astonishing foliage, I beheld luxuriant flowers, each composed of numerous petals, which passed in alternate tints from pure white to rose and pink.

And in the *Victoria regia* tank, under its giant leaves, I was later to learn, resided a strange animal, a small medusa – *Craspedacusta* by name. This was found in 1880 and considered to be the first-ever freshwater jellyfish (though it was subsequently realized to be the medusoid form of a hydrozoan, *Limnocodium*). For many years, *Craspedacusta* was found only in artificial environments –

tanks in botanical gardens – but it has now been found in several lakes, including Lake Fena in Guam.

*

79. A favourite book of mine, one of a delightful series ('Britain in Pictures') published during the Second World War, was *British Botanists* by John Gilmour. Gilmour gives a particularly vivid and moving portrait of Joseph Hooker as a grand botanical explorer and investigator, as the son of his renowned botanist father, William Jackson Hooker (who after his years teaching in Glasgow became the first director of Kew Gardens) – and above all, in his relationship with Darwin:

'You are the one living soul from whom I have constantly received sympathy,' Darwin wrote to him. From the time when [Hooker] slept with the proofs of the *Voyage of the Beagle* under his pillow so as to read them the moment he woke up, to the day when he helped to bear Darwin's pall to its last resting place in the Abbey, [he] was Darwin's closest and most frequent confidant. It was to Hooker that Darwin, in 1844, sent the first hint of his theory of natural selection and, fifteen years later, Hooker was his first convert. In 1858, when Darwin received one morning from Alfred Russel Wallace an essay setting out the identical theory of natural selection which he himself was about to publish, it was Hooker, overruling Darwin's quixotic desire to resign his undoubted priority to Wallace, who arranged for the famous double communication of the theory to be read at the Linnean Society. And at the centenary of Darwin's birth in 1909, Hooker, then

92, his tall figure still full of vigour, was present at Cambridge to do homage to the friend he had helped so much.

But quite apart from his role in the history of Darwinism, Sir Joseph Hooker stands head and shoulders above his contemporaries as systematic botanist, plant geographer and explorer.

'Few ever have known, or ever will know, plants as he knew them,' wrote Professor Bower. His early years were spent at Glasgow, during his father's professorship. The house, in which were accumulating the herbarium and library later to form the basis of the Kew collections, was near to the botanic garden, and he must have lived and breathed botany from morning to night. The intense love of plants acquired at Glasgow dominated his life.

*

80. Philip Henry Gosse, in his (anonymous) 1856 guide, *Wanderings through the Conservatories at Kew*, describes the cycads:

Clustered at the south-east extremity of the house, a considerable area of which they occupy, we see a group of plants having a common character, notwithstanding the various botanical appellations that we read on their labels. They bear, in their arching pinnate leaves, radiating from the summit of a columnar stem, a certain resemblance to palms, and also to the tree-ferns, but have neither the stately grace of the one, nor the delicate elegance of the other, while their excessive rigidity, and the tendency of their leaves to form spinous points, give them a repulsive aspect.

ENCEPHALARTOS.

A year later, in his bizarre book *Omphalos* – published just two years before the *Origin of Species* – Gosse, who was both a brilliant naturalist and a religious fundamentalist, attempted to reconcile the existence of fossils (which seemed to testify to former ages) with his belief in a single, instantaneous act of Creation. In his theory of 'Prochronism' he suggested that the entire crust of the earth, complete with its cargo of fossil plants and animals, was created in an instant by God and had only the appearance of a past, but no real past going with it: thus there had never been any living forms corresponding to the fossils. In the same way that Adam had been created in an instant as a young man (never a child, never born, with no umbilical cord – though none the less with an umbilicus, an omphalos), he argued, so a cycad, full of leaf-scars, seemingly centuries old, might also be quite newly created.

Taking an imaginary tour of the earth, a single hour after the Creation, he invites the reader to look at a panorama of animals and plants:

> I wish you to look at this Encephalartos. A horrid plant it is, a sort of caricature of the elegant Palms, somewhat as if a founder had essayed a cocoa-nut tree in cast iron. Out of the thick, rough, stiff stem spring a dozen of arching fronds, beset with sharp, sword-shaped leaflets, but having the rigidity of horn, of a greyish hue, all harsh and repulsive to excess. In the midst of this rigid coronal sits the fruit, like an immense pine-cone. . . . It would be no unreasonable conjecture to suppose that this great Cycadaceous plant is seven or eight centuries old . . . Nay, for this also has been created even now!

This extraordinary notion – one cannot call it a hypothesis, for it cannot in principle be either proved or disproved – had the distinction of earning the derision of palaeontologists and theologians alike.

*

81. In his guide to Kew, Gosse includes a whimsical note on the *Cibotium* there:

> [It is] a singular vegetable production, of which, under the name of Scythian Lamb, many fabulous stories are told. It was said, among other things, to be part animal, part vegetable, and to have the power of devouring all the

other plants in its vicinity. It is in reality nothing but the prostrate hairy stem of a fern, called *Cibotium barometz*, which, from its procumbent position and shaggy appearance, looks something like a crouching animal.

*

82. One cannot look at the cycads in Kew or in the Hortus without a sense of their frailty too, the extinction which constantly threatens species which are special and rare. This came home to me especially in the Kirstenbosch Gardens in Cape Town, where more than fifty species of the African cycad *Encephalartos* grow. Some of these are common, some are rare. One is unique, because it comes from a single (male) plant, *E. woodii*, discovered by Dr Medley Wood in 1895. Though cuttings of the original have been cultivated (propagated asexually and thus clones of the original), no other trees of this species, male or female, have ever been found – and unless an unknown female exists somewhere, *E. woodii* will never pollinate or mate; it will be the last of its kind on earth.

Seeing the magnificent solitary specimen at Kirstenbosch, unlabelled and surrounded by an iron fence to discourage poachers, reminded me of the story of Ishi, the last of his tribe. I was seeing here a cycad Ishi, and it made me think of how, hundreds of millions of years ago, the numbers of tree lycopods, tree horsetails, seed ferns, once so great, must have diminished to a critical extent until there were only a hundred, only a dozen, only a single one left – and finally, one day, none at all; only the sad, compressed memory held in the coal.

(Another unique cycad, a female Ishi, *Cycas multipinnata*, has recently been found in a temple garden in China; no other specimens are known to exist. It is portrayed, with others, in a set of postage stamps issued in May 1996, commemorating cycad species native to China.)

*

83. In the northern part of Guam, there is a tropical dry forest, dominated by cycads; in Rota the cycad forest is wetter, 'mesic', though not true rainforest such as one sees on Pohnpei. The last few years have seen the destruction of Rota's unique forests on a fearful scale, most especially with the building of Japanese golf courses. We encountered one such development as we were walking through the jungle – huge bulldozers tearing up the earth, mowing down an area of several hundred acres. There are now three golf courses on the island, and more are planned. Such clear-cutting of virgin forest causes an avalanche of acidic soil into the reef below, killing the coral which sustains the whole reef environment. And it may break up the jungle into areas too small to sustain themselves, so that within a few decades there will be a collapse of the entire ecosystem, flora and fauna alike.

*

84. Chamberlain, in *The Living Cycads*, described how he estimated the age of a *Dioön edule*, which reaches maturity (in the wild) around the age of fifty, and then puts out a new crown of leaves every other year on

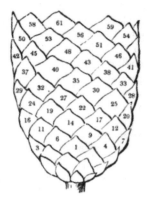

average. By counting the number of leaf scales on the stem, and dividing by the number of leaves produced each year, he arrived at the age of the tree. He described one beautiful specimen which, by this criterion, was 970 years old, even though less than five feet in height. Indeed, Chamberlain wondered whether some cycads might approach the sequoias in age.

*

85. The cones of cycads vary in character and shape and size: the vast cones of *Lepidozamia peroffskyana* and *Encephalartos transvenosus* may weigh more than a hundred pounds, and the cones of the smallest *Zamia*s no more than thirty milligrams. But all of them exhibit, in the arrangement of their cone scales, intricate geometric patterns similar to the corkscrew spirals or helices we see in pinecones, the leaf arrangement of cylindrical stems, or the whorling florets of sunflowers. The study of these patterns, this phyllotaxis, has intrigued botanists and mathematicians for centuries, not only because the spirals

300

themselves are logarithmic, but because there are numbers of accessory helices (or parastichies) running in the opposite direction and these two sets of helices occur in a fixed ratio to one another. Thus in cycad cones, as in pinecones, we almost always see spirals in five and eight rows, and if we express as fractions the number of parastichies, we find a series of 2/1, 3/2, 5/3, 8/5, 13/8, 21/13, 34/21, and so on. This series, named after the thirteenth-century mathematician Fibonacci, corresponds to a continued fraction which converges to 1.618, the numerical equivalent of the Golden Section.

These patterns probably represent no more and no less than an optimum way of packing leaves or scales together while avoiding their superimposition (and not, as Goethe and others thought, some mystical archetype or ideal), but they are a delight to the eye and a stimulus to the mind. Phyllotaxis fascinated the Reverend J. S. Henslow (professor of botany at Cambridge, and Darwin's teacher), who discussed and illustrated it in his *Principles of Descriptive and Physiological Botany*, and it is pondered at length in an eccentric (and very favourite) book, D'Arcy Thompson's *On Growth and Form*. It is said that Napier's discovery of logarithms at the start of the seventeenth century was stimulated by a contemplation of the growth of horsetails, and the great botanist Nehemiah Grew, later in the century, observed that 'from the contemplation of Plants, men might first be invited to Mathematical Enquiry'.

This sense of the mathematical determination (or constraints) of nature, especially of organic form and growth, divested of idealism or idiosyncrasy, is very strong now, especially with the development of chaos and complexity theory in the last few decades. Now that fractals are, so to speak, part of our consciousness, we see them every-where – in mountains, in landscapes, in snowflakes, in migraines, but above all in the vegetable world – just as Napier, four centuries ago, saw logarithms in his garden, and Fibonacci, seven centuries ago, found the Golden Section all about him.

*

86. The forms of plants exercised Goethe endlessly – we owe the very word 'morphology' to him. He had no sense of evolution, but rather of a sort of logical or morpholog-ical calculus whereby all higher plants might be derived from a simple primordial type, a hypothetical ancestral plant he called an *Ur-pflanze*. (This idea came to him, he recorded, while he was gazing at a palm in the Orto at Padua, and 'Goethe's palm', as it is now called, still grows there in a house of its own.) His hypothetical *Ur-pflanze* had leaves, which could metamorphose into petals and sepals, stamens and anthers, all the complex parts of flowers. Had Goethe concerned himself with flowerless plants, I could not help feeling, he might have seized on *Psilotum* as his *Ur-pflanze*.

A specific analogue of Goethe's theory which traces how higher plants might be derived morphologically from primitive psilophytes has been proposed by W. Zimmer-man in his theory of telomes, and a general analogue to Goethe's morphology in some of the current theories of universal morphogenesis, as Kauffman, Lindenmayer, Mandelbrot and others are exploring.

*

87. Such a feeling of transport to the distant past struck Safford when he saw the cycad forests of Guam: their 'cylindrical, scarred trunks, and stiff, pinnated, glossy leaves,' he wrote, suggested 'ideal pictures of the forests of the Carboniferous age'.

A very similar feeling is described by John Mickel, writing of horsetails:

> To wander among them is a kind of science-fiction experience. I well remember the first time I encountered a stand of the giant horsetail in Mexico. I had the feeling that I had found my way backward into a Carboniferous forest, and half expected dinosaurs to appear among the horsetails.

Even a walk in the streets of New York can evoke the Palaeozoic: one of the commonest trees here (apparently well able to resist pollution) is the maidenhair tree, *Ginkgo biloba*, a unique survivor little changed from the ginkgo-phytes of the Permian. But the ginkgo exists now only in cultivation; it is no longer found in the wild.

*

88. The unexpected adaptation of crabs to coconut eating fascinated Darwin, who describes them in the *Beagle*:

> I have before alluded to a crab which lives on the cocoa-nuts: it is very common on all parts of the dry land, and

grows to a monstrous size: it is closely allied or identical with the Birgos latro. The front pair of legs terminate in very strong and heavy pincers, and the last pair are fitted with others weaker and much narrower. It would at first be thought quite impossible for a crab to open a strong cocoa-nut covered with the husk; but Mr Liesk assures me that he has repeatedly seen this effected. The crab begins by tearing the husk, fibre by fibre, and always from that end under which the three eye-holes are situated; when this is completed, the crab commences hammering with its heavy claws on one of the eye-holes till an opening is made. Then turning round its body, by the aid of its posterior and narrow pair of pincers, it extracts the white albuminous substance. I think this is as curious a case of instinct as ever I heard of, and likewise of adaptation in structure between two objects apparently so remote from each other in the scheme of nature, as a crab and a cocoa-nut tree. . . .

It has been stated by some authors that the Birgos crawls up the cocoa-nut trees for the purpose of stealing the nuts: I very much doubt the possibility of this; but with the Pandanus the task would be very much easier. I was told by Mr Liesk that on these islands the Birgos lives only on the nuts which have fallen to the ground.

(In fact, coconut crabs do climb tall palm trees, and cut off the coconuts with their massive claws.)

*

89. It used to be held that cycads were wind-pollinated, like ferns and conifers, though early authors (including Chamberlain) had occasionally been struck by the pres-

ence of certain insects in or near the male cones at the time of pollination.

In 1980, Knut Norstog and Dennis Stevenson, working at the Fairchild Tropical Garden in Miami, were struck by the failure of many introduced cycads there to produce fertile seeds, even though healthy male and female plants had been planted just a yard or two apart, whereas the native *Zamia* was quite fertile. They found that snout weevils would feed as larvae on the male *Zamia* cones, emerging as adults by boring through the microsporophylls, covered with pollen. Could this be the way in which the female cones were pollinated?

Stevenson and Norstog, along with other researchers (Karl Niklas, Priscilla Fawcett, and Andrew Vovides) have confirmed this hypothesis in great detail. They have observed that weevils feed and mate on the outside of the male cone and then enter it, continuing to feed not on the pollen, but on the bases of the microsporophylls. Their eggs are laid, and larvae hatched, inside the microsporophylls, and the adult weevils finally chew their way out through the tips of the sporophylls. Some of these weevils go to the female cones, which exude a special warmth and aroma when they are ready for pollination, but the weevils cannot feed here, since the female cones are toxic to the insects. Crawling into the female cone through narrow cracks, the weevils are divested of their pollen and, finding no reason to stay longer, they return to the male cones.

The cycad thus depends on the weevil for pollination, and the weevil on the cycad cones for warmth and shelter – neither can survive without the other. This intimate relationship of insects and cycads, this coevolution, is the most primitive pollination system known and probably goes right back to the Palaeozoic, long before the evolution of flowering plants, with their insect-attracting scents and colours.

(A variety of insects can pollinate cycads, mostly beetles and weevils, though one species of *Cycas* is pollinated by a bee – giving the possibility, one likes to think, of a delicious cycad honey.)

*

90. One cannot think of these beautiful adaptations without feeling how excellent cycads are, in their own way, and how meaningless it is to see them as 'primitive' or 'lower' plants, inferior in the scale of life to 'higher', flowering plants. We have this almost irresistible sense of a steady evolutionary advance or progress (culminating, of course, in nature's 'highest' product – ourselves), but there is no evidence of any such tendency, any global progress or purpose, in nature itself. There is only, as Darwin himself insisted, adaptation to local conditions.

No one has written of our illusions about progress in nature with more wit and learning than Stephen Jay Gould, especially in his recent book, *Full House: The Spread of Excellence from Plato to Darwin.* They lead us, he writes, to a false iconography of the world, so that we see the Age of Ferns succeeded by the Age of Gymnosperms, succeeded by the present Age of Flowering Plants, as if the earlier forms of life had ceased to exist. But while many early species have been replaced, others continue to survive as highly successful, adaptable life forms, as with ferns and gymnosperms, which occupy every niche from rainforest to desert. If anything, we are really, Gould insists, in the Age of Bacteria – and have been for the last three billion years.

One cannot look at a single lineage, whether of horses or hominids, and come to any conclusions about evolution or progress, as Gould shows. We must look at the total picture of life on earth, of every species, and then we will see that it is not progress which characterizes nature but rather infinite novelty and diversity, an infinity of different adaptations and forms, none to be seen as 'higher' or 'lower'.

*

91. Darwin was the first to argue that dispersal of seeds by sea water might be an important means of their distribution, and made experiments to explore their ability to float and survive salt water. Many seeds, he found, had first to dry but then might float for remarkably long periods: dried hazelnuts, for example, floated for ninety days and afterwards germinated when planted. Comparing these time periods with the rates of ocean currents, Darwin thought that thousand-mile ocean journeys might be common for many seeds, even if they had no special flotation layer (like cycad seeds). 'Plants with large seeds or fruit,' he concluded, 'generally have restricted ranges, [and] could hardly be transported by any other means.'

Driftwood, he noted, might sometimes serve as a transport across the seas, and perhaps icebergs too. He speculated that the Azores had been 'partly stocked by ice-borne seeds' during the glacial epoch. But there is one form of oceanic transport, Lynn Raulerson suggests, which Darwin did not consider (though he would have been fascinated had it come to his attention), and this is transport by rafts of pumice, blown into the ocean by volcanic eruptions. These may float for years, providing transport not only for large seeds but for plants and animals as well. A vast pumice raft, stretching across the horizon, with coconut palms and other vegetation, was reportedly seen off Kosrae three years after Krakatau blew.

It is not enough, of course, for seeds to arrive; they must find conditions hospitable for colonization. 'How small would be the chance of a seed falling on favourable soil and coming to maturity!' Darwin exclaimed. The Northern Marianas – Pagan, Agrihan, Alamagan, Anatahan, Asuncion, Maug and Uracas – are doubtless visited by cycad seeds, but are too unstable, too actively volcanic, to allow them to survive and establish a viable colony.

*

92. The history and naming of the oceanic cycads is a story at once picturesque and confused. Surely Pigafetta, sailing with Magellan, must have obseved the cycads of Guam and Rota, but if he did, his descriptions are too vague for us to be certain. It needed a botanical or taxonomic eye to demarcate cycads in the first place from the circumambient palms around them. It was not until the next century that such botanical skills appeared, and

Encephalartos woodii, by Douglas Goode

then they appeared, with a sort of synchronicity, in two men, Rheede and Rumphius, whose lives and interests ran parallel in many ways. Both were officers of the Dutch East India Company. It was Rumphius who first described a cycad, on the Malabar coast in 1658. It was Rheede, his younger contemporary, who was to become governor of Malabar and publish a *Hortus Indicus Malabaricus* in the 1680s (after Rumphius' own manuscript for his *Hortus Malabaricus* was destroyed in a fire). Rumphius' and Rheede's cycads were taken to be the same, and both were called *Cycas circinalis* by Linnaeus. All the coastal and island cycads were called *C. circinalis* at first, so when the French botanist Louis du Petit-Thouars identified a cycad on the east coast of Africa in 1804, it was natural that he should call this *C. circinalis* too, though it would be recognized as a distinct species and renamed *C. thouarsii* a quarter of a century later. And Rumphius's name, a century and a half after his death, was first used in 1859 to denote the cycad he had originally described in the Moluccas.

In the past few years, there has been an effort to re-examine the taxonomy of the Pacific cycads, a task made peculiarly complicated, as Ken Hill notes, by 'the successive recolonization of areas by genetically distinct forms . . . facilitated by aquatic dispersal of the buoyant seeds'.

Most botanists now are disposed to confine the name *C. circinalis* to the tall Indian cycad (that originally figured in Rheede's *Hortus*), which grows inland and lacks buoyant seeds. This at least is Hill's formulation; he sees the Western Pacific cycads as belonging to the *C. rumphii* complex, and the Marianas cycad, which he has named *C. micronesica*, as a unique species within this complex. David de Laubenfels, a cycad taxonomist at Syracuse, agrees that *C. circinalis* occurs only in India and Sri Lanka, but feels that the Guam cycad belongs to an earlier-named species, *C. celebica*. Since, however, the Guam cycad has been called *C. circinalis* for two centuries, the likelihood is that it will continue to be called this, and that only botanists will insist on using its 'correct' name.

*

93. Aboriginal forests, cycad forests, seem to excite feelings of awe and reverence, religious or mystical feelings, in every culture. Bruce Chatwin writes of Cycad Valley, in Australia, as 'a place of immense importance' on some aboriginal songlines and a sacred place to which some aboriginals make their final pilgrimage before death. Such a scene, of final meetings and dyings beneath the cycads ('like magnified treeferns'), forms the ending of *The Songlines*.

*

94. The term 'deep time' was originated by John McPhee, and in *Basin and Range* he writes of how those most constantly concerned with deep time – geologists – may assimilate a sense of this into their inmost intellectual and emotional being. He quotes one geologist as saying, 'You begin tuning your mind to a time scale that is the planet's time scale. For me, it is almost unconscious now and is a kind of companionship with the earth.'

But even for those of us who are not professional geologists or palaeontologists, seeing ferns, ginkgos, cycads, forms of life whose basic patterns have been conserved for aeons, must also alter one's inmost feelings, one's unconscious, and produce a transformed and transcendent perspective.

Journals

Ahlskog, J. E.; S. C. Waring; L. T. Kurland; R. C. Petersen; T. P. Moyer; W. S. Harmsen; D. M. Maraganore; P. C. O'Brien; C. Esteban-Santillan; and V. Bush. 'Guamanian neurodegenerative disease: investigation of the calcium metabolism/ heavy metal hypothesis.' *Neurology* 45, 1340–1344 (July 1995).

Anderson, F. H.; E. P. Richardson, Jr.; H. Okazaki; and J. A. Brody. 'Neurofibrillary degeneration on Guam: frequency in Chamorros and non Chamorros with no known neurological disease.' *Brain* 102, 65–77 (1979).

Bailey-Wilson, Joan E.; Chris C. Plato; Robert C. Elston; and Ralph M. Garruto. 'Potential role of an additive genetic component in the cause of amyotrophic lateral sclerosis and parkinsonism-dementia in the Western Pacific.' *American Journal of Medical Genetics* 45, 68–76 (1993).

Brody, Jacob A.; Irene Hussels; Edward Brink; and Jose Torres. 'Hereditary blindness among Pingelapese people of Eastern Caroline Islands.' *Lancet*, 1253–1257 (June 1970).

Carr, Ronald E.; Newton E. Morton; and Irwin M. Siegel. 'Achromatopsia in Pingelap islanders.' *American Journal of Ophthalmology* 72 (4), 746–756 (October 1971).

Chen, Leung. 'Neurofibrillary change on Guam.' *Archives of Neurology* 38, 16–18 (January 1981).

Cody, Martin, and Jacob Overton. 'Short-term evolution of

reduced dispersal in island plant populations.' *Journal of Ecology* 84, 53–62 (1996).

Cox, Terry A.; James V. McDarby; Lawrence Lavine; John Steele; and Donald B. Calne. 'A retinopathy on Guam with high prevalence in lytico-bodig.' *Ophthalmology* 96, no. 12, 1731–1735 (December 1989).

Crapper McLachan, D.; C. McLachlan; B. Krishnan; S. Krishnan; A. Dalton; and J. Steele. 'Aluminum and calcium in Guam, Palau and Jamaica: implications for amyotrophic lateral sclerosis and parkinsonism-dementia syndromes on Guam.' *Environmental Geochemistry and Health* 11, no. 2, 45–53 (1989).

Cuzner, A. T. 'Arrowroot, cassava and koonti.' *Journal of the American Medical Assoc.* 1, 366–369 (1889).

de Laubenfels, D. J. 'Cycadacées.' In H. Humbert and J.-F. Leroy, eds., *Flora de Madagascar et des Comores. Gymnosperms*. Paris: Museum National d'Histoire Naturelle. 1978.

de Wit, H. C. D. 'In memory of G. K. Rumphius (1702–1952).' *Official News Bulletin of the International Association for Plant Taxonomy* 1, no. 7, 101–110 (1952).

Diamond, Jared M. 'Daisy gives an evolutionary answer.' *Nature* 380, 103–104 (14 March 1996).

—— 'The last people alive.' *Nature* 370, 331–332 (4 August 1994).

Duncan, Mark W.; John C. Steele; Irwin J. Kopin; and Sanford P. Markey. '2-Amino-3-(methylamino)-propanoic acid (BMAA) in cycad flour: an unlikely cause of amyotrophic lateral sclerosis and parkinsonism-dementia of Guam.' *Neurology* 40, 767–772 (May 1990).

Futterman, Frances. *Congenital Achromatopsia: A guide for professionals*. Berkeley: Resources for Limited Vision, 1995.

Gajdusek, D. Carleton. 'Cycad toxicity not the cause of high-incidence amyotrophic lateral sclerosis/parkinsonism-dementia on Guam, Kii peninsula of Japan, or in West New Guinea.' In Arthur J. Hudson, ed., *Amyotrophic Lateral Sclerosis: Concepts in Pathogenesis and Etiology,* Toronto: University of Toronto Press, 1987.

—— 'Foci of motor neuron disease in high incidence in isolated populations of East Asia and the Western Pacific.' In Lewis P. Rowland, ed., *Human Motor Neuron Diseases, 363–93.* New York: Raven Press, 1982.

—— 'Motor-neuron disease in natives of New Guinea.' *New England Journal of Medicine* 268, 474–476 (1963).

—— 'Rediscovery of persistent high incidence amyotrophic lateral sclerosis/parkinsonism-dementia in West New Guinea (Irian Jaya, Indonesia).' *Sections of the 1993 Journal of D. Carleton Gajdusek,* 489–544. Bethesda: National Institutes of Health, 1996.

—— and Andres M. Salazar. 'Amyotrophic lateral sclerosis and parkinsonian syndromes in high incidence among the Auyu and Jakai people of West New Guinea.' *Neurology* 32, no. 2, 107–126 (February 1982).

Garruto, Ralph M. 'Early environment, long latency and slow progression of late onset neurodegenerative disorders.' In S. J. Ulijaszek and C. J. K. Henry, eds., *Long Term Consequences of Early Environments.* Cambridge: Cambridge University Press, in press.

——; Richard Yanagihara; and D. Carleton Gajdusek. 'Cycads and amyotrophic lateral sclerosis/parkinsonism dementia.' Letter to the editor, *Lancet,* 1079 (November 1988).

Geddes, Jennian F.; Andrew J. Hughes; Andrew J. Lees; and Susan E. Daniel. 'Pathological overlap in cases of parkinsonism associated with neurofibrillary tangles.' *Brain* 116, 281–302 (1993).

Gibbs, W. Wayt. 'Gaining on fat.' *Scientific American* 8, 88–94 (August 1996).

Hachinski, V. C.; J. Porchawka; and J. C. Steele. 'Visual symptoms in the migraine syndrome.' *Neurology* 23, 570–579 (1973).

Haldane, J. B. S. 'Suggestions as to quantitative measurement of rates of evolution.' *Evolution* 3, 51–56 (March 1949).

Hansen, Egil. 'Clinical aspects of achromatopsia.' In R. F. Hess, L. T. Sharpe, and K. Nordby, eds., *Night Vision: Basic, Clinical and Applied Aspects*. Cambridge: Cambridge University Press, 1990.

Hill, K. D. 'The *Cycas rumphii* (Cycadaceae) in New Guinea and the Western Pacific.' *Australian Systematic Botany* 7, 543–567 (1994).

Hirano, Asao; Leonard T. Kurland; Robert S. Krooth; and Simmons Lessell. 'Parkinsonism-dementia complex, an endemic disease of the island of Guam. I: clinical features.' *Brain* 84, Part IV: 642–661 (1961).

——; Nathan Malamud; and Leonard T. Kurland. 'Parkinsonism-dementia complex, an endemic disease on the island of Guam. II: pathological features.' *Brain* 84, Part IV: 662–679 (1961).

Hubbuch, Chuck. 'A queen sago by any other name.' *Garden News*, Fairchild Tropical Garden, Miami, Fla. (January 1996).

Hudson, Arthur J., and George P. A. Rice. 'Similarities of Guamanian ALS/PD to post-encephalitic parkinsonism/ALS: possible viral cause.' *The Canadian Journal of Neurological Sciences* 17, no. 4, 427–433 (November 1990).

Hughes, Abbie. 'Seeing cones in living eyes.' *Nature* 380, 393–394 (4 April 1996).

Hussels, I. E., and N. E. Morton. 'Pingelap and Mokil atolls: achromatopsia.' *American Journal of Human Genetics* 24, 304–307 (1972).

Jacobs, Gerald H.; Maureen Neitz; Jess F. Degan; and Jay Neitz. 'Trichromatic color vision in New World monkeys.' Letter to the editor, *Nature* 385, 156–158 (July 1996).

Kauffman, Stuart. 'Evolving evolvability.' *Nature* 382, 309–310 (25 July 1996).

Kisby, Glen E.; Mike Ellison; and Peter S. Spencer. 'Content of the neurotoxins cycasin and BMAA in cycad flour prepared by Guam Chamorros.' *Neurology* 42, no. 7, 1336–1340 (1992).

Kisby, Glen E.; Stephen M. Ross; Peter S. Spencer; Bruce G. Gold; Peter B. Nunn; and D. N. Roy. 'Cycasin and BMAA: candidate neurotoxins for Western Pacific amyotrophic lateral sclerosis/parkinsonism-dementia complex.' *Neurodegeneration* 1, 73–82 (1992).

Kurland, Leonard T. 'Geographic isolates: their role in neuroepidemiology.' *Advances in Neurology* 19, 69–82 (1978).

—— '*Cycas circinalis* as an etiologic risk factor in amyotrophic lateral sclerosis and other neurodegenerative diseases on Guam.' In Dennis W. Stevenson and Knut J. Norstog, eds., *Proceedings of CYCAD 90, the Second International Conference on Cycad Biology*, 29–36. Milton, Australia: Palm & Cycad Societies of Australia, Ltd., June, 1993.

Lebot, Vincent, and Pierre Cabalion. 'Les kavas de Vanuatu: cultivars de *Piper methysticum* Forst.' Trans. R. M. Benyon, R. Wane and G. Kaboha. Noumea, New Caledonia: South Pacific Commision, 1988.

McGeer, Patrick L.; Claudia Schwab; Edith G. McGeer; and

John C. Steele. 'The amyotrophic lateral sclerosis/parkinsonism-dementia complex of Guam: pathology and pedigrees.' *Canadian Journal of Neurological Sciences* (in press).

Miller, Donald T.; David R. Williams; G. Michael Morris; and Junzhong Liang. 'Images of cone photoreceptors in the living human eye.' *Vision Research* 36 (8), 1067–1079 (1996).

Mollon, J. D. '"Tho' she kneel'd in that place where they grew . . .": the uses and origins of primate colour vision.' *Journal of Experimental Biology* 146, 21–38 (1989).

Morton, N. E.; R. Lew; I. E. Hussels; G. F. Little. 'Pingelap and Mokil atolls: historical genetics.' *American Journal of Human Genetics* 24 (3), 277–289 (1972).

Mulder, Donald W.; Leonard T. Kurland; and Lorenzo L. G. Iriarte. 'Neurologic diseases on the island of Guam.' *U. S. Armed Forces Medical Journal* 5, no. 12, 1724–1739 (December 1954).

Niklas, Karl. 'How to build a tree.' *Natural History* 2, 49–52 (1996).

Nordby, Knut. 'Vision in a complete achromat: a personal account.' In R. F. Hess, L. T. Sharpe, and K. Nordby, eds., *Night Vision: Basic, Clinical and Applied Aspects*. Cambridge: Cambridge University Press, 1990.

Norstog, Knut. 'Cycads and the origin of insect pollination.' *American Scientist* 75, 270–279 (May–June 1987).

——; Priscilla K. S. Fawcett; and Andrew P. Vovides. 'Beetle pollination of two species of *Zamia*: evolutionary and ecological considerations.' In B. S. Venkatachala, David L. Dilcher, and Hari K. Maheshwari, eds., *Essays in Evolutionary Plant Biology*. Lucknow: Birbal Sahni Institute of Palaeobotany, 1992.

——; Dennis W. Stevenson; and Karl J. Niklas. 'The role of

beetles in the pollination of *Zamia furfuracea* L. fil. (Zami-
aceae).' *Biotropica* 18, no. 4, 300–306 (1986).

Norton, Scott A., and Patricia Ruze. 'Kava dermopathy.' *Journal of the American Academy of Dermatology* 31, no. 1,
89–97 (July 1994).

Proceedings: 'Toxicity of cycads: implications for neurodegenerative diseases and cancer.' In Marjorie Grant Whiting,
ed., *Transcripts of Four Cycad Conferences.* [1st, 2nd, 4th,
5th] New York: Third World Medical Research Foundation,
1988.

—— 'Third conference on the toxicity of cycads.' *Federation
Proceedings* 23, no. 6, Part I, 1336–1388 (November–December 1964).

—— 'Sixth international cycad conference.' *Federation Proceedings* 31, no. 5, 1465–1546 (September–October 1972).

Raynor, Bill. 'Resource management in upland forests of Pohnpei: past practices and future possibilities.' *ISLA: A Journal
of Micronesian Studies* 2, no. 1, 47–66 (Rainy season 1994).

Sacks, Oliver. 'Coelacanth dated.' Letter to the editor, *Nature*
273, 463 (9 February 1995).

—— 'The divine curse: Tourette's syndrome among a Mennonite family.' *Life*, 93–102 (September 1988).

—— and Robet Wasserman. 'The case of the colourblind
painter.' *New York Review of Books* (19 November 1987).

Sharpe, Lindsay T., and Knut Nordby. 'Total colorblindness:
an introduction.' In R. F. Hess, L. T. Sharpe, and K. Nordby,
eds., *Night Vision: Basic, Clinical and Applied Aspects.*
Cambridge: Cambridge University Press, 1990.

Small, John K. 'Seminole bread – the conti.' *Journal of the New
York Botanical Gardens* 22, 121–137 (1921).

Spencer, Peter S. 'Are neurotoxins driving us crazy? Planetary
observations on the causes of neurodegenerative diseases of

old age.' In Roger W. Russell, Pamela Ebert Flattau, and Andrew M. Pope, eds., *Behavorial Measures of Neurotoxicity: Report of a Symposium*. Washington, DC: National Academy Press, 1990.

—— 'Guam ALS/parkinsonism-dementia: a long-latency neurotoxic disorder caused by "slow toxin(s)" in food?' *Canadian Journal of Neurologic Sciences* 14, no. 3, 347–357 (August 1987).

—; and Glen E. Kisby. 'Slow toxins and Western Pacific amyotrophic lateral sclerosis.' In Richard Alan Smith, ed., *Handbook of Amyotrophic Lateral Sclerosis*. New York: Marcel Dekker, 1992.

—; and H. H. Schaumburg. 'Lathyrism: A neurotoxic disease.' *Neurobehavioral Toxicology* 5, 625–629 (1983).

—; R. G. Allen; G. E. Kisby; and A. C. Ludolph. 'Excitotoxic disorders.' *Science* 248, 144 (1990).

—; Glen E. Kisby; and Albert C. Ludolph. 'Slow toxins, biologic markers, and long-latency neurodegenerative disease in the western Pacific region.' *Neurology* 41, 62–66 (1991).

—; Peter B. Nunn; Jacques Hugon; Albert Ludolph; and Dwijendra N. Roy. 'Motorneurone disease on Guam: possible role of a food neurotoxin.' Letter to the editor, *Lancet* 1, 965 (April 1986).

—; Valerie S. Palmer; Adam Herman; Ahmed Asmedi. 'Cycad use and motor neurone disease in Irian Jaya.' *Lancet* 2, 1273–1274 (1987).

Steele, John C. 'Guam seaweed poisoning: common marine toxins.' *Micronesica* 26, no. 1, 11–18 (June 1993).

—— 'Historical notes.' *Journal of Neural Transmission* 42, 3–14 (1994).

—— 'Micronesia: health status and neurological diseases.' In K.

M. Chen and Yoshiro Yase, eds., *Amyotrophic Lateral Sclerosis in Asia and Oceania*. Taiwan: National Taiwan University Press, 1984.

— and Tomasa Quinata-Guzman. 'The Chamorro diet: an unlikely cause of neurofibrillary degeneration on Guam.' In F. Clifford Rose and Forbes H. Norris, eds., *ALS: New advances in toxicology and epidemiology*, 79–87. London: Smith-Gordon, 1990.

— and Tomasa Quinata-Guzman. 'Observations about amytrophic lateral sclerosis and the parkinsonism-dementia complex of Guam with regard to epidemiology and etiology.' *The Canadian Journal of Neurological Sciences* 14, no. 3, 358–362 (August 1987).

—; J. Clifford Richardson; and Jerzy Olszewski. 'Progressive supranuclear palsy. A heterogeneous degeneration involving the brain stem, basal ganglia and cerebellum with vertical gaze palsy and pseudobulbar palsy, nuchal dystonia and dementia.' *Archives of Neurology* 10, 333–359 (April 1964).

Steele, Julia. 'Umatac.' *Pacifica 5*, no. 1, 20–27 (Spring 1996).

Stopes, Marie C. 'On the double nature of cycadean integument.' *Annals of Botany* 19, no. 76, 561–566 (October 1905).

Weisler, M. I. 'The settlement of marginal Polynesia: New evidence from Henderson Island.' *Journal of Field Archaeology* 21, 83–102 (1994).

Whiting, Marjorie Grant. 'Toxicity of cycads.' *Economic Botany* 17, 270–295 (1963).

— 'Food practices in ALS foci in Japan, the Marianas, and New Guinea.' *Fed Proc* 23, 1343–1345 (1964).

Yanagihara, R. T.; R. M. Garruto; and D. C. Gadjusek. 'Epidemiological surveillance of amyotrophic lateral sclerosis and parkinsonism-dementia in the Commonwealth of the

Northern Mariana Islands.' *Annals of Neurology* 13, No. 1, 79–86 (January 1983).

Yase, Y. 'The pathogenesis of amyotrophic lateral sclerosis.' *Lancet* 2, 292–295 (1972).

Yoon, Carol Kaesuk. 'Lake Victoria's lightning-fast origin of species.' *The New York Times*, C1–4, 27 August 1996.

Zhang, Z. X.; D. W. Anderson; N. Mantel; G. C. Román. 'Motor neuron disease on Guam: geographic and familial occurrence, 1956–85.' *Acta Neurologica Scand.*, 1996 (in press).

Zimmerman, H. M. 'Monthly report to medical officer in command.' *USN Medical Research Unit No. 2* (June 1945).

Zimmerman, W. 'Main results of the "telome theory."' *The Paleobotanist*, Birbal Sahni Memorial Volume, 456–470. 1952.

Bibliography

Arago, J. *Narrative of a Voyage Round the World in the Uranie and Physicienne Corvettes, Commanded by Captain Freycinet*. 1823. Reprint, Bibliotheca Australiana, vol. 45; Amsterdam: N. Israel and New York: Da Capo Press, 1971.

Ashby, Gene. *Pohnpei: An Island Argosy*. 1983. Revised ed., Rainy Day Press, P. O. Box 574, Kolonia, Pohnpei, F.S.M., 96941.

— *Some Things of Value ... : Micronesian Customs and Beliefs*. 1975. By the Students of The Community College of Micronesia. Revised ed., Kolonia, Pohnpei: Rainy Day Press, 1993.

Barbour, Nancy. *Palau*. San Francisco: Full Court Press, 1990.

Beaglehole, J. C. *The Exploration of the Pacific*. 1934. Reprint, third ed. Stanford: Stanford University Press, 1966.

Bell, Alexander Graham. *Memoir Upon the Formation of a Deaf Variety of the Human Race*. New Haven: National Academy of Science, 1883.

Bornham, Chris H. *Welwitschia: Paradox of a Parched Paradise*. Capetown: C. Struik, 1978.

Botting, Douglas. *Humboldt and the Cosmos*. London: Sphere Books, 1973.

Bower, F. O. *The Origin of a Land Flora*. London: Macmillan and Co., 1908.

Browne, Janet. *Voyaging: Charles Darwin*. vol. 1. New York: Alfred A. Knopf, 1995.

Cahill, Kevin M., and William O'Brien. *Tropical Medicine: A Clinical Text*. London: Heinemann Medical Books, 1990.

Carr, D. J., ed. *Sydney Parkinson: Artist of Cook's* Endeavour *Voyage*. Canberra: Australian National University Press, 1983.

Chamberlain, Charles Joseph. *The Living Cycads*. 1919. Reprint, New York: Hafner, 1965.

Chatwin, Bruce. *The Songlines*. New York: Viking Penguin, 1987.

Cook, James. *The Explorations of Captain James Cook in the Pacific: As Told by Selections of His Own Journals, 1768–1779*. New York: Dover, 1971.

Crawford, Peter. *Nomads of the Wind: A Natural History of Polynesia*. London: BBC Books, 1993.

Critchley, Macdonald. *Sir William Gowers, 1845–1915: A biographical appreciation*. London: William Heinemann, 1949.

Dampier, William. *A New Voyage round the World*. 1697. Reprint, London: Adam and Charles Black, 1927.

Darwin, Charles. *The Autobiography of Charles Darwin (1809–1882), with original omissions restored*. Nora Barlow, ed. London: William Collins, 1958.

— *Diary of the Voyage of H.M.S. Beagle*. Unpublished letters and notebooks. Nora Barlow, ed. New York: Philosophical Library, 1946.

— *On the Origin of Species by Means of Natural Selection*. 1859. London: Everyman's Library, J. M. Dent & Sons, 1951.

— *On the Structure and Distribution of Coral Reefs* [1842]; *Geological Observations on the Volcanic Islands* [1844] *and parts of South America: Visited during the Voyage of H.M.S. Beagle* [1846]. John W. Judd, ed. London: Ward, Lock, and Co., 1890.

—— *The Voyage of the Beagle.* 1839, revised ed. 1860. Reprint, Leonard Engel, ed. New York: Doubleday and Co., 1962.

Dawkins, Richard. *Climbing Mount Improbable.* London: Viking, 1996.

De Pineda, Antonio. *Descripciones de la Isla de Cocos (Islas Marianas).* 1792. Marjorie G. Driver, ed. Guam: Micronesian Area Research Center, 1990.

Dibblin, Jane. *Day of Two Suns: U.S. Nuclear Testing and the Pacific Islanders.* NewYork: New Amsterdam, 1988.

Edelman, Gerald M. *Bright Air, Brilliant Fire: On the Matter of the Mind.* New York: Basic Books, 1992.

Eldredge, Niles. *Dominion: Can Nature and Culture Co-Exist?* New York: Holt, 1995.

Farrell, Don A. *The Pictorial History of Guam.* 3 vols. Tamuning, Guam: Micronesian Productions. Vol. 1, *The Americanization: 1898–1918.* 1986; Vol. 2, *The Sacrifice: 1919–1943.* 1991; Vol. 3, *Liberation–1944.* 1984.

Figuier, Louis. *Earth before the Deluge,* fourth revised edition, 1865.

Freycinet, Louis-Henri de Saulces de. *Voyage Autour du Monde.* 13 vols. Paris: Pillet Aine, 1824–44.

Gilmour, John. *British Botanists.* London: William Collins, 1944.

Le Gobien, Charles. *Histoire des Isles Marianes, Nouvellement convertiées àla Religion Chrétiennes & de la mort glorieuse des premiers Missionaires qui y ont prêché la Foy.* Paris: Nicolas Pepie, 1701.

Goethe, Johann Wolfgang. 'The Metamorphosis of Plants.'

1790. In *Goethe's Botanical Writings*. Woodbridge, CT.: Ox Bow Press, 1989.

Goode, Douglas. *Cycads of Africa*. Capetown: Struik Winchester, 1989.

Gosse, Philip Henry. *Omphalos: An Attempt to Untie the Geological Knot*. London: John van Voorst, 1857.

[Gosse, Philip Henry.] *Wanderings through the Conservatories at Kew*. London: Society for Promoting Christian Knowledge, 1856.

Gould, Stephen Jay. *Dinosaur in a Haystack: Reflections in Natural History*. New York: Harmony Books, 1995.

—— *Full House: The Spread of Excellence from Plato to Darwin*. New York: Harmony Books, 1996.

—— *Time's Arrow, Time's Cycle*. Cambridge: Harvard University Press, 1987.

Grimble, Arthur. *A Pattern of Islands*. London: John Murray, 1952.

Groce, Nora Ellen. *Everyone Here Spoke Sign Language: Hereditary Deafness on Martha's Vineyard*. Cambridge: Harvard University Press, 1985.

Henslow, J. S. *The Principles of Descriptive and Physiological Botany*. London: Longman, Rees, Orme, Brown & Green; and John Taylor, 1835.

Hess, R. F.; L. T. Sharpe; and K. Nordby, eds. *Night Vision: Basic, Clinical and Applied Aspects*. Cambridge: Cambridge University Press, 1990.

Holder, Charles Frederick. *Living Lights: A Popular Account of Phosphorescent Animals and Vegetables*. London: Sampson Low, Marston & Co., 1887.

Holland, G. A. *Micronesia: A Paradise Lost? A Surgeon's Diary of Work and Travels in Oceania, the Joys and the Pains*. Montreal: G. A. Holland, 1993.

Bibliography

Hough, Richard. *Captain James Cook*. London: Hodder & Stoughton, 1994.

Humboldt, Alexander von. *Personal Narrative of Travels to the Equinoctial Regions of America during the Years 1799–1804*. London: George Routledge and Sons, 1852.

—— *Views of Nature: Or Contemplations on the Sublime Phenomena of Creation*. 1807. London: Henry G. Bohn, 1850.

Hurd, Jane N. *A History and Some Traditions of Pingelap, An Atoll in the Eastern Caroline Islands*. University of Hawaii, unpublished master's thesis, 1977.

Isely, Duane. *One Hundred and One Botanists*. Ames, Ia.: Iowa State University Press, 1994.

Jones, David L. *Cycads of the World*. Washington, DC: Smithsonian Institution Press, 1993.

Kahn, E. J., Jr. *A Reporter in Micronesia*. New York: W. W. Norton & Co., 1966.

Kauffman, Stuart. *At Home in the Universe: The Search for the Laws of Self-Organization and Complexity*. Oxford: Oxford University Press, 1995.

Kroeber, Theodora, and Alfred Kroeber. *Ishi in Two Worlds: A Biography of the Last Wild Indian in North America*. Berkeley: University of California Press, 1961.

Lessard, W. O. *The Complete Book of Bananas*. Miami: W. O. Lessard, 19201 SW 248th Street, Homestead, FL 33031, 1992.

Levi-Strauss, Claude. *The Savage Mind*. Chicago: University of Chicago Press, 1968.

Lewin, Louis. *Phantastica: Narcotic and Stimulating Drugs – Their Use and Abuse*. 1931. Reprint, London: Routledge & Kegan Paul, 1964.

—— *Über Piper methysticum (kawakawa)*. Berlin: A. Hirschwald, 1886.

London, Jack. *The Cruise of the Snark: A Pacific Voyage.* 1911. Reprint, London: Kegan Paul International, 1986.

— *The House of Pride and Other Tales of Hawaii.* New York: Macmillan & Co., 1912.

Lyell, Charles. *Principles of Geology.* 3 vols. London: John Murray, 1830–1833.

Marche, Antoine-Alfred. *The Mariana Islands.* Robert D. Craig, ed. Mariana Islands: Micronesian Area Research Center, 1982.

Mariner, William. *An Account of the Natives of the Tonga Islands in the South Pacific Ocean,* 2 vols. Edinburgh: Constable & Co., 1827.

McPhee, John. *Basin and Range.* New York: Farrar, Straus & Giroux, 1980.

Melville, Herman. *Journals, 1849–1860.* In Howard C. Horsford & Lynn Horth, eds. *The Writings of Herman Melville,* vol. 15. Evanston and Chicago: Northwestern University Press and The Newberry Library, 1989.

— *Omoo.* 1847. *The Writings of Herman Melville,* vol. 2. Evanston and Chicago: Northwestern University Press and The Newberry Library, 1968.

— *Typee.* 1846. *The Writings of Herman Melville,* vol. 1. Evanston and Chicago: Northwestern University Press and The Newberry Library, 1968.

— *The Encantadas.* 1856. Reprinted in *Shorter Novels of Herman Melville.* New York: Liveright, 1978.

Menard, H. W. *Islands.* New York: Scientific American Books, 1986.

Merlin, Mark; Dageo Jano; William Raynor; Thomas Keene; James Juvik; and Bismark Sebastian. *Tuhke en Pohnpei: Plants of Pohnpei.* Honolulu: Environment and Policy Institute, East-West Center, 1992.

Mickel, John, and Evelyn Fiore. *The Home Gardener's Book of Ferns.* New York: Holt, Rinehart and Winston, 1979.

O'Connell, James F. *A Residence of Eleven Years in New Holland and the Caroline Islands: Being the Adventures of James F. O'Connell. Edited from his Verbal Narration.* 1836. Reprint, Canberra: Australian National University Press, 1971.

Orliac, Catherine & Michel Orliac. *Easter Island: Mystery of the Stone Giants.* 1988. New York: Harry N. Abrams, 1995.

Peck, William M. *A Tidy Universe of Islands.* Honolulu: Mutual Publishing Co., 1996.

Peck, W. M. *I Speak the Beginning: Anthology of Surviving Poetry of the Northern Mariana Islands.* Commonwealth Council for Arts and Culture, Saipan, Northern Mariana Islands 96950, 1982.

Pigafetta, Antonio. *Magellan's Voyage Around the World by Antonio Pigafetta: Three Contemporary Accounts.* Charles E. Nowell, ed. Evanston, Ill.: Northwestern University Press, 1962.

Prusinkiewicz, P. and A. Lindenmayer. *The Algorithmic Beauty of Plants.* New York: Springer Verlag, 1990.

Quammen, David. *The Song of the Dodo: Island Biogeography in an Age of Extinctions.* New York: Scribner, 1996.

Raulerson, Lynn, and Agnes Rinehart. *Ferns and Orchids of the Mariana Islands.* Guam: Raulerson & Rinehart, P. O. Box 428, Agana, Guam 96910, 1992.

—— *Trees and Shrubs of the Northern Mariana Islands.* Coastal Resources Management, Office of the Governor, Saipan, Northern Mariana Islands 96950, 1991.

Raup, David M. *Extinction: Bad Genes or Bad Luck?* Intro. by Stephen Jay Gould. New York: W. W. Norton & Co., 1992.

Rheede tot Draakestein, Hendrik A. van. *Hortus Indicus*

Malabaricus. Amsterdam: J. v. Someren & J. v. Arnold Syen, 1682.

Rogers, Robert F. *Destiny's Landfall: A History of Guam*. Honolulu: University of Hawai'i Press, 1995.

Rose, June. *Marie Stopes and the Sexual Revolution*. London and Boston: Faber and Faber, 1992.

Rossi, Paolo. *The Dark Abyss of Time: The History of the Earth and the History of Nations from Hooke to Vico*. Chicago: University of Chicago Press, 1984.

Rudwick, Martin J. S. *Scenes from Deep Time*. Chicago: University of Chicago Press, 1992.

Rumphius, Georg Everhard. *Herbarium Amboinensis*. Amsterdam: J. Burmann, 1741.

Sacks, Oliver. *An Anthropologist on Mars*. London: Picador, 1995.

— *Awakenings*. 1973. Revised ed., London: Picador, 1990.

— *Migraine*. 1970. Revised ed., London: Picador, 1992.

Safford, William Edwin. *The Useful Plants of the Island of Guam*. Contributions from United States National Herbarium, Volume IX. Washington, DC: Smithsonian Institution, 1905.

Scott, Dukinfield Henry. *Studies in Fossil Botany*. London: Adam & Charles Black, 1900.

Simmons, James C. *Castaways in Paradise: The Incredible Adventures of True-Life Robinson Crusoes*. Dobbs Ferry, NY: Sheridan House, 1993.

Stanley, David. *Micronesia Handbook: Guide to the Caroline, Gilbert, Mariana, and Marshall Islands*. Chico, CA: Moon Publications, 1992.

— *South Pacific Handbook*. Fifth ed., Chico, CA: Moon Publications, 1994.

Stevenson, Dennis, ed. *Memoirs of The New York Botanical*

Garden, Vol. 57: The Biology, Structure, and Systematics of the Cycadales. Symposium Cycad 87, Beaulieu-sur-Mer, France, April 17–22. New York: New York Botanical Garden, 1987.

Stevenson, Robert Louis. *In the South Seas: The Marquesas, Paumotus and Gilbert Islands.* 1900. Reprint, London: Kegan Paul International, 1986.

Stopes, Marie C. *Ancient Plants: Being a Simple Account of the Past Vegetation of the Earth and of the Recent Important Discoveries Made in this Realm of Nature Study.* London: Blackie, 1910.

Theroux, Paul. *The Happy Isles of Oceania: Paddling the Pacific.* New York: Ballantine Books, 1993.

Thompson, D'Arcy Wentworth. *On Growth and Form,* 2 vols. 1917. Reprint, Cambridge: Cambridge University Press, 1959.

Thornton, Ian. *Krakatau: The Destruction and Reassembly of an Island Ecosystem.* Cambridge: Harvard University Press, 1996.

Turrill, W. B. *Joseph Dalton Hooker: Botanist, Explorer, and Administrator.* British Men of Science Series. London: Thomas Nelson and Sons, 1963.

Unger, Franz. *Primitive World.* 1858.

von Economo, Constantin. *Encephalitis Lethargica: Its Sequelae and Treatment.* 1917. Reprint, Oxford: Oxford University Press, 1931.

Wallace, Alfred Russel. *Island Life, or The Phenomena and Causes of Insular Faunas and Floras including a Revision and Attempted Solution of the Problem of Geological Climates.* 1880. Third ed., London: Macmillan and Co., 1902.

—— *The Malay Archipelago: The Land of the Orang-Utan and the Bird of Paradise, A Narrative of Travel with Studies of*

Man and Nature. 1869. Tenth ed., New York: Macmillan and Co., 1906.

Warming, E. *A Handbook of Systematic Botany.* 1895. London: Swan Sonnenschein, 1904; New York: Macmillan and Co., 1904.

Weiner, Jonathan. *The Beak of the Finch: A Story of Evolution in Our Time.* New York: Alfred A. Knopf, 1994.

White, Mary E. *The Nature of Hidden Worlds.* Balgowlah, Australia: Reed Books, 1990.

—— *The Greening of Gondwana.* Balgowlah, Australia: Reed Books, 1986.

Wieland, G. R. *American Fossil Cycads*, 2 vols. Washington, DC: Carnegie Institution of Washington, vol. 1: 1906; vol. 2: 1916.

Wilson, Edward O. *Biophilia.* Cambridge: Harvard University Press, 1984.

—— *The Biophilia Hypothesis.* Washington, DC: Island Press, 1993.

—— *Naturalist.* Washington, DC: Island Press, 1993.

Index

333

Index

Index

Index

Index

Index

Index

Index

Index

Index

Index

Index

For further information contact:

The Achromatopsia Network
P. O. Box 214
Berkeley, CA 94701-0214
Tel: 510-540-4700
E-mail: Futterman@achromat.org
Web site: http://www.achromat.org